THE SHIMMERING IS ALL THERE IS

On Nature, God, Science, and More

Heather Catto Kohout
Edited by Martin Donell Kohout

TEXAS A&M UNIVERSITY PRESS
COLLEGE STATION

This paper meets the requirements
of ANSI/NISO Z39.48–1992 (Permanence of Paper).
Binding materials have been chosen for durability.
Manufactured in the United States of America

Library of Congress Cataloging-in-Publication Data

Names: Kohout, Heather Catto, 1959–2014, author. | Kohout, Martin Donell,
    1959– editor, writer of introduction. | Jones, Nancy Baker, writer of
    foreword.
Title: The shimmering is all there is : on nature, God, science, and more /
    Heather Catto Kohout ; edited by Martin Donell Kohout.
Other titles: Women in Texas history series.
Description: First edition. | College Station : Texas A&M University Press,
    [2021] | Series: Women in Texas history | Includes index.
Identifiers: LCCN 2020053642 | ISBN 9781623499501 (cloth) | ISBN
    9781623499518 (ebook)
Subjects: LCSH: Kohout, Heather Catto, 1959-2014—Philosophy. | Human
    ecology—Texas—Texas Hill Country—Philosophy. | Human
    ecology—Religious aspects—Christianity. | Human ecology—Texas—Texas
    Hill Country—Poetry. | Environmental ethics. | Ecotheology. | LCGFT:
    Essays. | Poetry.
Classification: LCC PS3611.O375 S55 2021 | DDC 814/.6—dc23
LC record available at https://lccn.loc.gov/2020053642

Contents

ESSAYS

POEMS

Foreword

Her entire life was a dialogue with the world, whether the world knew it or not.
These words, spoken by Heather Catto Kohout's son, Christopher Henry
(Tito) Kohout, at her memorial service at All Saints' Episcopal Church in
Austin, Texas, on October 23, 2014, perfectly describe her outlook on life.
She drew strength and inspiration from the natural world around her, and
this collection of prose and poetry reveals her keen intellect, boundless
curiosity, optimism, and deep appreciation of the tangible and intangible
aspects of life she encountered every day.

For this volume to appear in a series about Texas women's history will
strike some as odd, since it is not a history in the traditional sense. However,
history can be defined in various ways. It is nothing if not human expe-
rience, recorded. Memoir is a form of history, written by the participant
at ground zero. In this case, we have a collection of essays and poetry that
require the reader to work a bit to distill how a life was constructed and
what it meant in the end.

This book offers a unique perspective by a talented writer, a Texas woman
to the core, with a mind and heart that capture an essence of Texas in prose
so captivating that it seems to break the mold of even the classic Texas and
environmental writers of the past. She takes on remarkably complex topics
and relies not only on biblical passages, but also on Alexis de Tocqueville,
Henry David Thoreau, and Mary Oliver, among others. She travels; she
eats meat and cares about the animals from which it comes; she thinks
about being and nothingness, comparing what may superficially seem odd
pairings, yet always finding common ground. She writes as both owner and
steward of the land and notices its beauty and its difficulties. Through this
very wide-ranging approach to what is at the bottom of an environmen-
talist's view of living, she reveals humor, compassion, occasional fear, and
thoughts of both God and the quotidian.

Heather Catto Kohout's roots run deep in Texas. Born in 1959, she was the daughter of Henry E. Catto Jr., who had a long diplomatic career under four different presidents, and Jessica Hobby Catto, who was herself the daughter of Oveta Culp Hobby, one of the most distinguished and powerful women in Texas history, and William P. Hobby Sr., a former governor of the state. The oldest of four siblings, Heather grew up in San Antonio and in McLean, Virginia. She earned a bachelor's degree in English literature from Williams College in Massachusetts, and master's degrees in English literature from the University of Texas at Austin and in religion from the Episcopal Theological Seminary of the Southwest. She was a published poet, a dedicated rower, and a passionate lover of nature and her native state, as is evident through her writings in this book.

Heather married San Francisco native Martin Kohout, a Williams class-mate and fellow English major, in 1985. They lived in Austin for most of the next thirty years and raised three children, Elizabeth, Tito, and Thea, all of whom inherited their mother's intelligence and giving spirit. As Tito said, "She gave of herself freely and completely to good and just causes, from immigration to environment, and insisted that her children do the same." They do, and she was fiercely proud of the remarkable adults they became.

The Kohouts founded Madroño Ranch: A Center for Writing, Art, and the Environment on their 1,500-acre spread in the Texas Hill Country near Medina. Over a five-year period, Madroño Ranch hosted some sixty residents in a variety of disciplines, including painting, music, poetry, photography, fiction, journalism, printmaking, paleontology, sculpture, filmmaking, fiber arts, marine biology, book arts, drama, and forest history. Heather always believed that, as a child of privilege, she had an obligation to live a life imbued with generosity and humility. She also inherited a profound love of the Lone Star State that remained obvious even when she was most exasperated by the foibles of its political leaders (everything is bigger in Texas). To quote Martin, "The writings collected here offer the merest taste of her astonished delight in unexpected connections, always recounted with grace, passion, and self-deprecating humor."

Heather died in October 2014, three years after receiving a diagnosis of metastatic cancer in her spine and pelvis. After her death, her husband and children reached the difficult decision to sell the ranch, but their resulting charitable enterprise, the Madroño Foundation, is in many ways a tribute to Heather's spirit and her active engagement with and insatiable curiosity about the world.

Heather Kohout was so many things—public intellectual, mother, wife, friend, philosopher, comedian, supporter of the arts—that it is difficult to define her. The environment was certainly one of her passions, but so were things spiritual. Collected and edited by Martin Kohout, these essays and poems reveal the essence of an extraordinary Texas woman and her outlook on a life filled with wonder. We are proud and honored to include this volume in the Women in Texas History book series sponsored by the Ruthe Winegarten Foundation for Texas Women's History.

—Cynthia J. Beeman and Nancy Baker Jones
General Editors

As a child, date unknown.

Heather with her great-aunt Lizabeth Pritchett, sister Isa, and father Henry E. Catto Jr., El Salvador, early 1970s.

With her women's soccer club, Austin, mid-1980s.

Introduction

In these remarkable essays and poems, I believe the reader can chart the development of an extraordinarily talented and thoughtful writer. Always a sophisticated, generous thinker, Heather's confidence grew and the power of her prose increased over the roughly four years (2009–2013) in which she wrote these essays, years during which we operated a residency program for environmental writers and artists at Madroño Ranch: A Center for Writing, Art, and the Environment, near Medina, Texas.

One thing that did not change over the course of those four years was Heather's absolute refusal to let herself off the hook, or take herself too seriously. Despite her years of experience as a teacher, she never stopped thinking of herself as a student, as someone who would always have more to learn. She was never—well, rarely—prescriptive; her default rhetorical stance was one of astonishment and delight, and she sought to make the reader share in the wonder and joy of her discovery. At the same time, she had an absolutely astonishing ability to think beyond conventional disciplinary boundaries, to make cosmic connections that would never occur to most people. At least, they never would have occurred to me. And yet, once she pointed them out in her thoughtful, frequently hilarious way, they seemed, if not obvious, inevitable. Again and again, when she would give me one of these pieces to post on our website, I would find myself asking, "How in the world does she do that?"

But no one was less full of herself than Heather; perhaps that's why her heart and mind had so much room for others. Sometimes her stubborn refusal to let herself off the hook in even insignificant matters drove me crazy. But the more I reflect on her life, her writing, and her gift for relationship, the more I admire her. She moved through the world with grace and humility and tolerance and insatiable curiosity. I hope these writings can inspire in the reader the desire to do the same.

Heather's literary idols included Wendell Berry and Mary Oliver, two truth-tellers who create works of towering beauty. I believe that Heather, in her own modest way, belongs in their company, though she herself would call such a statement blasphemous. She was concerned, as they are, with what it means to live a good life on this earth, to make the most of the gifts we are given, and how best to show our appreciation for them. She was, like them, showing us how to be better humans.

For all of her brilliance as an essayist, poetry was Heather's first and deepest literary love; when we attended the annual Poetry at Round Top festival, she was agog at the opportunity to rub elbows with literary heroes. I'm not sure she was ever more nervous than when she was asked to introduce Gregory Orr before one of his readings (he is a lovely and gracious man, by the way). Her own poems are knotty and thoughtful, filled as they are with subtle rhythms and internal rhymes; they are occasionally very funny, but always, I believe, worthy of serious contemplation. In them, as in her essays, she wrestles with fundamental questions of existence and belief: what does it mean to be human? To be religious? To be sinful? To be alive? She often bewailed how long it took her to produce these gems, and how hard they were to understand, but that complexity and attention to detail are exactly what make them so extraordinary.

I hope that, for those who did not have the singular good fortune to know Heather during her all-too-brief life, the essays and poems will provide at least some idea of the warmth, humor, goodness, curiosity, and intelligence that shone forth from her.

I may not exactly be objective, but to me these essays and poems exemplify the best of Texas womanhood: stubborn independence, fierce conviction, great good humor, and instinctive kindness. I hope you enjoy them.

THE SHIMMERING IS
ALL THERE IS

With her father,
Henry E. Catto Jr.,
ca. 1980.

With Martin on
graduation day,
Williams College,
Williamstown,
Massachusetts,
1981.

With sister Isa and
brother Will at cousin
Laura Hobby's wedding,
Houston, 1984.

ESSAYS

1

The Wonder and Power of Water

SEPTEMBER 13, 2009

The wonder and power of water in a time of drought are, oddly, matched only in times of flood. The Texas Hill Country is in the grip of a drought unparalleled at least since the 1950s. This drought has been so fierce that cattle going to drink at their accustomed (and empty) tanks have found themselves mired in mud so viscous and vicious that they are unable to extricate themselves from it. Even if ranchers find the cattle before they die of dehydration, they're often as helpless as the foundered cows, unable to do anything but shoot them to relieve their misery.

While at Madroño we've been surveying parched rangeland and dropping water tables with dismay, yet we still have what now is revealed to be the astonishing gift of running water. At the far northwest corner of the property, our intrepid ranch manager Robert Selement and his gang of workers—comprised mostly of his own children—have been cleaning out what we call the trout ponds, which have been choked with silt and vegetation for several decades.

The trout ponds are three dammed pools, each about 70 feet long and 5 to 8 feet deep, which spill over at the end into Slippery Creek, which snakes its way southward down the valley until it flows into Wallace Creek. The water for Slippery Creek comes straight out of the rocks and is mostly routed through a series of lovingly crafted stone holding pens built in the 1970s and intended for raising brown trout.

As it emerges from its heavily shaded, ferny grotto, the water is astonishingly cold, cold enough to make you gasp if you have the nerve to sit in it. By the time it becomes a shallow Slippery Creek, it's pleasantly cool—to anyone but a trout, that is; the breeding venture petered out pretty quickly.

(Much to their mutual surprise, our son Tito managed to pull a trout out of Wallace Creek about ten years ago, but that was the last one we've seen.)

But the beautiful stonework, the soothing sound of falling water, and the rich coolness remain. During this wretchedly hot summer, Robert keeps his workers motivated by working elsewhere during the (relatively) cool mornings and saving work at the trout ponds for the worst of the afternoon's heat. Several of the cracks in the rock that usually leak water are dry now, making the small, steady flow that rises from underground even more remarkable, its apparently modest output sustaining the life and well-being of countless creatures and plants. What a blessing!

2

Dreaming Time

SEPTEMBER 18, 2009

In the mission statement for Madroño Ranch: A Center for Writing, Art, and the Environment ("Inspired by the rhythms of the Texas Hill Country, Madroño Ranch offers writers and artists focused on nature and the environment a source and resource for work and rest, solitude and communion"), the inclusion of the word "rest" is no accident. Here's why:

Joel Salatin, a farmer in Virginia, has developed a philosophy and practicum of farming that is simple and radically countercultural: use the needs and desires of the land, the plants, and the animals to direct farming decisions. As a consequence, his Polyface Farm is not only phenomenally productive, it annually increases the amount of chemical-free topsoil on the land and allows its animals to lead comfortable, healthy, chemical-free lives.

Here's the real point of interest: the farm consists of about 550 contiguous acres, and Salatin and his family intensively farm only about 100 acres. The rest is "unused" forest; his pigs do forage for acorns there, and some of the trees are selectively milled, but about 80 percent of his land is apparently ignored.

This unused land is considered wasted by conventional farming standards, which would have Salatin cut down the forest and expand his operation, but he's convinced that the productivity of his actively farmed land *requires* all those unused acres. They provide the ecological ballast for his doughty craft, helping reduce evaporation in the fields, providing wind breaks, permitting the existence of a complexity of interaction between flora and fauna that supports the entire operation.

Salatin's insistence on the need for this apparently unproductive forest seems to have a parallel in the rhythms of sleeping and waking and the perception in our culture that sleep is time wasted, time that could be used "productively." While some people seem to have a genetic mutation that allows them to sleep less than the general population and still function well, most of us become significantly *less* productive, not more, when we try to cut back on our sleep. Studies show that people become psychotic when deprived of uninterrupted sleep over extended periods; forced wakefulness is a well-known torture technique. (Any college student can tell you this.) Even so, our out-of-kilter culture continues its assault on this maddeningly "unproductive" necessity.

Just as they need to eat, to work, to worship, people—and maybe all creatures—need time dedicated not just to sleeping but to dreaming as well. People whose sleep is subtly interrupted at the dream phase eventually develop the symptoms of those denied all sleep. (I don't think I'm making this up.) Dreaming time, like Salatin's untouched acreage, is necessary to the health and integrity of individual organisms and their ecosystems. I've come to think of the planet's shrinking wilderness as its dreaming time. The list of activities or places declared unproductive by the market culture has grown significantly during my lifetime: time to cook, to play (if you aren't a child, and sometimes if you are), to make music or art (if you're not an expert), to observe a sabbath, to allow plants and animals to grow at their own pace, to make money that benefits whole communities rather than just a few individuals. By consciously using the word "rest" in our mission statement, we want to mount the ramparts and defend the borders of dreaming time.

3

A Mother's Legacy

OCTOBER 16, 2009

The first sparks for the idea of Madroño Ranch: A Center for Writing, Art, and the Environment were kindled about a year ago in conversations with my mother, Jessica Hobby Catto. She has listened carefully and thoughtfully to my sometimes wildly utopian ideas, offering hard-earned practical advice and persistent encouragement.

Her death on September 30 has left me so stunned that I'm having trouble relegating her to the past tense. I am struggling to stay in the present perfect, which refuses to point to a specific time, preferring instead to drift between the present and the past. This grammatical eddy allows me to dawdle a little longer before I face a present and future without her. At the same time, I know that at Madroño her spirit is always present, always past, always future.

My mother's love for the outdoors shaped my life. The first house I remember was on a bluff north of the San Antonio airport, terrain that didn't qualify as even remotely suburban at the time. Since my three siblings and I arrived within six years of each other, my mother must have deemed it a survival strategy to push us out of doors as much as possible. We had no immediate neighbors and spent our time pretending to be lost in the woods, investigating the draws and seasonal creeks that occasionally flooded and kept us home from school, and sliding down the cliff (strictly forbidden) to visit the nearest neighbors who rewarded us with butterscotch candies. The gravel road on which we lived was rural enough that people felt comfortable dumping trash on it. Every few months my mother would send us to drag a large trash can and pick up the trash on the road that we could pick up: we were permitted to leave the large appliances and dead livestock. Her point was—and is—clear: some human interactions with the landscape are unacceptable.

She also taught me that love of place is a perfectly reasonable principle by which to order a life. Converted to the Church of High Altitudes at Cimarroncita Ranch Camp in New Mexico, she began proselytizing to her children in the mid-1960s when we began annual summer treks to Aspen, Colorado. In the requisite station wagon filled with pillows, the reek of Panhandle oil and cattle, and squabbling children, we always stopped at the top of then-unpaved Independence Pass (12,000-plus feet above sea level) to play in the snow.

Aspen then had one paved street, one stop sign, a drug store with a soda fountain, and two fine old movie theaters. What more did we need? On days we didn't hike, my mother shooed us outside to play in the puddles if it was raining or to climb up nearby Aspen Mountain with raincoats or pieces of cardboard upon which we would slide back down the meadow grasses. When my father's career took us away from Texas and to other interesting venues, Colorado was the place we always returned to, my mother's spiritual center. Despite her peripatetic life, she had a profound love of the Roaring Fork Valley, its smells and flowers, its imperious weather changes, the varieties of its wildness. These never ceased to sustain her, and she in turn worked to sustain them through her involvement with various environmental causes, particularly land conservation.

When she was diagnosed with metastatic colon cancer in 2007, my parents began spending more time at their San Antonio home to be near the doctors she most trusted. Since she had long since given her heart and energy to Colorado, I was worried that she would feel unmoored during her time in San Antonio, adding to the discomforts of treatment. As we talked about ways in which she could stay connected to the conservation world she loved, especially in a state like Texas that so dearly values its private property rights, the idea of creating a gathering place for people passionate about nurturing the natural world was born.

I know I will eventually move out of the strange timelessness that hovers around times of death, but never completely. Despite her preference for the mountains, she saw the beauties of the Texas Hill Country and bought the original piece of what has become Madroño Ranch more than fifteen years ago. The blessings she bestowed on me—awareness of human limits, love of place, the place itself—are with me as long as I am here to receive them.

4

Growing Hope

OCTOBER 23, 2009

This summer we attended a screening of *Fresh*, a documentary that highlights the efficiency and productivity of organic farming and the casual cruelty and hidden costs of industrial agriculture. Along with about a hundred others, we watched the film under the pecan trees at Boggy Creek Farm while eating locally sourced vegetarian picnic dinners provided by the Alamo Drafthouse, one of the screening's cosponsors. (The others were *Edible Austin* and our friend Steve Kinney's Front Porch Project.)

This kind of setting induces feelings of satisfaction that can all too easily morph into self-righteousness, and there's no question that this event was a classic case of preaching to the choir. One of Boggy Creek's neighbors' front yards frequently sports a sign demanding housing for the homeless, not food for the rich. There's no question that the momentum behind the local/sustainable food movement has been slowed by the argument that it's a movement for the dainty tastes of the economic elite.

Fresh delivers a powerful counterpunch—maybe even a KO—in the person and work of Will Allen, whose nonprofit Growing Power Inc. operates two acres of greenhouses in working-class Milwaukee, producing mountains of affordable, healthy food, and trains countless inner-city residents to convert empty lots into thriving organic food centers.

The son of a sharecropper, Allen believes with every fiber of his six foot seven inch body that healthy food is primarily a social justice issue: income should have no bearing on access to quality food. He himself is a happy consumer of doughnuts and doesn't condemn those who have no alternative to KFC, but his passion for fresh food is altering the urban landscape and the food choices of thousands of people who might otherwise face a future of obesity and diabetes.

We're no experts on food pricing, but we would guess that Growing Power enjoys a pricing "advantage" over other organic farmers because of grant money and a sizable volunteer labor pool. Agribusiness is able to control costs through government subsidies. What if the playing field on which organic and industrial agriculture compete were level? If organics were subsidized? If the costs of the ecological devastation caused by agribusiness monocultures, manure cesspools, and the health issues resulting from fast foods were factored into the cost of "cheap" food?

Before the 1962 publication of Rachel Carson's *Silent Spring*, many considered conservation a hobby for the wealthy. Carson made clear the connection between environmental issues and civil rights. We hope that people like Will Allen and movies like *Fresh* will do the same for the local/sustainable food movement.

After the screening at Boggy Creek, *Edible Austin* sold copies of the movie on DVD, along with licensing agreements allowing purchasers to show it to groups of up to twenty people—neighborhood gatherings, church groups, book clubs, etc. Through this bottom-up, grassroots, guerilla marketing campaign, the producers hope to spread the word far beyond those hundred or so predominantly White, relatively wealthy faces under the trees. We bought two copies, one for Robert and one for us.

5

"Everywhere There's Lots of Piggies ..."

OCTOBER 30, 2009

I sometimes find myself feeling a little defensive about the Texas Hill Country. In the summer of 1981, after we graduated from college in Massachusetts, Martin, a San Francisco native, and I drove across the country via Texas. Somewhere around Bastrop, I said, "Well, we're at the eastern edge of the Hill Country."

"Really?" he said. "So where are the hills?"

Okay, so our hills are a little stumpy and our landscape a little scruffy, and most of the fauna (and much of the flora) will scratch, sting, or bite you. But at least we can proudly boast that nobody's got more feral hogs than we do.

Hogs are always lurking in the background of life at Madroño—and frequently in the foreground as well. They're smart, secretive, social, fierce, and remarkably fecund; a sow can have two, and sometimes three, litters of eight a year. Robert, the ranch manager, figures that his wife Sherry shot the Madroño heavyweight title holder, which tipped the scales at about 400 pounds, and they can get significantly bigger than that. They have no predators other than humans, whom they generally leave alone. Dogs, however, they consider fair game. These hogs are expert at slashing their tusks in an upward arc, where they can easily intersect a dog's jugular or stomach with deadly results.

One fall day a couple of years ago, my brother-in-law Daniel and I, along with his intrepid dog Mojo, were walking along the top of the property. Mojo is an unspecified breed, maybe part wolverine, low to the ground with a long heavy coat, and utterly fearless. The minute he heard porcine snorting in a nearby cedar brake, he charged, even as Daniel and I screamed for him to stop. For the next few heartbeats of eternity we yelled and listened to the invisible fight as it receded down a draw. Sure that Mojo was a goner, we trudged sadly downhill to break the horrible news to my sister Isa—Daniel's wife—and their young children.

So when Mojo popped out of the brush halfway down, he received an ecstatic and extended hero's welcome. His ruff was stiff with pig spit; his thick fur had saved him from what were doubtless multiple tusk slashes. Many dogs aren't so lucky.

Here's one good thing about hogs: they make delicious sausage. Here's another good thing about them: they're omnivorous, eating even snakes. Here's a(nother) bad thing: they love grubs, especially if those grubs are under wet grass. Carefully tended yards can look like a demonic rototiller has let loose its evil fury after a rain or a watering, the grass torn up and plowed under in great sheets. Robert once got so furious at the persistent destruction of the lawn he'd tended so carefully at the lake house that he vowed to sleep there until he'd hunted the culprits down. After four nights and increasingly plaintive appeals from the family he'd abandoned, Robert admitted defeat. "Those pigs outsmarted me and whupped my ass in the lake house yard," he said ruefully. "It was a humbling experience."

6

Carnivorocity

NOVEMBER 13, 2009

Since we're in the early planning stages for our first Madroño Ranch bison harvest, I've been reflecting on issues of carnivorocity, which my spell-checker tells me isn't a word. It suggests "carnivorousness" instead. But I prefer my neologism because it retains echoes of the ferocity that undergirds all meat eating.

I have been a happy meat eater all my life, with the exception of my senior year in college, when I chose to be a vegetarian for financial and lifestyle rather than ethical reasons. Although I still eat meat, I've grown increasingly troubled by the system that produces most of it in the United States, and no longer eat meat at most restaurants or from supermarkets.

In some ways, I think that vegetarians may be more evolved than meat eaters. According to Genesis, *all* creatures—not just humans—were vegetarians in the beginning. God said, "See, I have given you every plant yielding seed that is upon the face of the earth, and every tree with seed in it for fruit. And to every beast of the earth, and every bird of the air, and to everything that creeps on the earth, everything that has the breath of life, I have given every green plant for food" (Genesis 1:29–30). Thus modern vegetarians are hearkening back to their Edenic roots, to a human dominion over nature that reflected the aboriginal harmony and mutual respect among species—unless, of course, you happened to be a green plant.

But the story became more complicated, as good stories always do. As punishment for various transgressions, God sent a flood that only Noah and the passengers on his ark survived. In thanksgiving, Noah built an altar to the Lord and made of every clean animal and bird (although this was before the laws differentiating clean from unclean) a burnt offering. When

God "smelled the pleasing odor, he said in his heart, 'I will never again curse the ground because of humankind'" (Genesis 8:21). From that time on, humans were given animals for food, with the stipulation that they should not eat flesh that still had blood in it.

Complicated? My goodness, yes. Eating meat is God's concession to the fact that something in the original balance of the world has been thrown out of whack—and that the smell of cooking meat is profoundly satisfying. Those who can resist the lure of barbecue are made of sterner stuff than God! The line between vegetarians and meat eaters is the line between self-identified utopianists and realists—or between utopianists and people who don't think about the issue. I tend toward the utopian end of the spectrum. So why do I eat meat?

In his fascinating book *The River Cottage Meat Book*, British chef and farmer Hugh Fearnley-Whittingstall points out that scripture has been used to justify the most heinous acts, including the abuse of animals for human consumption. He finds the "commitment to eliminate the pain and suffering of animals at the hands of humans . . . to be morally superior to the commitment to ignore it." But he also finds the pro-vegetarian argument based on the desire to eliminate the pain and suffering of animals unconvincing. Animals inevitably suffer, even without human intervention. He points out that "dying of old age" rarely occurs in nature, and that wild animals are quite likely to end their lives as food for something.

Eating meat is a reminder that we belong to the system over which we exercise dominion. We are not above the law that ordered the universe; we do not lie outside the natural order. Not long ago I took a cooking class from Jesse Griffiths of Dai Due, one that took a chicken "from *gallina* to *pollo*," as our daughter Elizabeth put it. We started with two live roosters, which we were to kill, pluck, and clean. After Jesse showed us how to hold a rooster upside down—which disorients and calms it—he put it headfirst into a lopped-off traffic cone and slit its jugular. The whole business took ten seconds or less per bird and was strangely intimate, giving me an insight into some of the labyrinthine dietary and purity laws in Leviticus. Surely we are meant to eat meat with a profound awareness of the sacrifice that doing so entails. As usual, no one has said it better than Wendell Berry:

> *I have taken in the light*
> *that quickened eye and leaf.*

May my brain be bright with praise
of what I eat, in the brief blaze
of motion and of thought.
May I be worthy of my meat.

Though it is tempting to let St. Wendell have the last word, there's much more to be said on the topic of eating meat. Jonathan Safran Foer's new book, *Eating Animals*, has generated a significant buzz; if you Google "foer eating animals," you get 961,000 results. Foer spent three years investigating meat production in the United States, factory farming in particular. Although he himself is a vegan, he says that he has no interest in converting anyone to veganocity; he just wants people to think about where their food—specifically, their meat—comes from.

Although I haven't come to his vegan, or even vegetarian, conclusions, I think Foer is right. (Ahem. I haven't read the book.) In fact, awareness of and gratitude for the sacrifice required to satisfy the appetite of the meat eater—awareness that demands, for those who are to be sacrificed, a life of comfort in the world to which they are adapted—should be extended to vegetables as well; after all, even vegans require sacrifice—it's just not as messy. By the very act of eating, all creatures—including, most emphatically, humans—participate in the circle of sacrifice, and a circle it most assuredly is; in nature, there is no such thing as a free lunch.

What sacrifice, then, is demanded of us? This year's edition of *The Best American Essays*, edited by Mary Oliver, includes an essay by Wendell Berry titled "Faustian Economics," originally published in *Harper's Magazine*. In it, Berry rails against the American propensity to confuse personal freedom with unlimited consumption, a fantasy that perhaps arose due to the intersection of the Industrial Revolution with the discovery of vast natural resources in the American West. As a nation, we're confronting the end of this fantasy and "entering a time of inescapable limits"—an opportunity, according to Berry, to become reacquainted with traditional definitions of humanness. By their very nature, humans are, well, natural, and therefore limited. What distinguishes us from other animals (although I think this topic is being hotly debated) is our capacity for *self*-limitation, *self*-restraint, particularly as it is "implied in neighborliness, stewardship, thrift, temperance, generosity, care, kindness, friendship, loyalty, and love."

As long as we base our identity on limitlessness, we deny an essential—

and liberating—element of our humanity. As long as we base that funda-
mentally human activity, commerce, on fantasies of limitlessness, it will
be inhuman and inhumane, what Berry calls an "economy of community
destruction." Instead, he would have us cultivate a mindfulness of human
limits—agricultural, economic, medical, technological, scientific—in order
to reclaim "the knowledge that some things, though limited, are inexhaust-
ible." He cites intact ecosystems like working forests and farms that give
inexhaustibly, given the practice of human self-restraint. He compares this
practice to the willing submission of artists to the constraints of their art
forms—the poet to the sonnet, the painter to the canvas. The work that
arises from this sort of discipline has the capacity to feed us inexhaustibly, a
capacity we've all experienced when revisiting favorite novels or symphonies
or buildings.

The title of Berry's essay comes from Christopher Marlowe's *Tragical
History of Doctor Faustus*, first published in 1604, in which Faustus sells
his soul to Lucifer in exchange for knowledge and power. What Faustus
learns—or, more accurately, refuses to learn—is that the human mind
and soul are and ought to be subject to limits. When creatures refuse to
acknowledge limits, hell is born.

So how do we practice the self-restraint necessary to maintain our
humanity? Some, like Foer, argue that abstaining from eating meat is a
logical and reasonable sacrifice. I don't disagree with him, but I don't think
there's a single way to humane self-restraint. Many indigenous cultures
have focused on—even worshipped—the animals that fed them, Native
Americans and bison being a case in point.

I'm not sure any of this will mean much to those people and businesses
that value scale and efficiency over humanness. Nor will it mean much
to most Americans accustomed to the availability of cheap meat at every
meal. But, with Berry, I believe that our humanity is at stake in the choices
we make when we eat. When we choose to abet the suffering of animals
and ecosystems to feed ourselves, we whittle away at our own humanness.
When we choose to limit our choices, we paradoxically open ourselves to
the possibility of inexhaustible plenty.

Sounds like a deal to me.

7

James Cameron, Alexis de Tocqueville, and the Nature of Nature

JANUARY 15, 2010

In a recent op-ed column in the *New York Times*, Ross Douthat examines the underlying values of James Cameron's movie *Avatar* and links it to a tide of pantheism coursing through Hollywood in particular and America in general. As a nation, Douthat argues, we have almost from our inception tended to collapse distinctions and seek unity, a tendency Alexis de Tocqueville noted in the 1830s:

> *When the conditions of society are becoming more equal . . . [t]he idea of unity so possesses man and is sought by him so generally that if he thinks he has found it, he readily yields himself to repose in that belief. Not content with the discovery that there is nothing in the world but a creation and a Creator, he is still embarrassed by this primary division of things and seeks to expand and simplify his conception by including God and the universe in one great whole.*

We Americans, it seems, are born to pantheism as the sparks fly upward. Douthat believes that we should fight, or at least question, this impulse. He doubts whether nature "actually deserves a religious response." The traditional monotheistic religions confront the problem of evil, struggling to reconcile a loving creator with suffering and death. Pantheism can't address this basic human concern, according to Douthat, because nature "*is* suffering and death. Its harmonies require violence. Its 'circle of life' is really a cycle of mortality." Religion, he believes, exists in part to pull self-conscious humanity, simultaneously of nature and outside it, out of this tragic cycle. Without religion—Christianity, for Douthat—there is no escape "upward," only a downward abandonment of our consciousness. Pantheism leaves us with only dust and ashes.

Since the Madroño Ranch mission and vision statements[1] rest comfortably on a foundation of Christian pantheism—defined as finding God in all things—I can't help but respond. Here's why I think Douthat's definition of Christianity and its relationship to the material world—i.e., nature—needs to be questioned.

Christianity arose at the confluence of two distinct and, in some ways, contradictory traditions: Judaism, which tended to see the divine as simultaneously transcendent and thoroughly enmeshed with created matter, and Platonism, which opposed the corruption of the material to the purity of the eternal. The Nicene Creed, adopted in 325, endorsed the latter view by asserting the doctrine of *creatio ex nihilo*, which asserts that creation did not arise from eternally preexisting materials and that God created the universe from scratch.

The poetic cosmology of the creed, however, left room for multiple interpretations. My personal favorite comes from Maximus the Confessor (c. 580–662), who set the scene for Eastern Orthodoxy and declared that Jesus was the first person to become fully human and thus, paradoxically, divine. Jesus thereby reopened the clogged conduit between the created and divine realms, and his call to humanity is to live fully, as he did, into the image of the divine imprinted in all of us. Western Christianity, however, preferred a top-down model in which the initiative for divine-mortal interaction was exclusively unilateral, leaving humanity in the dust, so to speak.

I present this radically reductive, tongue-in-cheek summary to suggest that the relationship between God and creation (and humanity and the rest

---

1. *Mission*: Inspired by the rhythms of the Texas Hill Country, Madroño Ranch: A Center for Writing, Art, and the Environment offers writers and artists focused on the environment a source and resource for work and rest, solitude and communion.

Vision: Believing in the intelligence and elegance of nature, we envision a world in which creative thinkers devise and articulate ways of aligning human commerce and consciousness more closely with the environment that nourishes and sustains us. Madroño Ranch: A Center for Writing, Art, and the Environment supports this vision by bringing people together to work, eat, converse, and rest in a setting that resonates with the rhythms of the land, water, and sky. The operations and activities of Madroño Ranch will be economically self-sustaining, to the greatest degree possible, and will exemplify balanced respect for and awareness of community and place.

of creation) may be more complicated than some Western Christians (like Douthat) believe. Shortly after reading Douthat's column, I read another recent *New York Times* article by Natalie Angier. In it, she describes research being conducted on the complexity of plants, specifically on "their keen sensitivity to the environment, the speed with which they react to changes in the environment, and the extraordinary number of tricks that plants will rally to fight off attackers and solicit help from afar." Says one researcher, "Even if you have quite a bit of knowledge about plants, it's still surprising to see how sophisticated they can be." Attributes we've always ascribed to humans alone seem to be much more widely spread than anyone imagined, moving out of the animal kingdom, even. Using and eating plants may be a much more fraught enterprise than we'd supposed. If the right relationship between humans and animals has inspired a multigenerational series of philosophical and theological contortions, what will happen when we find that algae are, like us, just a little lower than the angels?

One of the things that's becoming clear to this utter nonscientist and spastic theologian is that the created order becomes more intricate and surprising the more we study it, repeatedly requiring us to question assumptions that we had thought were beyond questioning. "Your job as a scientist is to find out how you're fooling yourself," says astrophysicist Saul Perlmutter. I would say this is true in most human endeavors, most particularly if you're claiming knowledge of God. (Which I do all the time. I figure God has got to be a bossy oldest daughter, like me.) Does nature deserve a religious response? How can it not?

Douthat may have been saying that nature is not worthy of worship, but worship is not the only religious response available to us. According to many Christian thinkers (and doers), we are called to love even our enemies because they too are formed in the image of God. What might it mean to find the image of God outside the narrow confines of humanity? Surely we would need to love that image with the same constancy and self-discipline required to love our irritating fellow humans. Rather than trapping us in the tragic cycle of mortality, this kind of commitment—to love the natural world as we would love God, our neighbors, and ourselves—strikes me as precisely what leads to wisdom, even if it means collapsing traditional distinctions (sorry, Alexis!) between heaven and earth.

8

Massachusetts, Part I
Of Books and Houses and Hospitality

JANUARY 29, 2010

On our very brief trip to Massachusetts last weekend, Martin and I drove straight from Boston's Logan Airport to Concord in hopes of glimpsing one of the hotbeds of American utopian thinking before the winter sun set. Driving through snowy woods and by quaint (and probably drafty) colonial homes, it was clear that we were a loooong way from Texas.

On the plane, Martin was reading a compilation of Henry David Thoreau's writings. Martin reading is not an unusual sight. Noteworthy was the fact that he was underlining in the book, something I have never seen him do in nearly thirty years of pretty continuous association. (Our ongoing "discussion" over the propriety of marking up books could well be the subject of another essay.) For the first time, he just couldn't help himself; Thoreau's aphoristic and slyly funny prose begged for some kind of physical interaction. In the same vein, he required me to listen or read for myself what so tickled him. Thoreau's spirit, utterly inaccessible to Martin (and me) when *Walden* was assigned reading in high school, was suddenly uncontainable and had to be shared.

I found this slightly annoying. The snippets I heard and read clashed with what I was reading on the plane, Lorrie Moore's *A Gate at the Stairs*, a somewhat dystopian novel about post-9/11 life in a midwestern university town, narrated by a woman student raised on a nearby farm by early organic-minded parents. Thoreau's mid-nineteenth-century voice felt arch and artificial in comparison, and the contrast was grating, like walking from a quiet, dim study into the brightly lit noise of a teenager's room. But the shock of seeing Martin underline in a book stunned me into keeping, just barely, a receptive ear.

We conquered the tangle of highways to Concord with only a few wrong turns. Walking into Orchard House, the Alcott home (Louisa May, Bronson, et al.), at 2:58 and knowing that it closed at three, we played the we've-traveled-so-far card and won a wonderful private tour with a sympathetic and knowledgeable docent. Although *Little Women* may have a sentimental ring to twenty-first-century ears, it resonates with the profoundly utopian thinking—and physically taxing reality—of the world Louisa May Alcott lived in. Orchard House showed signs of both worlds: charming eccentricities (Louisa's sister May's sweet pre-Raphaelite pencil drawings on her bedroom walls) and structural frailties (buckling floors, chilly drafts).

Bronson Alcott, Louisa's father, was a visionary of the first order, rarely concerning himself with such practicalities as earning enough money to feed and shelter his family, and thereby propelling Louisa into the unusual role of supporting her family financially with her writing. As a teacher, Alcott developed a race- and gender-neutral child-centered pedagogy that most people found scandalous, even immoral, and that most Americans today take for granted. He helped establish a commune, Fruitlands, an early back-to-nature effort, which failed quickly but interested many other questing spirits of the time, Ralph Waldo Emerson, Nathaniel Hawthorne, and Thoreau among them. He was a frequent contributor to the Transcendentalist journal *The Dial* and was often mocked for his opaque prose, and yet the influence of American Transcendentalism, especially in the environmental movement, is still alive and kicking today. It was a tour worth taking and a house worth visiting.

From the Alcott home we drove to Walden Pond in the waning light. I've heard many people express the same dismay on seeing Walden Pond they do when they see the Alamo ("it's so small!"), but it's several times the size of the "lake" at Madroño Ranch, so I wasn't at all disappointed. We crunched through the snow along the edge, noting the space between the pond's ice and the shore while watching two men out on the ice doing something indecipherable with unidentifiable equipment. As the heatless sun began to sink behind the trees, we came to the spot where Thoreau built his cabin, now marked only by low concrete posts, although his words remain carved on a nearby wooden sign: "I went to the woods because I wished to live deliberately, to front only the essential facts of life, and see if I could not learn what it had to teach, and not, when I came to die, discover that I had not lived." As I stood there beating my hands together and stamping my frozen feet, I wondered if on a monochromatic winter afternoon like this Thoreau would have hightailed it to Emerson's house for a little warm food and company, as apparently he was wont to do.

Later, as we sat in a blessedly warm house in Wellesley, I began reading Martin's volume of Thoreau and found myself beguiled, first by the slightly fustian voice of Joseph Wood Krutch, who wrote the introduction, and then by Thoreau's own words, until Martin rather selfishly reclaimed his book. I went back to my literary farm girl, reading about the role of her father's farm in her recovery from multiple heartbreaks.

This week, while waddling around Austin's Lady Bird Lake (a body of water as beloved to me as Walden Pond was to Thoreau), I found myself thinking about Martin's spontaneous overflow of powerful underlining and the odd stability of words, their capacity to be sturdy dwelling places despite their formless origins in the tohubohu of the human spirit. (Isn't "tohubohu" a word you can live in? I do, actually, since it means chaos.) Martin's invitation on the plane for me to join him in Thoreau's house was a kind of evangelism, the best kind: a delighted discovery that clamors to be shared. Even though I was seated happily in Lorrie Moore's house (which, with its love of place, is built on top of Thoreau's) with all the doors closed and blinds drawn, Martin convinced me that the house Thoreau built was so splendid that I had to go in—which I did, grudgingly at first, but with increasing pleasure.

Hospitality from so many quarters: from the kind docent at Orchard House; between the walls of books; from my tickled husband; from the friend of a friend who opened her house to us; even in the cold empty space in Walden Woods marked off by the Massachusetts Department of Conservation and Recreation. Thoreau reached out from the past and invited us into its tohubohu, asking for our response and drawing from us a tiny new creation. Not bad for a crusty, allegedly misanthropic Yankee.

9

Massachusetts, Part II

Take a Walk on the Wild Side

FEBRUARY 19, 2010

A Very Long Time Ago, my mother brought home a Peter Max–style poster with this quotation from Henry David Thoreau: "In wilderness is the preservation of the world." Each time we moved, its reappearance was an indication that I was home again despite the bewildering newness of my surroundings. Thanks to this poster, I associated "wilderness" with "home."

During our recent and ongoing Thoreau binge, I discovered, disconcertingly, that the poster has it wrong. The quotation comes from Thoreau's essay "Walking," initially delivered as a (very long) lecture in 1851 and published posthumously in the *Atlantic Monthly* in 1862. "I wish to speak a word for nature, for absolute Freedom and Wildness, as contrasted with a freedom and Culture merely civil," he begins. Walking is civilized humanity's entrée into nature, but Thoreau's notion of walking is highly particular: "I have met with but one or two persons in the course of my life who understood the art of Walking, that is, of taking walks, who had a genius, so to speak, for *sauntering*." For Thoreau, to walk in nature was to be a pilgrim, a *sainte-terrer*, simultaneously seeking the holy land and already graced: "It requires a direct dispensation from heaven to become a walker." Clearly, according to Thoreau, hoofing it to the neighborhood grocery store to pick up a loaf of bread does not qualify as walking.

Nor does walking have anything to do with exercise or taking a break. Walking requires attention. "It is of no use to direct our steps to the woods, if they do not carry us thither. I am alarmed when it happens that I have walked a mile into the woods bodily, without getting there in spirit. . . . The thought of some work will run in my head, and I am not where my body is; I am out of my senses." Rather, he says, "you must walk like a camel, which is said to be the only beast which ruminates when walking." (That's a joke, I think.)

Thoreau found that his preferred direction for a walk was almost always southwestward. "It is hard for me to believe that I shall find fair landscapes or sufficient Wildness and freedom behind the eastern horizon. . . . I must walk toward Oregon, and not toward Europe." There is something specifically American in his way of walking, and he predicts that walks through the American landscape will form the American soul: "I trust that we shall be more imaginative; that our thoughts will be clearer, fresher and more ethereal, as our sky—our understanding more comprehensive and broader, like our plains—our intellect generally on a grander scale, like our thunder and lightning, our rivers and mountains and forests—and our hearts shall even correspond in breadth and depth and grandeur to our inland seas."

He has nothing against civilization, culture, education, the arts, but he felt that they all rely on something unexpected: "The West of which I speak is but another name for the Wild; and what I have been preparing to say is, that in Wildness is the preservation of the world."

Here is where this Thoreauvian saunter has led us, gentle reader—back to that poster. In *Wildness*, not wilderness, is the preservation of the world.

I think the distinction is enormously important. "Wilderness" implies an external state; "wildness" is as easily internal as external. Thoreau didn't want to erase human culture; rather, he sensed that it required wildness, both psychic and physical, in order to flourish.

In one of those beneficent coincidences, I put down Thoreau's essay a couple of Sundays ago and discovered an article in the *New York Times Magazine* titled "Is There an Ecological Unconscious?" The article described a somewhat inchoate field of study in which a clear link is made between human mental health and the health of wild nature. Glenn Albrecht, a philosopher and professor of sustainability at Murdoch University in Perth, Australia, has coined the term "solastalgia" to designate "the pain experienced when there is recognition that the place where one resides and that one loves is under immediate assault . . . a form of homesickness one gets when one is still at home." A growing number of psychologists agree with Albrecht's assertion that there is a direct connection between environmental degradation and mental illness. One of them calls not just for intact ecosystems that include large predators but for a "re-wilding of the psyche," a term perhaps more appealing to poets and transcendentalists than to funders of academic research.

It's an interesting proposition. What does a re-wilded psyche look like? In his book *Monster of God: The Man-Eating Predator in the Jungles of History and the Mind*, David Quammen muses on the merits of what he calls "alpha predators," among them lions, grizzly bears, Nile crocodiles, reticulated pythons, and white sharks. He considers mythical creatures as well, particularly Leviathan as he appears in the book of Job. In examining this uncomfortable perspective on humanity as meal instead of master, Quammen wants us to consider the crucial role this perspective has played "in shaping the way we humans construe our place in the natural world." In short, it's important for us to know ourselves as part, not masters, of the food chain. Why? For the same reason God beats Job over the head with questions about Leviathan: who can tame such a furious beast? Can Job? Duh, no. The man-eaters remind us of the life-promoting necessity of humility. As dangerous as they are, the destruction of man-eaters, or even their relegation to zoos, would be more dangerous: we might thus be further encouraged to behave as if we were masters of the universe—a time-tested guarantee for misrule if there ever was one.

A human psyche that resonates with, or trembles at, the roars of actual alpha predators is likely to be awake in a particular way, awake to its own contingency. (If you haven't read Mary Oliver's "Alligator Poem," now is definitely the time to do so.) Years ago, walking in the back reaches of Madroño Ranch, Martin and I heard the unmistakable scream of a mountain lion. I've never reentered that canyon—especially when I'm alone—without taking a deep breath.

So back to the misquotation. As much as I love that old poster, and as vital as I think wilderness is, I think Thoreau got it right. Without access to wildness, without knowing the necessity of bowing before it, we cease to be fully human. And if we can't fully inhabit our humanity, what home is left for us?

10

Mapping the Geography of Hope
Our Place in the Wilderness
MARCH 12, 2010

Last week, during a visit to San Francisco that also took us to the nearby Djerassi Resident Artists Program, Martin and I spent a day exploring the Point Reyes National Seashore with his childhood friends Brad and Hans. Before setting off on our hike, we wandered into Point Reyes Books and wandered out again with the first two volumes of the *West Marin Review*, a nifty literary journal whose inaugural issue considers Wallace Stegner's claim that

> *we simply need . . . wild country available to us, even if we never do more than drive to its edge and look in. For it can be a means of reassuring ourselves of our sanity as creatures, a part of the geography of hope.*

Even if I can't give coordinates for the geography of hope, I like the idea that it might exist on some map buried deep under the mess in my brain's glove compartment. In current mainstream environmental thinking, however, humans and wilderness cannot exist together because humans are an inevitable contaminant. Having spent the drive from San Francisco to Point Reyes with my face glued to the car window taking in an enticing new vocabulary of birds, I'd like to think that the geography of hope includes a place where humans are part of wilderness, not set off from it.

Our hike took us north between Tomales Bay and the ocean, through herds of tule elk, watching waves crash on the rocky shore and tender crocuses and poppies huddled in the chilly wind. As we returned to the parking lot at Pierce Point Ranch, we heard the whine of chainsaws; the Park Service was taking down an enormous Monterey cypress, maybe 75 feet tall. The presence of rot in some branches posed a threat to the uninhabited cluster of historic ranch buildings at the head of the trail. The decision to cut down the tree seemed iconic of the destruction endemic to human activity in the natural world.

So it was with interest that I saw an essay in the *West Marin Review* titled "The Fiction of Wilderness," by Mark Dowie, the former editor and publisher of *Mother Jones*. Dowie suggests that the Wilderness Act of 1964 set in stone the idea that wilderness was best preserved by balkanizing large tracts of land and ejecting any permanent residents who might have lived there, as the Miwok tribe was ejected from Yosemite. He says this creates "a commodified wilderness . . . a deliberate charade, a culturally constructed neo-Edenic narrative played out for weary human urbanites yearning for the open frontier their ancestors 'discovered' then tamed—a place to absorb the sounds and images of virgin nature and forget for a moment the thoroughly unnatural lives they lead." (Ouch.)

But Dowie suggests an alternative. His research revealed that many aboriginal peoples have nothing analogous to the Western conception of wilderness and were stumped when he tried to explain it to them. The closest equivalents in their languages were domesticated ones: "backyard," "big farmyard," "food," or "pantry." There was, in other words, no sense of separation between the people and the landscapes they lived in. Dowie quotes a Tarahumaran ethnoecologist from Mexico who says that in his culture the landscape is granted the same love and affection as family, resulting in a "kincentric ecology."

Dowie hopes that environmentalist notions of wilderness can change to include the possibility of human activity intimately embedded within the land in a mutually profitable relationship. When we see ourselves as apart from a pristine nature that exists outside the bonds of kinship, we are more likely to commodify and exploit it.

Serendipitously, my reading took me from the *West Marin Review* to a publication that our friends Hugh and Sarah Fitzsimons of Thunder Heart Bison gave me just before we left for San Francisco. Titled *Five Ways to Value the Working Landscapes of the West*, it may not rise immediately to the top of the *New York Times* best-seller list, although it makes for compelling reading. The first essay, "In Praise, and in Appraisal, of the Working Landscapes of the West," begins with this heartening pronouncement: "The simplest fact about Western ranches tends to be the one which most folks tend to forget: raising range-fed livestock is one of the few economic activities that produces food—and potentially ecosystem health and financial wealth—by keeping landscapes relatively wild, diverse, and resilient."

We're planning our first bison harvest in the near future and have hopes of developing a food culture that will feed whoever happens to be staying at Madroño Ranch and perhaps others in the immediate community as well. Our concern can't stop at our bellies, though; what feeds us must be fed as well, and well fed. The essay's authors, Gary Paul Nabhan and Ken Meter, write of working landscapes:

> If we commit ourselves to eating their bounty, we derive a good portion of our nourishment from the very ground on which we stand. We do not stand apart [my emphasis] from the energy and water flows of our home ground. Instead, they work through us, and we work because of them. The land is not mere scenery suitable only for tourism and leisure. It is a functioning community in which we either live well or poorly, depending on how efficiently and conservatively we participate in the land's work.

And then, as the clincher, they quote my new hero Henry David Thoreau: "Perhaps we are here to 'meet the expectations of the land' and not the other way around."

This whole essay may be nothing more than a stem-winding rationalization for contaminating the rapidly disappearing Texas wilderness. But I hate the idea that there is no room for an ongoing and mutually satisfying exchange between the landscape and its human inhabitants. We need guides to lead us from here to there, though, guides who know both the intimate history of the land and the capacities and limits of new technologies. Increasingly, these guides are ranchers like Hugh and Sarah who cherish their working landscapes and who, in return, receive its abundance, even in lean times. We'd like Madroño Ranch to find its own place in this geography of hope.

11

Sorry, Dad
Wilderness and Government Regulation
MARCH 26, 2010

Harmonic convergences have ordained that I'm not done pondering wilderness yet.

For my recent piece on "Mapping the Geography of Hope: Our Place in the Wilderness," I once again used a quotation without having read its source. My latest hit-and-run involved Wallace Stegner's oft-repeated phrase "the geography of hope." I didn't think I'd left the phrase gasping for the air of its original context, but this week I backtracked and read Stegner's famous 1960 "Wilderness Letter," which argued powerfully that the federal government should set aside sweeping tracts of wilderness to remain largely untouched by human hands. Since my piece had expressed the modest hope that private landowners, especially responsible ranchers, could be full participants in, rather than obstacles to, wilderness preservation, I thought, "Oh, help and bother!"

Then my sister forwarded me a lovely email from her friend Karin Teague, who noted that "we as a species are SO far from understanding and practicing living harmoniously with the land, with all our technological toys and need for speed and basic greed, THANK GOODNESS we had visionary thinkers like John Muir and Aldo Leopold who advocated for wilderness protection, otherwise we would have lost forever so many extraordinary landscapes." Help and BOTHER.

Finally came the news of Stewart Udall's death. As secretary of the interior, Udall presided over the passage of the Wilderness Act of 1964, the act that Stegner's letter helped bring into existence, the act by which the government protected millions of acres from our "need for speed and basic greed"—a piece of legislation that not only kept foundational landscapes untouched but advanced the idea that such landscapes have been necessary to the formation of the American character. Alright already!

To move ahead, I first need to move back. I am the product of a politically mixed marriage (Democratic mother, Republican father), though I have generally landed on my mother's side, or somewhat to her left, most of the time. But learning about the hoops that our friends who are small farmers, ranchers, and chefs must jump through in order to keep up with rules designed primarily for agribusiness, I've begun foaming at the mouth over government regulation, which pleases my father. Our Madroño adventure has taught me about the daunting bureaucratic gauntlet through which community-minded entrepreneurs must run, and it gets my dander, hackles, and dyspepsia up.

These producers often see their customers every day and consequently feel a profound personal connection and responsibility to them. But they're forced to run the same maze of regulations as do the agribusiness giants who don't know me from Adam. Agribusiness's faceless relationships with its customers are driven by the bottom line, a much more tangible measure of success than the idealistic-sounding yardsticks of community or environmental well-being. But my farming and ranching friends, whom I see every week at market, know that we are intricately bound together at many levels, not merely at the bottom line. Our health—economic, environmental, familial, personal—is a package deal. None of us prospers unless we all do.

So, yes, I've learned to be skeptical of government regulation. And yet, and yet . . . government shapes not just the reality of America but the idea of America as well. As much as I hate stupid regulations, I hate even more the possibility that, without some external restraints, our apparently insatiable appetites might destroy the very source of our richest symbols and concrete sense of liberty.

In his Wilderness Letter, Stegner wrote,

> *Something will go out of us as a people if we ever let the remaining wilderness be destroyed; if we permit the last virgin forests to be turned into comic books and plastic cigarette cases; if we drive the few remaining members of the wild species into zoos or to extinction; if we pollute the last clean air and dirty the last clean streams and push*

our paved roads through the last of the silence, so that never again
will Americans be free in their own country from the noise, the ex-
hausts, the stinks of human and automotive waste. And so that never
again can we have the chance to see ourselves . . . [as] part of the
environment of trees and rocks and soil, brother to the other animals,
part of the natural world and competent to belong in it. Without
any remaining wilderness we are committed wholly, without chance
for even momentary reflection and rest, to the headlong drive into
our technological termite-life, the Brave New World of a complete-
ly man-controlled environment. We need wilderness preserved—as
much of it as is still left, and as many kinds—because it was the
challenge against which our character as a people was formed.

Flying over West Texas not long ago, I noticed that parts of the Permian Basin have been carved up into thousands of—well, I'm not sure what. I saw a network of dirt roads leading to what looked like empty squares of bare earth, which I presume are somehow connected to the oil and gas industry.

I know, I know: it's not as if the Permian Basin was the Garden of Eden before. So what have we lost by carving up this cussedly dry and famously inhospitable landscape? Back to Stegner:

Let me say something on the subject of the kind of wilderness worth
preserving. Most of those areas contemplated are in the national for-
ests and in high mountain country. . . . But for spiritual renewal,
the recognition of identity, the birth of awe, other kinds will serve
every bit as well. Perhaps because they are less friendly to life, more
abstractly nonhuman, they will serve even better.

Texans have traditionally prided themselves on their ability to subdue and conquer even the most unpromising land—to make it pay, whether through cotton or cattle or petroleum. One of the unfortunate effects of this pride has been to minimize the value of the land as it exists before being "improved." We treat it like, well, dirt, and not like our patrimony. In such cases, it seems that government, as Udall and his allies saw, is the only answer to our apparently endless "need for speed and basic greed." Until we demonstrate that we (both Texans and Americans) are able as a people to restrain ourselves from devouring what sustains us, I continue to support (wise) government intervention to save us from our grotesque appetites. There's astonishingly little legislation that encourages us to feed our neighbors and the land that sustains us as we would have ourselves fed: with mutual respect and self-restraint. But I'll support it when I see it and push for it when I don't. (Sorry, Dad.)

Stegner quotes Sherwood Anderson as saying that the wild nature of the prairie has the capacity to "take the shrillness out of" us. Maybe I need to go spend the night under the vast West Texas sky to lose some of my own shrillness. But I've quoted Sherwood Anderson without ever having read anything by him, so at least I know what my next topic will probably be.

12

Purity, Ambiguity, and the Investment Portfolio

APRIL 23, 2010

This week I'll begin with a parable from my favorite set of wise weirdos, the desert fathers, forerunners of Christian monasticism.

A brother said to Abba Poimen, "If I give my brother a little bread or something else, the demons tarnish these gifts, saying it was only done out of a desire for praise." The old man said to him, "Even if it is out of a desire for praise, we must give the brother what he needs." He told the following parable:

> *Two farmers lived in the same town; one of them sowed and reaped a small and poor crop, while the other, who did not even trouble to sow, reaped absolutely nothing. If a famine comes upon them, which of the two will find something to live on?*

The brother replied, "The one who reaped the small, poor crop." The old man said to him, "So it is with us. We sow a little poor grain, so that we will not die of hunger."

In the life that sought to be perfect in the love of God, neighbor, and self, the seeker had to give up the need to be beyond reproach and simply do the best he or she could. Early church scholar Roberta Bondi, an Episcopal priest, has written of this eccentric collection of early Christians whose baffling exodus into the Egyptian desert began in the fourth century. She says,

It must have been a great temptation to the early Christian monastic to try to codify the moral law for himself or herself in such a way that there would be no ambiguity left, that one could always know what to do without having to take responsibility for the suffering of others that might result from one's moral action.

Unfortunately, there was no way to avoid having to use one's own judgment then, just as there is no way now, once it is granted that the goal is love rather than fulfilling a legal code.

Virtuous actions could even be roadblocks on The Way if the actor's motive was simply to feel pure or, worse, look down his Roman nose at his apparently less virtuous brother.

With all that said, I'd like to make a narrative- and logic-defying leap to John Tierney's column in last Tuesday's *New York Times*. In it, he approvingly reviews a new book by Stewart Brand, the compiler of the *Whole Earth Catalog*, which came out in 1968 and helped inspire the original Earth Day. In his new book, titled *Whole Earth Discipline*, Brand urges the environmentally minded to "question convenient fables" and offers up seven lessons, updating what he sees as myths to be discarded. Among them are several that immediately got my back up, including (as summarized by Tierney) "'Let them eat organic' is not a global option"; "Frankenfood, like Frankenstein, is fiction"; and "'New Nukes' is the new 'No Nukes.'"

Heresy, right?

On Wednesday, Martin and I attended a conference at city hall on the Slow Money movement in Austin. The keynote speaker was Woody Tasch, author of *Inquiries into the Nature of Slow Money: Investing as If Food, Farms, and Fertility Mattered*. Tasch, a venture capitalist, foundation treasurer, and entrepreneur, hopes to update nineteenth- and twentieth-century notions of fiduciary responsibility to reflect the economic, social, and environmental realities of the twenty-first century, largely by devising ways to invest in local food economies. Although he is idealistic, Tasch offers some trenchant assessments of the nature of risk in conventional bottom-line investment strategies. The conference also featured several panel discussions with various local organic food entrepreneurs, expounding on the possibilities for investment opportunities based on local businesses. At one point, one of the panelists—who sells beautiful eggs and organic chicken feed—exclaimed to the audience: We can feed the world with organic principles, and we don't need genetically engineered foods to do it, either! Raise your hand if you agree! And many in the standing-room audience raised their hands and cheered.

Orthodoxy, right?

One of the things I like about Tasch is his pragmatism, despite his utopian goals. As someone who has been lost in the fog of literature, religion, and family for many years, I was glad to hear his analysis of the market as neither good nor bad, but simply an elemental force that, like water or fire, can work for good or ill. He doesn't believe that any single scheme (even his own) will save the world, but rather calls for an economic polyculture that includes various ways of and goals for investing, not just the usual American emphasis on maximum monetary return on investment without regard for the consequences.

A question from the audience arose: I want to invest in strictly local businesses. How do I find the ones that won't sell out to national or international companies later? How do I stay pure? His response: you can't. And why would you? Some companies will, and some won't. The market has its seasons and needs multiple species of business in order to flourish in times of plenty and times of drought. There is no one "right" way to participate that is beyond reproach. If your goal is to invest in your community with a moderate rate of return, you can't worry too much about purity. "Don't let the perfect be the enemy of the good," Tasch admonished, hearkening back to the high-minded pragmatism of Voltaire.

As a recovering perfectionist and helpless idealist, I find this to be good news: that the ideal of purity in the world of investment—and elsewhere—can work against good and genuine change. To be honest, I have no idea whether organics are the only way, whether genetically modified crops are required in the global battle against hunger; whether the benefits of nuclear power outweigh the risks. Nor do I have a very clear idea of how I've arrived at a conception of purity that rejects these possibilities. I have always found John Tierney—the *New York Times* reporter—to be a lively and reliable source of information. In my local food community, I've found a fount of practical wisdom about the world in which small, independent producers must run three times as fast over rougher regulatory terrain than larger (and largest) producers to keep their place in the economic culture, even as it becomes clear that a flourishing economic ecosystem requires the presence of small farmers. How do I choose between these divergent views, when I find each of their expounders to be trustworthy guides?

American culture currently encourages, even celebrates, the immediate rejection of ideas that aren't genetically identical to the ones commonly held. In this harsh monoculture, I find relief in the generosity of the desert fathers. Do the best you can, even if you don't always meet your own—or your peers'—standards. Question those standards regularly to see why you have them, especially when they become shining purity badges that encourage you to condemn others. As soon as you condemn your fellow traveler, you've wandered off the road. Remember that there's no way to produce any kind of crop without getting dirty.

13

The Devil's Bargain
On Gardening and Violence

MAY 7, 2010

I spent last weekend at the ranch planning a new garden—or, rather, watching our dear friend Glee Ingram, an Austin landscape designer; Steve Diver, a horticulturist with Sustainable Growth Texas; and Robert Selement, Madroño's redoubtable manager, plan a new garden as I poked at bugs, stared at the sky, and occasionally said, "Huh?"

Despite me, we made good progress. Using Glee's initial design, we flagged the perimeter of a beautiful labyrinth-inspired shape. We thought about armadillo-, feral hog-, bison-, and raccoon-proof fencing (ha!); permaculture; gates and traffic patterns; rainwater collection; hoop-house placement; compost systems and leaf corrals; how to integrate the activities of the residents of the adjacent Chicken Palace; planting fruit trees as wind barriers; and soil and amendment ratios. We (well, some of us) got really sunburned. We felt that we'd really earned that cold beer on the porch as we watched the afternoon light turn golden while scores of swallows dove and swooped around us.

If this makes Madroño sound like Paradise and us like laborers in Eden, well, that's what it felt like. At the same time, however, these things also happened: I watched a hungry red-tailed hawk flying low over the Chicken Palace, hoping for yet another carry-out chicken dinner. I awoke at dawn's first glimmering to operatic squawking from the Chicken Palace but, unable to find a flashlight, had to wait until it was light to investigate. (Robert has killed more rattlers this spring than in his seven previous years at the ranch combined.) In fact, there was a dead hen, but we're not sure what killed her; she may have been egg-bound. During my morning perambulation on the road above the lake, a dozen buzzards wheeled just overhead. I couldn't smell anything dead, nor could I see the focus of their activity, but I remembered the shrieking white-tailed doe I'd heard at this same spot last spring. It was a heart-stopping noise. I glimpsed her thrashing through the underbrush on the cliff below me but was unable to find her again when I returned with reinforcements. Paradise it may be, but Madroño's beauty is woven with the warp of nature's potential and actual violence.

A good friend emailed me the following after reading my last piece:

> *I have read that if all the ants were eliminated from the planet it would cease to exist. My thought is that if all the humans somehow disappeared the earth would flourish.*

I've had that thought as well, but I also think that, with or without us, earth's flourishing has always involved violence and suffering. Predation, disease, floods, volcanic eruptions, earthquakes, tornadoes, and drought preceded human enviro-tinkering and will continue once we're gone.

Given that humans are part of the natural order, it's also a given that we will engage in violence. My definition of violence is idiosyncratic and personal: I define it as existing on a spectrum involving the imposition of one being's (or group's) will on another being (or group). So when you order your lollygagging child to stop staring at the ceiling and put on her school clothes, you are, according to my definition, moving into the realm of violence, albeit at the lowest possible vibration. If, as in this case, the imposition of said will is done to enable or assist the flourishing of the one imposed upon, maybe you get a free pass. I'm not sure about this. Nor am I sure how to word my definition to include violence against self, surely as invidious and terrible as violence against another. And of course violence is not restricted to the physical realm, nor is it directed only against humans. Our species' casual, thoughtless violence against the natural world is relentless.

Unique to humans in this violent world, however, is the capacity to restrict the reach of our violence. Christians and Jews have been commanded to do so in no uncertain terms (as have the followers of virtually every faith tradition; it's just that I'm most familiar with those two). Repeated several times in the Pentateuch is the phrase "an eye for an eye," often misunderstood as an incitement to violent retribution. In fact, the point of the phrase was to minimize violence, not incite it; the loss of an eye could not be redeemed by murder. Leviticus 19:18 is even more to the point: "You shall not take vengeance or bear a grudge against any of your people, but you shall love your neighbor as yourself." Jesus thought this a good enough line to use in the Sermon on the Mount and reinforced it by instructing his followers to rein in their violent tendencies even more tightly: "If anyone strikes you on the right cheek, turn to him the other also" (Matthew 5:39). Human violence against nature is less of an issue in the Bible, as the capacity to inflict permanent damage on our world wasn't ours at that point. But scripture does specifically address the correct treatment of animals; they were considered part of the community and were to enjoy a Sabbath rest (Exodus 20:10).

Restricting the reach of violence requires recognizing its ubiquitous footprint. I see its size 7 1/2 tracks all around me: in my sarcasm, in my imperious demands that things be done my way, in my constant consideration of my own comfort, in my need to have reality ordered in a particular way. Having spent the last couple of weeks in my garden at home in Austin, I've become aware of the arbitrary nature of life and death: what have those cute little flowering clovers ever done to me that they should be so unceremoniously yanked up? And don't get me started on pill bugs.

Gardens are great places for contemplating unsolvable mysteries. How else are you going to keep your mind occupied when pulling weeds? But I think there's a deep and distinctive link between restricting our carbon footprints and our violence footprints. When we accept that our flourishing always comes at the expense of someone or something else's flourishing, it's hard not to be humbled. What better place than a beautiful, infuriating garden to watch such a serious drama play itself out?

14

Still More on Violence
There Will Be Blood

MAY 28, 2010

The other day, I stopped my car to chat with neighbors (a frequent occurrence in our chatty neighborhood). We quickly got to the topic of the Deepwater Horizon oil spill and its spreading devastation. D. told me that he'd heard an interview on National Public Radio with a worker at an oil and gas pipe factory in Youngstown, Ohio, after President Obama had spoken there to promote his economic policies. This worker was notably unimpressed with the president's moratorium on offshore drilling. (According to the transcript on the NPR website, the worker, Larry Collins, actually said, "I'd like for [President Obama] to say it's a go and let's start drilling. The more rigs we have out there drilling, the more demand for our product.")

To D., I snorted something snarky about Mr. Collins's self-centeredness and shortsightedness and then realized in the midst of sneering that I had left my car running while we were chatting. Once I got home, I turned off lights that had been left on all day, presumably so our dogs and cats wouldn't need to use their reading glasses. I remembered my father doing the same thing during the energy crisis of the 1970s, usually while asking, "Do you think your daddy owns the electric company?"

I recount this unremarkable scenario as part of my ongoing musings about violence and our usually invisible participation in and promulgation of it. This seems like a precious way to continue the conversation about our individual and collective violence footprints, but after turning off the ignition and the lights, I realized that Mr. Collins and I had more in common than I had initially acknowledged. Am I prepared to examine my energy consumption—from the mechanical pencils in my desk drawer, to the food I eat, to the trash I throw away, to the investments I make—and change my expectations and habits? Am I Just Saying No to habits that keep drilling an attractive option to companies like British Petroleum? Well, no, not really. I keep hoping someone will invent something that will painlessly neutralize my energy cravings, sort of like those diet pills advertised in women's magazines. But as Bill McKibben points out in the latest issue of the *Christian Century*, we are addicted to cheap oil: "You think maybe, just maybe, that the needle BP stuck into the bottom of the sea flows straight into our veins?"

To me, one of the most appealing facets of the American character is our buoyant sense of optimism. Our hopefulness attracts hopeful people of all other nationalities, like Saul Griffith, featured in the *New Yorker*'s May 17 "Innovators Issue." Born and raised in Sydney, Australia, he came to the United States in 1998 as a doctoral student at MIT, initially to work on electronic ink—the idea that eventually became the Kindle. The author of the *New Yorker* article, David Owen, describes Griffith thusly: "His hair, which is reddish brown, is usually an omnidirectional mess, and he often looks as though he had dressed from the bottom of the laundry pile." I love that "omnidirectional," which apparently describes Griffith's brain as well as his hair: in 2004, he won the $30,000 prize awarded to the MIT student who shows great promise as an innovator, and in 2007 he received a MacArthur Foundation "genius grant." Since then, among other things, he has been thinking about and working on energy efficiency.

My favorite anecdote in the article describes Griffith, who now lives in San Francisco, riding to his lab on the prototype of an electricity-assisted tricycle he had designed. The tricycle included an enclosure for carrying cargo, and on the rainy morning in question the cargo was his infant son Huxley. The rain caused a short circuit in the tricycle's wiring, resulting in a small fire under Huxley's seat, which Griffith extinguished after hauling the baby off the trike. Writes Owen, "Huxley had reacted placidly to the crisis, as though, at eight months, he was already accustomed to life as the child of an inventor." Genetic buoyancy and hopefulness at work here, clearly.

But the article charts Griffith's growing disenchantment with technology as a means of avoiding the ecological disasters lying ahead. The things that he and his colleagues produce, while ingenious, often aren't addressing the actual problems, because the problems aren't fundamentally technological in nature. Griffith believed, for example, that waste from discarded cell phones could be reduced by the production of hand-cranked cell phones, using technology developed in the 1920s. But the problem of discarded cell phones isn't technological, he realized, it's cultural; people discard their cell phones because they want the latest model, not because their old phones stop working.

Griffith also notes that the nations with the lowest energy needs and highest standards of living, like Portugal, built their infrastructures long ago, when energy was much more costly than it is today. Houses built before the advent of cheap coal and oil were (and remain) energy efficient because they had to be; they are small, with small windows and thick walls. So here's the kicker: "Such low-tech ideas are crucial to forming viable environmental strategies, Griffith believes, because implementing more complicated technologies . . . would consume natural resources and generate greenhouse gasses at unsustainable rates." Griffith currently lives in what he describes as a "thermodynamic nightmare" of a house in San Francisco's Mission District. "If I were building a house from scratch," he says, "I could totally design a thermodynamically amazing, almost zero-energy house—but a huge amount of energy would go into building it, just in the materials, and right now most of that energy would come from burning fossil fuels." In other words, in trying to use technological innovation to solve the problems of our increasing demand for energy, we're more often than not acting like Wile E. Coyote, busily sawing off the branch of the tree we're sitting on.

Assuming that Griffith has a broader perspective on the issues of energy use than I do, I am coming to lose some of my American optimism. I'm thinking that if, like Mr. Collins in Youngstown, I as an individual and we as a nation continue to take a short-sighted, self-centered view of our energy needs, I and we will, in effect, be demanding that BP and its cohorts keep taking the kinds of risks for which the Gulf of Mexico and the countless beings in, around, and over it are now paying in blood. What do we consider acceptable losses? What will make us change before we kill what is most precious to us, including our sense of hope?

I'll try to write something cheerier next time, I promise.

15

Home with the Armadillo
Love Letter to Texas
JUNE 11, 2010

Recently we and our three kids went to Martin's native San Francisco to help celebrate his father's eighty-fifth birthday. The five of us spent an afternoon walking along the cliffs of Point Reyes National Seashore, where the ground was springy, the wind was fierce, and in some spots along the trail we pushed through wildflowers up to our shoulders. Hawks wheeled through the cloudless sky, elk sunned in the lees of the cliffs, and the ocean's shining hide swelled and stretched like the flanks of a well-groomed, self-satisfied, and very large cat. At one point, our son Tito turned to us and said incredulously, "You mean we had a choice between this and *Texas?*"

Yes, well. Martin has spent much of his time in the Lone Star State not entirely convinced that civilized life is possible here—certainly not from May to October, and frequently not after elections. I grew up spending summers in Colorado, where despising Texans is a competitive sport, and as a teenager and young adult I also got to spend time in places of unsurpassed beauty such as the highlands of Guatemala, the Swiss Alps, the Masai Mara, Paris, and the Canadian Rockies. And yet I love Texas and can't imagine living anywhere else. Time for that apologia, son.

Some of my love of Texas is just an old bad habit. Many fine writers have noted how people stubbornly cling to the smells and sounds of their childhood, sensations that undermine the idea that time moves only into the future. Much of my first decade was spent in the then-unbroken woods just north of the San Antonio airport. The uncanny whinny of the screech owl, the languid moan of the mourning dove, the overpowering sweetness of mountain laurel at Easter, the loneliness of the north wind on a clear winter day: each time I experience these now I'm reminded that the girl who was gripped by them forty years ago is still inside me. She isn't gone, despite all appearances to the contrary.

There's more to it than nostalgia, though. Texas tells stories about itself, some of them true. While I know that many find this self-conscious tale-telling irritating—maybe even pathological—I find it sort of comforting. So maybe we actually lost the battle of the Alamo. So maybe the Texas Rangers weren't a bunch of ethically ripped superheroes. So maybe every cowboy doesn't have the soul of a poet. But there seems to be a (nearly) conscious yearning for the power of myth to work among us with these stories. Of course, there are stories Texans tell about themselves that I loathe: bigger is better, we should each of us be our own posse, it's manly to kill animals with automatic weapons and spurn the meat—but this is a place that recognizes the power of stories to shape reality.

One of the stories told over and over in multiple variations is the power and variety of the land itself. One of my favorite signs is on Interstate 10 at the Louisiana-Texas state line. It reads something like this: Beaumont, 20 miles; El Paso, 937 miles. While I have lived only in Central Texas—in some ways the easiest part of the state to love—I've learned to respect and admire many of the landscapes between the ends, from east to west and from north to south. I make no claims to anything but the cursory knowledge that comes from road trips involving grumpy children—me and my siblings years ago, and more recently our own children. My parents drove us to Colorado every summer through the Panhandle; Martin and I chose instead to make our annual pilgrimage by way of Fort Stockton and then north through the Pecos wilderness. One hot summer day the gas tank light came on when we were halfway through the hundred inhospitable miles between Pecos and Loving, New Mexico. The prospect of running out of gas here at midday with a dog and several children concentrated the mind wonderfully and caused me to sweat through my clothes despite the car's air conditioning. (We managed to make it to the next filling station.) We passed by multiple examples of the land's indifference to human striving; we often threatened to abandon our squabbling children in Orla, an oil ghost town baked into dusty submission, if they didn't behave. (It didn't help.)

We always planned our route back to Austin through Balmorhea and Fort Davis and, inevitably, a thrashing summer thunderstorm would force us off the highway—or so we assumed, since we couldn't even see the highway through the mud on the windshield. But before the storm hit, you could see the Guadalupe Mountains to the west, and when we made it to Marfa and the high grasslands, we—well, some of us—were exhilarated by the wind and the shadows, by the pitilessness and delicacy of the Chinati Mountains.

At the other end of the spectrum, I love the featurelessness of the South Texas brush country, an admittedly perverse passion. In March, the mesquite bloom neon green. At least as many things will sting, bite, or poison you as won't. As our friend and mentor Hugh Fitzsimons of Thunder Heart Bison says, there are two seasons in South Texas: January and summer. At the rare watering holes, there are birds of remarkable beauty: green jays and hooded orioles and American widgeons. Once in April, on my way back from Piedras Negras and Eagle Pass, I drove through a migration of yellow sulphur butterflies that extended for dozens of miles. When I got back to Austin, probably a dozen people pointed out the grotesque beauty of my Suburban's grille, which had become an extravagant collage of dead butterflies.

I'm leaving a lot of verses out of my Texas love song, but the last verse here has to be the one about the Hill Country. Loving the Colorado Rockies as much as I love any landscape, I've been trained to seek out views, to climb and pant and strain and exult upon reaching the summit. Well, the Hill Country upends that paradigm. Once you make it to the top of the hill—at least at Madroño—the landscape sinks into an unexpected anonymity. The personality of the Hill Country is in its draws and canyons, the intimate interstitial places where oaks and pecans crowd together, and great slabs of limestone create undulating walls and pools, and ferns and cedar sage grow with the demure confidence of cloistered beauty. In February, the draws ring with the slurred chatter of hundreds of intoxicated robins and waxwings. The draws also snarl with the movements of feral hogs, coyotes, and mountain lions, and vibrate with the possibility of rattlesnakes on sunny shelves, the clatter of unseen hooves in caves and cedar brakes, and the songs of maddeningly invisible birds that suddenly move, shine, and disappear again before they can be named. The draws protect and expose, invite and terrify. You want stories? You'll find them here.

So, son, I'll be happy to spend time in California, especially in August, even if the locals make fun of how I talk and where I'm from. But I'll always want to come home.

16

The Gift Economy

JUNE 25, 2010

I've been thinking about our entertainingly (or so we hope) ill-prepared entry into the marketplace. (Martin says the most terrifying words in the world are "Honey, I've been thinking . . ." when they come out of my mouth. Reader, beware!)

In preparing for the seminar we're going to lead at the Gemini Ink Summer Lit Fest in San Antonio next month, I've been rereading Lewis Hyde's *The Gift: Creativity and the Artist in the Modern World*. The description of our seminar in the Gemini Ink catalog asks all the Big Questions about our hopes and plans for Madroño Ranch. I'm not sure what prompted me to look at *The Gift* again, but whatever it was, it was, well, a gift; Hyde beautifully untangles many of the ideas knotted in my head about those hopes and plans.

He begins by identifying the two distinct economies in which a work of art exists: the market economy and the gift economy. While a work of art can exist without a market, it cannot exist without a gift. Harlequin Romances, for example, follow guidelines set by market research and sell very well. But are they works of art? Probably not. While writing one requires a certain level of competence, a Harlequin Romance probably doesn't have a foot, or heaving bosom, in the gift economy.

Hyde develops a theory of the gift, which of course has multiple levels of significance. Its economy is marked by three related obligations: to give, to accept, and to reciprocate. Gift exchange is what one early theorist called a "'total social phenomenon'—one whose transactions are at once economic, juridical, moral, aesthetic, religious, and mythological." Gift exchange is an issue in medical ethics as well, especially with reference to organ transplants:

what is the status of body parts? Is it appropriate to commodify what has traditionally been regarded as a gift? What are the consequences when something moves from the gift economy to the market economy—when worth and value are confused?

Hyde cites the case of the Ford Pinto, a car that had a tendency to spill gas in low-speed collisions, a defect that killed at least five hundred people. An easy fix for this defect existed, but after a cost-benefit analysis that valued a human life at $200,000, Ford decided that the costs of fixing the Pinto exceeded the benefits. While the decision may have made sense from a market perspective, it ignored the fact that most of us participate in another economy as well, one in which the gift of life cannot be assigned a dollar value.

One of the marks of a gift is that it is always in motion, transferred from one individual or community to another. It must be consumed (i.e., eaten, immolated, thrown into the sea) or given away; otherwise, it ceases to become a gift and becomes mere property. A true gift is the antithesis of personal property. Hyde says that

> *a gift is consumed when it moves from one hand to another with no assurance of return. . . . A market exchange has an equilibrium or stasis; you pay to balance the scale. But when you give a gift there is momentum, and the weight shifts from body to body.*

Gift economies generally operate in relatively small communities like families, brotherhoods, or tribes; market economies tend to emerge at the limits of gift economies as a means of negotiating with outsiders. While my truncated description makes gift economies sound primitive, they aren't; Hyde cites the (ideally) unrestricted flow of ideas within the scientific community as an example. When ideas become remunerative for an individual or a portion of the community instead of free to the entire community, the gift economy dries up and the spirit of the group evaporates. The gift of ideas ceases to move.

Gift economies foment community; market economies fragment it— another iteration of the endless wrestling match between the Many and the One. One of the great benefits of a market economy—freedom from bondage—has significant limits. Where *the market alone rules, and particularly where its benefits derive from the conversion of gift property to commodities, the fruits of exchange are lost. At that point commerce becomes correctly associated with the fragmentation of community and the suppression of liveliness, fertility, and social feeling. For where we maintain no institutions of positive reciprocity, we find ourselves unable to . . . enter gracefully into nature, unable to draw community from the mass, and, finally, unable to receive, contribute toward, and pass along the collective treasures we refer to as culture and tradition.*

So here's what I've been thinking, honey: industrialized nations have converted the gift properties of nature into commodities. Any aboriginal people could have told us that disaster would ensue as a result of buying and selling what was pure gift, something not earned but given to us in abundance that the gift economy demands we pass on to our children in its original abundance.

I've also been rereading Bill McKibben's *The End of Nature*, in which he quotes the journals of the early American artist, writer, and wanderer George Catlin. Riding north to the Missouri River, Catlin found a campsite

in one of the most lovely little valleys I ever saw, and even far more beautiful than could be imagined by mortal man . . . an enchanting little lawn of five or six acres, on the banks of a cool and rippling stream, that was alive with fish; and every now and then, a fine brood of ducks, just old enough for delicious food and too unsophisticated to avoid an easy and simple death. This little lawn was surrounded by bunches and copses of the most picturesque foliage, consisting of leafy bois d'arcs and elms, spreading their huge branches as if in offering protection to the rounded groups of cherry and plum branches that supported festoons of grapevines with the purple clusters that hung in the most tempting manner over the green carpet that was everywhere decked out with wild flowers of all tints and various sizes, from the modest sunflowers, with their thousand tall and droopy heads, to the lilies that stood, and the violets that crept beneath them. . . . The wild deer were repeatedly rising from their quiet lairs, and bounding out and over the graceful swells of the prairies which hemmed it in.

McKibben comments, "If this passage had a little number at the start of each sentence, it could be Genesis."

So with Hyde and McKibben in the front of my mind, I was stunned to read of Judge Feldman's recent injunction against President Obama's moratorium on offshore drilling, which just proves that I live in a lovely little bubble along with fairies and elves and a herd of unicorns. I do not argue against the fact of the market economy any more than I argue against the changing seasons. Nor do I argue against the gravity of depriving tens of thousands of Gulf Coast residents of economic stability. But those who value the treasures of the Gulf through a market-driven cost-benefit analysis need to remember that they're operating in a gift economy as well, and that there will be an audit.

Back to Gemini Ink and Madroño's mission. We hope that Madroño will operate in a way that recognizes the beauty and necessity of both markets; after all, I'm out there hawking the virtues of bison meat. But I hope that in producing that meat we recognize the gift of abundance it brings us, that we honor that gift, and that we pass it on to our children and to the community in and around the ranch.

17

Made for You and Me
Some Thoughts on Private Property
JULY 9, 2010

Last week I went to Woody Creek, Colorado, to visit my father, sister, and brother and their posses. Among the many pleasures I find at the family place are my early morning walks up a trail that runs behind my sister and brother-in-law's house through Bureau of Land Management land. Known locally as the Buns of Steel Trail, it gallops up a southwest-facing slope dotted with scrub oak and sage. The soil is so red (*colorado* in Spanish) that if you wear white socks, you may be sure that they'll never be white again, even after repeated washings. From varying elevations, you can watch the entire Roaring Fork Valley unroll below you and note the stately procession of the valley's grand guardians, from the hulking Sawatch Range in the east to the ethereal Elk Mountains to the south to the comfortable bulk of Mount Sopris to the southwest and down to the gentler terrain (relatively speaking) toward Glenwood Springs. Because of bears, it's wise to walk with dogs or other noisemakers, but a flushed grouse can stop your heart just as effectively as the sudden appearance of a bear. Sometimes you walk through waist-high lupines, which can give a Texan a complex; even in a fabulous spring you can't walk in bluebonnets, first cousins to mountain lupines, any higher than your shins.

I came to the familiar circle of scrub oaks where I usually look down on my father's and sister's houses about a thousand feet below and then, delighted with the world, turn to go back down. Just imagine the oceanic depths of my outrage when I saw a sign that said "For Sale: Cabin Site." For SALE? Whose foul idea of a joke was this? This wasn't private property;

it was communal, open to all who would admire it and dream away the hidden bears.

My sister set me straight: we have been trespassing all these years, the fence marking the boundary of BLM land having fallen into disrepair several dozen yards before the turnaround spot. The dirt road next to the turnaround spot wanders for miles through the back country and is accessible to the public, but the relatively new owners of the land around the road (including the cabin site) regularly patrol it to be sure that what few walkers there are don't step off the public way onto their private property.

Still incensed the next evening as the dogs and I took our postprandial constitutional, I encountered a young man on a four-wheeler driving onto our property, which is at the end of Little Woody Creek Road. "Can I help you?" I asked. "Oh, no, ma'am," he said politely. "I'm just going to check my water. I do it twice a day." My eyebrows at my hairline, I said, perhaps not quite as politely, "YOUR water?" "Yes, ma'am," he said complacently.

I almost slugged him. In the politest, most Christian way, of course.

My sister explained (do you detect a pattern here?): Colorado's water laws are so Byzantine and obtuse that they make those in Texas, shockingly, look almost reasonable. (In Colorado, whichever property has the oldest claim to the water controls it, regardless of how many times that property has changed hands.) But water laws aren't really germane here. What I was struck by—and almost struck out in defense of—is my sense of what constitutes private property, especially when it comes to land that I love. I was furious to find that (A) land I thought was communal was, in fact, privately owned (and NOT by my family); and (B) land I thought was privately owned (by my family) was, in some respects, communal.

Having recently moved Lewis Hyde's *The Gift: Creativity and the Artist in the Modern World* to the top of my nonfiction top-ten list, I can't ignore the profound complications of ownership, especially of something like land, which clearly comes to humanity as gift. We did not make it, and yet somehow we (some very few of us) have come to claim it as our own—initially, at least, through arrogance and (often violent) appropriation. This makes me sad and uneasy, because I love the land that my family and I "own." And I hate those quotation marks, but I think they're a useful discipline for any landowner.

When I got back to hot, scruffy, sweaty Texas from cool, elegant Colorado,

I found a book waiting for me: Ellen Davis's *Scripture, Culture, and Agriculture: An Agrarian Reading of the Bible*. (Insert punch line here.) In the book's first line, Davis writes: "Agrarianism is a way of thinking and ordering life in community that is based on the health of the land and living creatures." Those may not sound like fighting words, but they are. Davis claims that the Bible is grounded in agrarian thought and practice, in which possession of the land—Israel—is dependent "upon proper use and care of land in community." One great irony is that America, steeped in the parallels between its own westward expansion and the Hebrews' crossing the Jordan to the Promised Land, has completely missed the point by ignoring the holiness of the land given (and received by its first residents) as unmitigated gift. Buying and selling land for rapacious personal profit, poisoning it, cutting down ancient trees in order to build highways, polluting waters, killing for sport, abusing the animals given for nourishment, leaving the land for dead—these behaviors were and still should be open to emphatic prophetic censure as clear violations of the spirit in which the Earth's tenants were given such gifts, and clear invitations for divine retribution that included (and still includes) such weapons as whirlwinds, drought, flood, and famine.

In his introduction to Davis's book, Wendell Berry writes,

> *We have been given the earth to live, not on, but with and from, and only on the condition that we care properly for it. We did not make it, and we know little about it. In fact, we don't, and will never, know enough about it to make our survival sure or our lives carefree. Our relation to our land will always remain, to a certain extent, mysterious. Therefore, our use of it must be determined more by reverence and humility, by local memory and affection, than by the knowledge we now call "objective" or "scientific." Above all, we must not damage it permanently or compromise its natural means of sustaining itself.*

As seriously as I take Wendell Berry, Ellen Davis, and the Bible, though, I can't ignore that very noisy part of me that wanted to deck that polite young man on "our" property checking on "his" water. The part of me that understands ownership as power isn't going to disappear in a puff of high-mindedness. Nor am I sure it should; I don't know of any compellingly desirable alternative to private landownership as it currently exists. The government? Don't think so. The Church, whatever that is? Ditto. Communal ownership? Only if I have my own bathroom. And while well-thought-out policies are a necessary component of land stewardship, they can't force the conversion experience that moves our relationship with the land from that of owner and chattel to that of respectful, fruitful, loving partnership. How do we become married to the land?

By this point in most of my essays, I've managed to tie myself into emotional knots: dear God, there's no way out of whichever mess I've decided needs fixing this week. So this is the time I usually go outside and stew about it. And I'll start pulling weeds and notice a volunteer melon plant spilling its way out of the pile of compost I forgot to spread. And I'll see one of the crowd of long-armed sunflowers fluttering and waving under a dozen investigative goldfinches so bright they look like flowers themselves. And I'll watch the power plays at the hummingbird feeders, and listen to the mockingbirds make fun of the wrens. I'll find that damn grasshopper that's been eating my basil. (We shall say no more of him.) I'll find a really cool-looking bug I haven't seen before, or maybe shriek a little shriek when I come upon one of those terrifying large and harmless (oh, sure) yellow garden spiders. I'll hear a chuck-will's-widow emphatically tuning up in the draw behind our house. And I'll tell someone how much I love "my" garden, how lucky I am, how lucky we are to live on this earth. Isn't that how converts are made?

18

Double Vision

Prophets, Tribalism, Eugenics, and the Environment

JULY 23, 2010

Recently, as I dog-paddled through the sea of books threatening to drown not just me but the overwhelmed shores of my bedside table, I found these sentences:

> *For those who draw near and offer themselves before God, satisfaction of hunger is neither an end in itself nor a wholly "secular" event. . . . [E]ating is a worshipful event, even revelatory; it engenders a healthful knowledge of God.*

When I read this, I thought, "Ah, I am a member of the tribe that believes this."

I briefly met Ellen F. Davis, author of *Scripture, Culture, and Agriculture: An Agrarian Reading of the Bible* and professor of Bible and practical theology at Duke Divinity School, when she spoke at our church about ten years ago, and I immediately developed a helpless intellectual crush on her. The crush is not diminished by the fact that Our Hero Wendell Berry wrote the foreword to the book and is quoted at the beginning of each chapter.

Davis's basic claim is that the fertility and habitability of the Earth—and particularly of Israel—are the best indexes of the health of the covenant relationship between God and his people. She writes beautifully about dominion, that stickiest of words in Genesis 1, when mankind is given "dominion" over the earth. Made in God's image, we are meant to exercise dominion as God does, and in Genesis 1, the way God exercises dominion is to exclaim in delight over the goodness of his work, and then to declare a day of rest for his delightful creation. Reckless topsoil depletion, toxic pesticides, and Confined Animal Factory Operations, among many other current agricultural practices, would probably not pass the Delight Test.

I read all this with a double vision: on the one hand, I underline passages, write notes, and spray exclamation points in the margins. On the other hand, I think about my neighbors in the Hill Country, many of whom are very conservative Christians, and I wonder how they would react to Davis's scathing comparison of pharaonic agricultural and economic policies (the ones that made God really, really mad) with the practices of American agribusiness. I'm not sure the book will get a lot of traction here. (Well, or anywhere; the book's title is so unsexy it might as well be wearing a suit of armor.) And yet it seems to me so clear that Davis's analysis is Right and needs to be broadcast.

So how do you convince someone you're right? Well, here's how not to do it: the way the American conservation movement sounded its earliest notes, at least politically. The current issue of *Orion* magazine carries a feature story titled "Conservation and Eugenics: The Environmental Movement's Dirty Secret." Charles Wolforth, the author, links Teddy Roosevelt's New Nationalism, with its emphasis on patriotism and conservation, to the propagation of "higher races," as opposed to Native Americans, Eskimos, and other "lower races."

Wolforth writes:

> *These ideas had been developed at Ivy League and other universities, at museums of natural history and anthropology in New York and Washington, in learned societies and in scientific literature. When . . . world's fairs focused on the West, the link between natural resources, morality, and racism was drawn ever more explicitly.*

Pointedly, Wolforth quotes from Roosevelt's New Nationalism speech, arguably the launching of the modern conservation movement:

> *Of all the questions which can come before this nation, short of the actual preservation of its existence in a great war, there is none which compares in importance with the great central task of leaving this land even a better land for our descendants than it is for us, and training them into a better race to inhabit the land and pass it on.*

Conservation is a great moral issue, for it involves the patriotic duty of insuring the safety and continuance of the nation.

It also, apparently, involved practicing eugenics.

Awash in my sea of books, I am a descendent of this tribe. No wonder it's hard to convince many people I'm right.

When I walk through my beloved Austin neighborhood, I'm often beset with the same double vision I have when reading the prophetic environmental writing I'm prone to read. I walk through my neighborhood pleased—delighted—with my wonderful neighbors and their well-tended homes and gardens. As I have mentioned before, walking a couple of blocks can take forty-five minutes or more, depending on who else is out and about and what news needs to be exchanged, which dogs need to be admired, whose children are doing fabulously or exasperatingly nutty things. How can this be a bad thing? And yet I can't help but be aware of the multitudes of cars, the endless whir of air conditioners, the trucks bearing pesticides that fertilize lawns, the lights that are on all night, the sprinklers running even as it rains. (We, too, are guilty of some of these.) How do you convince people without double vision that the goodness they're seeing in their way of life is resting on something destructive?

In the fruit of the American environmental movement there is a noxious worm: a sense of righteousness that often gnaws its way into self-righteous tribalism. The ways in which we eat and live are often markers of who we are; when told (or bullyragged) to change these ways, it can seem as if something essential in us has been condemned, most particularly when judgment comes from outside the tribe. Like triumphalist Christians who refuse to acknowledge the ugliness and violence that comes bundled with the hope and beauty of Christian history, triumphalist environmentalism will foment ill-will from people whose health and livelihoods could be enhanced or saved by its message.

Every movement must have its prophets. Traditionally, prophets haven't been the sort of people you want to invite home for dinner; they eat locusts, dress in skins or nothing at all, sit in cisterns, moan a lot—that sort of thing. We listen to the true prophets not because they're scaremongering but because they always have an accurate sense of their tribe's history, an acute awareness of when it has fallen away from its original goodness. They include themselves in their judgments. Despite their very visible eccentricities, there is an essential humility to them. When I pull up behind a pickup truck with a bumper sticker that says "Drill Here Drill Now Pay Less" (along with a Rick Perry sticker) and my first impulse is to jump out of my car and bash in the windshield, I know I'm no prophet. We're both driving, after all, and I need that gas as much as the other driver does. I'm not passing that humility test.

So where does that leave my tribe, the irritable non-prophets of the environmental persuasion? As an oldest child, I always like to have the right answer to pass on—and enforce, whenever possible. My tribe is frequently stymied. But here's one thing: invite someone over for dinner, someone not of the tribe. Feed them something that's beautiful, that's grown in accordance with the revelatory economy of food kindly produced. And think about this passage from one of Wendell Berry's Sabbath poems:

> *Leave your windows and go out, people of the world,*
> *go into the streets, go into the fields, go into the woods*
> *and along the streams. Go together, go alone.*
> *Say no to the Lords of War which is money*
> *which is Fire. Say no by saying yes*
> *to the air, to the earth, to the trees,*
> *yes to the grasses, to the rivers, to the birds*
> *and the animals and every living thing, yes*
> *to the small houses, yes to the children. Yes.*

19

Cleaning Out the Mental Refrigerator
Niebuhr, McKibben, and Band-Aids

AUGUST 6, 2010

I've been surveying the multitude of leftovers in the refrigerator of my mind. When was the last time this thing was cleaned out? Jeez. Prodded into further examination of my last piece by subsequent emails, conversations, and readings, I've concluded that my thinking is a little moldy and needs either to have the fuzz shaved off or be thrown out. *Caveat lector*: slightly smelly smorgasbord on the way.

Fuzzy thought number one: Chiding me for a Band-Aid approach to life-threatening environmental crises, a friend emailed this:

> *I actually think democratic control of the world through political action must be established. For me that means crushing the power of corporations.*

On the one hand, I agree fully. The sheer, concentrated force of most multi-national corporations is flabbergasting. The fact that British Petroleum still enjoys reasonable financial health despite the costs of the oil spill cleanup beggars the imagination. That much money is as good as a private militia, if not a private nuclear arsenal. Like anything powerful and willful, corporations need constant skeptical scrutiny.

Fuzzy thought number two: Bill McKibben, environmental prophet extraordinaire, was the first speaker a few weeks ago in a new annual lecture series endowed by my father in my mother's memory at the Aspen Center for Environmental Studies. Martin and I were unable to attend, but my sister told me that the evening was beautiful, the talk was inspiring, and McKibben was a passionate and humble witness to the planet- (and therefore self-) destructive path we're currently running down. (A few days later he gave a more formal version of his lecture at the Aspen Ideas Festival.)

Likening the scope of climate change to the devastation of nuclear warfare, he says that Americans "have so far failed to imagine that the explosion of a billion pistons and a billion cylinders each minute around the world could wreak the same kind of damage on the same scale." Contributing to this failure of imagination are national inertia (we like the way we live); the divide between wealthy and poor nations (how do we tell others not to do what we have done when we are so comfortable?); and, unsurprisingly, the defensive position of the fossil fuel industry, which has hefted its mighty bulk directly on top of anything that might derail profits as usual. Imagine the public response to a campaign by the munitions industry downplaying the effects of nuclear warfare; one assumes that most of us would be thunderstruck. We should be as horrified by an industry that uses "the atmosphere as an open sewer for the effluent of their product" and makes more money than any industry in the history of money. But apparently we're not. Yet.

Fuzzy thought number three: corporations aren't going away, nor should they. They (can/should) provide the infrastructure that local and sustainable economies need to thrive. The problem comes when mighty corporate bulk squishes the little guys flat, which is what usually happens. Governmental regulations meant to restrain the mighty corporate bulk often squish the little guys even flatter. (That's about the most sophisticated economic observation I'm capable of producing, so I hope you enjoyed it.)

Fuzzy thoughts numbers four through six, which come from the very back of the bottom shelf: when faced with complex, apparently insoluble problems, my tendency is to go for a walk. Or pull out Band-Aids. Or make a big messy meal requiring lots of cleaning up. (Martin, as chief dishwasher, gets tired of this one.) But having spent the week reading Reinhold Niebuhr, one of the great Christian theologians of the twentieth century, and listening to Bill McKibben, I must sadly conclude that mine are inadequate responses. Writing with the stench of World War II still in the air, Niebuhr rebuked those Christians who had concluded that the only response to evil in the world was pacifism, trusting in the power of human goodness to counteract evil. Nor did he allow those who act against evil to trust fully in their own righteousness. Rather, he said, we need to be acutely aware that

> *political controversies are always conflicts between sinners and not between righteous men and sinners. [The Christian faith] ought to mitigate the self-righteousness which is an inevitable concomitant of all human conflict. The spirit of contrition is an important ingredient in the sense of justice.*

As tempting as it is to preen, when we choose to fight the bully power of corporations, we need to be clear about our own implication in the tangled web of environmental injustice.

Add Niebuhr's words to these: McKibben, a mild-mannered science writer, published a column titled "We're hot as hell and we're not going to take it anymore" on the TomDispatch.com website this week that immediately went viral. Furthermore, our mild-mannered hero writes specifically about the refusal of our political leaders even to consider climate legislation last week:

> *So what I want to say is: This is fucked up. The time has come to get mad, and then to get busy.*

This from a Methodist Sunday School teacher!

The organization he started in 2008 with seven recent Middlebury College graduates—350.org—was a ragtag effort to organize a worldwide response to climate change. The results of that effort were astonishing. It turns out that the term "environmentalist" does not apply just to a bunch of over-educated, effete white Americans; in fact, the rest of the world—most of it brown, young, poor, and powerless—knows something we Americans still aren't willing to confront: climate change, driven by fossil fuels, has crippled the regularity of the natural order we rely on for everything. Everything. *Everything.*

Through 350.org, we have an opportunity on October 10, 2010— 10/10/10—to tell the powers that be that we're hot as hell and we're not going to take it anymore. We should still walk through our neighborhoods and chat with our neighbors. We should still introduce people to the profound pleasures of eating locally and according to the seasons. Acts like these will give us sustenance for the battle ahead, especially those of us who don't feel much like fighters, who don't want to crush anyone or anything, and most especially those of us who don't want to clean out our refrigerators.

20

"A Cup of Tea, a Warm Bath, and a Brisk Walk"

AUGUST 20, 2010

A path is little more than a habit that comes with knowledge of a place.

—Wendell Berry

If you are ready to leave father and mother, and brother and sister, and wife and child and friends, and never see them again; if you have paid your debts, and made your will, and settled all your affairs, and are a free man; then you are ready for a walk.

—Henry David Thoreau

I'm an enthusiastic walker and believe firmly in walking's spiritual, psychic, and medicinal benefits. Whenever our kids were feeling puny, they were usually told that a cup of tea, a warm bath, and a brisk walk would put them in order—one of the reasons my family nickname is "Deathmarch." "We're DYING," they'd moan. "You'll feel better after a walk," I'd respond. After tugging a drooping daughter on one particularly frustrating foot-dragging outing, we discovered she had mono. But I'm sure the walk did her good.

Both nature and nurture have gone into creating this momster that is me: my mother used to frog-march my three siblings and me up the mountains around the Roaring Fork Valley in Colorado, hoping to create the conditions for quiet evenings in the little cabin we stayed in every summer. "It didn't work," she admitted. "The four of you never got worn out, but I sure did." So whether it's genetics or training, I walk, and Madroño has been—and surely will continue to be—a treasure trove of most excellent walks.

When we first started going to Madroño, when our youngest was a wee babe and the other two not much older, sneaking out for walks made me feel both guilty and liberated. For a brief time, at least, I was free to look at, listen to, think about, or not think about whatever I wanted, without interruption. Now that our youngest is leaving for college, I still feel that solitary walks are a guilty pleasure, albeit one about which I'm increasingly less apologetic, but I still feel the sense of release that comes when I head out the door with at least one ecstatic dog who's noticed I've put on my boots and my hat and picked up my binoculars. (Walking with unbelievably brave and stupid dogs could be the subject of an entire essay.)

For a long time, I went for what my dear friend Ellen calls the yodelaiEEoo pace of walking: trying to cover as much ground as quickly as possible, preferably headed up or down steep inclines. This is a really dumb way to walk in the Texas Hill Country, especially if you're not on a road and even if you are. First of all, if you're off-roading and going uphill, there's not a lot of purchase, given the rocks, leaves, and cedar detritus that cover the heavily wooded hills. There's even less purchase when you're coming downhill, which can look a lot like skiing, especially if you're a really spastic skier. But off-road descents can be easier than on-road ones. Once, when our youngest was about five or six, I bullied her into walking down the steepest road on the ranch with me, after we had driven up. She was so little that her relatively slight weight couldn't overcome the force of incline + scree; the final equation was an extremely sore little heinie from having her feet shoot out from under her every three steps or so.

Aside from the falling down problem, when you're moving at the yodelaiEEoo pace, it's very easy to miss all the Interesting Stuff to be found—or to run straight into it when you'd really rather not. I was walking on one of the roads on top one morning in June many years ago at a yodelaiEEoo pace only to find myself entangled in an enormous—no, I mean ENORMOUS—spider web. After shrieking, dancing, frantically patting my head, pulling my clothes off, etc., I slowed down enough to notice these spiders. I still don't know what kind they were—maybe golden orbs? As I walked along, twitching and squinting with every step I took, I saw their webs everywhere. Some of them spanned fifteen- to twenty-foot gaps. How had they done that? Parachuted? Hailed taxis to drive them across? Not only were the webs huge, but they were invisible until you were two inches away from them. They taught me to slow down AND to limbo.

Once the kids got big enough, we went for what we called scrambles, which involved walking up and/or down one of the many mysterious draws that pepper the ranch. Walking with children, of course, cannot occur at a yodelaiEEoo pace, at least not until they're bigger and stronger than you and you start calling plaintively: "Guys? Guys? Hey, wait for me!" But while I was still bigger and stronger than they were, we loved to go poke around in the draws, especially with some of our family's emergency back-up children. (We haven't actually outgrown this.) The kids were the ones who found all the Interesting Stuff: the rocks that looked like Swiss cheese or hearts, the iron bedsteads alongside a cast-iron Dutch oven, the fossils, the arrowheads and stone tools, the tiny flowers and ferns hiding in the shade, the little caves, the really weird bugs, the secret springs. And the snakes.

I must say a word about walking and snakes. I've climbed up, fallen down, and poked through a lot (though not nearly all) of the property, and I've concluded that snakes don't want to see me any more than I want to see them. I try to be sure I can see where I'm putting my hands and feet, and dogs (at least the smart ones, if any such exist) are often helpful, hopping sideways to let you know that you shouldn't step on that spot. Robert, the intrepid ranch manager, sees them all the time, but he does things like drain and dig around in the bottom of ponds. I've been lucky so far, with one notable exception.

One warm November day my then-fifteen-year-old son and I went walking to the back of the property. For some reason, he had brought a shotgun, and as we were walking through a patch of tall grass, he stopped and said calmly but urgently, "Mom. Snake." And one step ahead of me was the fattest, longest, ugliest water moccasin I had ever seen. As it slithered off, he shot it, securing his place in my heart (and my ankles, where I probably would have been bitten had he not been there) as a hero.

As I've become more interested in birds, my yodelaiEEoo pace has become a thing of the past, for a couple of reasons. One is the difficulty of trying to track the little boogers through thick live-oak canopies or heavy underbrush. Another is having to stop and listen to them over the clatter I make. Our beloved old black Lab Phoebe is too blind and creaky to walk with me now, but back in the day she hated these stop-and-listen moments;

if I paused for more than a minute or two she commenced with a low and pitiful moaning that wouldn't let up until we started again. Phoebe liked the yodelaiEEoo pace. But even she was stilled into silence that February day when we turned into a usually still canyon only to hear the voices of what turned out to be literally thousands of robins and cedar waxwings, feasting—and maybe drunk—on cedar berries. The noise level was on par with I don't know what: maybe a middle school hallway after the last class of the year, but considerably less smelly.

In fact, much to my family's astonishment, I've learned to walk places and then just sit, at least sometimes. Chula the Goggle-Eyed Ricochet Hound walks with me now that Phoebe can't, and Chula is fine with just sitting. (She has other issues that will be revealed in my walking-with-dogs essay.) Did you know that certain grasses snap and crackle when the sun first hits them on cold mornings? I must have spent twenty minutes on my hands and knees one morning trying to figure out what was making that noise. Bugs? The little creatures in my head? Nope, it was just the grass talking. We had a lovely conversation, while Chula looked on, quietly concerned.

Perhaps, finally, it's time for a new family nickname.

21

Stubbing the Giant's Toe
Thoughts on Midwestern Agribusiness

SEPTEMBER 3, 2010

Corn. Soybeans. Corn. Soybeans. Corn. Soybeans. Corn. Soybeans. Corn. Soybeans. Corn. Soybeans. Corn. Soybeans. Corn. Soybeans.

And did I mention corn?

We drove last week from Austin to Gambier, Ohio, to deliver our youngest to college, and then back to Austin. (Empty nest. Delight. Depression.) That this trip was my maiden voyage into the American Midwest was just one of many notable firsts. At about the time we crossed the line from Kentucky to Ohio, it began: fields of corn and soybeans on either side of the road stretching to the horizon, interrupted only occasionally by copses of oaks or by farmhouses and barns or by grain storage units. We started to joke about it by the time we got to Gambier, smack in the middle of Ohio. After installing our daughter in her new dorm room, we turned our noses west and drove from Gambier to Clarksville, Missouri, on the banks of the Mississippi River, in one endless, relentless, repetitive, mind- and butt-numbing 600-mile day. The joking stopped at about mile 100.

The landscape wasn't unpleasant by any means. The apparently unlimited fecundity of the earth was impressive, as was the system that ordered such abundance. The scope of it! And we didn't even make it into Iowa or Nebraska! No wonder the people behind this astonishing productivity are proud of it.

But there's another way to see that landscape, and those afflicted with the double vision I wrote about in an earlier piece might see the abundance as a tumor, or at least a spreading rash. The economic, cultural, and environmental damage imposed by the efficiencies of agribusiness have been well documented, most popularly by Michael Pollan in *The Omnivore's Dilemma: A Natural History of Four Meals* and Eric Schlosser's *Fast Food Nation: The Dark Side of the All-American Meal*, along with films like *Food, Inc.* and *Fresh*. The idea that inexpensive food can be grown only through the use of annuals and monocultures, efficiencies of scale, and heavy pesticide use has been seriously challenged by farmers like Joel Salatin and Will Allen. Along with the steady depletion of topsoil, the off-farm effects of conventional agriculture are also well documented, from depletion of local biodiversity to the rapidly growing "dead zone" in the Gulf of Mexico.

After spending the night in Clarksville, we drove through another scene of apparent abundance en route to Eureka Springs, Arkansas. Arkansas, of course, is the home of Tyson Foods, which began as a chicken wholesaler in 1935. In the interests of full disclosure, I have to admit that I love chickens for reasons that aren't entirely rational. Last year, we moved our chickens at Madroño from the nasty old chicken coop to the Chicken Palace and added substantially to their numbers. The Chicken Palace, built by Robert Selement, the ranch's redoubtable manager, could probably withstand a nuclear attack and has already foiled a whole lot of skunks, raccoons, coyotes, bobcats, hawks, and owls.

One of the great pleasures of a Madroño morning is to let the ladies (one of whom is named Fred, for reasons not entirely clear to us) out of the Palace and into the adjoining pasture and then to throw them the previous night's vegetable scraps. From the moment they see me coming down the hill, they begin an almost-intelligible running commentary that steadily increases in volume and intensity. ("Can you believe she wears boots with her nightgown?" "God, I hope there's no fennel in that scrap bowl." "Hasn't she ever opened a gate before? What's taking her so long?") Anticipation is so focused that by the time I open the door to the yard, and then the gate from the yard to the pasture, there's a charge in the air that surely rivals the first seconds of the running of the bulls in Pamplona. No, really. Those chickens are *moving*. And I'm laughing. And very happy to gather (and sell) their marigold-yolked eggs. (For the reflections of a true *chickenista*, be sure to check out the highly readable blog posts of Carol Ann Sayle, who owns and operates Austin's wonderful Boggy Creek Farm along with her husband Larry Butler. Carol Ann's chicken blogs are worthy of a BBC comedy of manners with period costumes.)

Given my tender feelings toward our chickens, seeing a Tyson truck rolling down an Arkansas highway carrying its cargo of tightly packed chicken cages made me tense. When we got to Eureka Springs, with its funky old boutiques and gingerbread houses, we found a restaurant that served local produce and whose waitress told us that she was a "universal soul." I relaxed a little, enough to start chatting with the friendly couple sitting next to us. As it turned out, the husband was a Tyson chicken farmer. The sixteen-year-old boy he had hired for the summer was worthless, he said, but the fourteen-year-old was great. He didn't have an attitude yet, and never complained about the hours he had to spend each day picking up dead chickens.

I got tense again.

How can something that seems so clearly wrong to one person seem perfectly acceptable to another? How can I have arrived at my advanced age and still be surprised that this is so? Even though we all technically speak the same language—the midwestern corn and soybean farmers, the Arkansas chicken farmer, and I—there seems to be an unbridgeable perceptual gulf between us.

When I'm feeling this kind of tension, I become almost ridiculously grateful for things like the *National Geographic* website, which describes the work of young scientists with big ideas that "show a potential for future breakthroughs." Among the chosen for 2010—and they are a fascinating group—is an agroecologist named Jerry Glover who works for the Land Institute in Salina, Kansas. His field of study, so to speak, is perennial grains, wheat in particular. Unlike annual crops, which need to be replanted every year, drain nutrients from the soil, and allow erosion when they die, perennial crops can be "harvested year after year and maintain excellent soil quality." Glover doesn't preach (at least not on the *National Geographic* website), and he doesn't point fingers at conventional farmers and say: Bad, bad, bad. He points to the evidence in the soils he works with, which speaks for itself—and in the same dialect as the farmers whose practices I find so confounding.

Seeing the scope of those midwestern cornfields is sobering. Thinking about the money, time, and corporate muscle they represent is daunting. Reading about the salmonella outbreak in factory farm-produced eggs is appalling. When you buy from your local farmers and humane producers, you're allying yourself with an entity so tiny it barely stubs the giant's toe when it gets kicked aside. But that tiny stumbling block gathers a little more heft with each kick. To mix my images, watching this process is like watch-ing a big pot of water boil: just when you think your stove is busted or your water's dead, you start seeing those tiny bubbles appear and get perceptibly more emphatic—especially when there are young scientists like Jerry Glover working next to the giant and turning up the heat. And if those of us who eat keep asking for it, the giant will eventually be able to put sweet organic (or at least less devastating) corn into the pot and feed the less-eroded world with it. Sounds like a fairy tale, I know, but maybe it's more of a parable—a story with an unexpected and revelatory twist at the end. Whatever it is, just think of the possible chicken commentary on giants in the kitchen. I'll bet their footwear choices are even more entertaining than mine.

22

Hall of Mirrors
The Lost Art of Conversation

SEPTEMBER 17, 2010

Last week I found myself in a conversation with someone who doesn't believe in AGW and has written a soon-to-be-published book explaining his position. AGW—which I had to look up—is short for anthropogenic global warming, or global warming caused by human activity. That idea is, he contends, "the biggest whopper sold to the public in the history of humankind."

Now, I've read a lot about people like this; they listen to Rush Limbaugh, watch Glenn Beck, think the Earth is six thousand years old, vote against the teaching of evolution in public schools, read the Bible literally, and vote Republican or Libertarian. I could probably pick them out in a crowd. They just have this *look*, right?

Except that this young man has a lot in common with, well, me. We're both English majors from small New England colleges. Both former (at least on my part) doctoral students in literature. Both rowers. Both writers (although he's been published in high-profile publications like the *New Yorker*, while I've been published in the *Anglican Theological Review*). Both voted for Obama. Both believers in "clean" energy, whatever that is. We most certainly don't have *that* look.

He gave me the basics of his argument, the science of which I followed imperfectly, as I follow all scientific arguments. He caught and retained my attention when he said this: science relies on narrative. In other words, scientists tell stories about their research. They articulate their theories and findings in a particular way, a way that relies on their own experiences, influences, and personal quirks. Facts are facts, but facts aren't self-interpreting. How the facts are articulated is essential to the final shape of the story.

So here's the question: why do I take one set of scientific conclusions as gospel and reject another set? I'm not qualified to evaluate the merits of most scientific assertions, period. On what grounds do I choose one interpretation over another? I have to conclude that I rely on considerations other than scientific ones, just as many people do who don't agree that climate change is caused by human activity, or that the earth is heating up at all. I tend to judge *those* people using criteria that I don't generally apply to myself, a predictably unscientific state of affairs that may tarnish the burnished glow of my intellectual honesty.

According to a recent Gallup poll, Democrats are twice as likely as Republicans to believe that the effects of global warming are underway. All of the GOP candidates currently vying for Senate seats doubt the evidence supporting global warming and oppose government action to limit warming pollution. It would seem that most of us in the debate about climate change—and environmental concerns in general—are driven at least as much by political ideology as by science.

One of my daily reads is *Grist*, an e-zine that calls itself "A Beacon in the Smog." Among the stories I read this week is one titled "Stupid Goes Viral: The Climate Zombies of the New GOP." Near the top of the story comes a staccato burst of single-sentence paragraphs that reads:

Meet the Climate Zombies.

They're mindless.

Their stupid is contagious.

And if they win, humanity loses.

While the tone is ironic, even flip, the message is clear: we need to be afraid of the politicians who refuse to acknowledge human participation in the destruction of the environment.

The tone of the story sounds very much like Glenn Beck's when he ridiculed Nancy Pelosi's anxiety about the rhetorical strategies of Tea Partiers:

This is how they are attempting to silence the Tea Partiers—they are just so hateful, they are going to get violent. During the Tea Parties, liberals in the media were trembling with fear and shaking in their boots. And they were right—see how scary they look? Oh, the horror! Parents, cover your children's eyes. Of course, no actual violence ever actually happened at any of the Tea Party rallies. But that didn't stop Nancy Pelosi from crying about the possibility.

While Beck's tone is ironic, even flip, the message is clear: we need to be afraid of the politicians who want to curtail our right to speak out.

Although I'm more willing to listen to one voice than the other, here's the problem: neither set of comments is intended to be part of an actual conversation. Both are speaking from within a hall of mirrors in which each auditor is imagined to be a mere projection of the speaker, or at most, a member of the speaker's monolithic tribe. I recently read a great blog about the "epistemic closure" in much current conservative thinking—the tendency to accept evidence only when it reinforces preexisting opinions—and this from someone who works for the libertarian Cato Institute! But I find evidence of epistemic closure on the left as well, frequently manifested by a tone that smirks, "If you don't agree with me you're a moron, and I refuse to converse with morons."

Well, this moron wants some conversation. In reading *Plurality and Ambiguity: Hermeneutics, Religion, Hope*, by David Tracy (very interesting, wretched title, periodically intelligible), I found this meaty sentence: "Conversation is a game with some hard rules: say only what you mean; say it as accurately as you can; listen to and respect what the other says, however different or other; be willing to correct or defend your opinions if challenged by the conversation partner; be willing to argue if necessary, to confront if demanded, to endure necessary conflict, to change your mind if evidence suggests it."

Of course, you can only have a conversation when all the participants agree to these rules, and the Glenn Becks of the world usually seem to want to talk only to themselves in their own halls of mirrors. But when those of us with passionate feelings about the fate of all Earth's residents, human and nonhuman alike, sound just like the conversation-stompers on the other side, then we become part of the problem, not the solution. As frustrating as it is to follow the rules—especially when your conversation partner has his back turned, his arms crossed, fingers in his ears and singing "lalalalala"—it becomes even more imperative to walk out of our own hall of mirrors willing to engage (again and again and again) in the hard and morally vital work of conversation in the open air.

Living as I do in my own little hall of mirrors in Austin, my conversational muscles are a tad underdeveloped. I may have to start with the AGW denier I mentioned above, the one who otherwise looks pretty much like me. I'll try not to call him a moron and try to be willing to change my mind, to leave my tribe and go outside, if evidence suggests that it's necessary.

Now *that's* scary.

23

Of Mothers and Mountains

OCTOBER 8, 2010

I've just introduced myself to the pleasures of Aldo Leopold's *A Sand County Almanac, and Sketches Here and There*. Called the father of wildlife conservation in the United States, Leopold heard in the revving of the great American economic and technological engines the death knell of what he called "the biotic community," in which humanity is merely a fellow passenger, not the driver. *A Sand County Almanac* was published posthumously in 1949; more than sixty years later, Leopold's ability to see where those engines would take us seems eerily prophetic.

Aside from what he says, I love his tone—warm and humble, courteous and scholarly. But what he says is compelling and important. In one essay, "Thinking Like a Mountain," he recounts an experience he had as a young man working for the Forest Service in Arizona, at a time when land managers "had never heard of passing up a chance to kill a wolf." One day, from a "high rimrock," he and his colleagues spotted a pack of wolves, including some pups, and opened fire. Leopold, having shot a female, climbed down and

> reached the old wolf in time to watch a fierce green fire dying in
> her eyes. I realized then, and have known ever since, that there was
> something new to me in those eyes—something known only to her and
> to the mountain. I was young then, and full of trigger-itch; I thought
> that because fewer wolves meant more deer, that no wolves would
> mean hunters' paradise. But after seeing the green fire die, I sensed
> that neither the wolf nor the mountain agreed with such a view.

Over the years, as he watched the destruction of the wolf population and the subsequent explosion of the deer population and disappearance of the mountain flora, Leopold came to understand the wolves' vital place in the biotic community. He became a passionate, but never strident, defender of predators and other despised or voiceless members of his tribe, like soil, water, flowers, and mountains.

I'm thinking about the mind of the mountains because last week my sister Isa, my brother John, and I walked into what we consider their heart. We climbed up to Buckskin Pass, our mother's favorite hike, on the first anniversary of her death. We agreed that one of her greatest gifts to us was a deep, abiding love for wild places, especially those in Colorado, a love she shared with everyone she could. I don't know if she ever read *A Sand County Almanac*, but I know that she, too, thought about her response to the inner life of mountains and encouraged us to do likewise.

At the end of "Thinking Like a Mountain," Leopold writes this: "We all strive for safety, prosperity, comfort, long life, and dullness. . . . A measure of this is all well enough, and perhaps is a requisite to objective thinking, but too much safety seems to yield only danger in the long run. Perhaps this is behind Thoreau's dictum: In wildness is the salvation of the world. Perhaps this is the hidden meaning in the howl of the wolf, long known among mountains, but seldom perceived among men."

I was particularly taken with his misquotation of Thoreau; in a previous piece I wrestled with my own misquotation of the same line. What Thoreau actually wrote was this: "In wildness is the preservation of the world." But I love Leopold's rendering, since the substitution of "salvation" for "preservation" gives the minds of wolves and mountains a distinctly theological dimension. (Coincidentally, I've also just discovered Thomas Berry, an ecology-minded priest and writer who proclaimed himself a "geologian.")

How might the wild minds of the mountains save us? I'm not sure there's a single answer to that question, especially since the mountains are just as capable of destroying as saving. I remember times during our childhood forced marches when we had to sprint down from above tree line to avoid summer storms that seemed to come out of nowhere, bristling lightning. Even as their come-hither beauty draws me to these high places, their monastic austerity keeps me in my place. My brother John, an alpinist by vocation and avocation, has spent more time dangling in very thin air than most normal people, and he confirms the almost erotic call and implacable heart of the mountains—or at least I feel sure he would if I asked him.

How might the wild minds of the mountains save us? Here's one answer: in *The Solace of Fierce Places: Exploring Desert and Mountain Spirituality*, Belden C. Lane recounts the parable of an Englishman visiting Tibet some years ago:

> *Only as the grandeur of the land drew him beyond himself did he begin to discover what he sought. Walking one day toward a remote monastery at Rde-Zong, he was distracted from his quest for spiritual attainment by the play of the sun on stones along the path. "I have no choice," he protested, "but to be alive to this landscape and light." Because of this delay, he never arrived at the monastery. . . .*

> *Most compelling to his imagination was the fact that the awesome beauty of this fierce land was in no way conditioned by his own frail presence. It was not there for* him. . . . . *Hence he declared, "The things that ignore us save us in the end. Their presence awakens silence in us; they restore our courage with the purity of their detachment." Becoming present to a reality entirely separate from his own world of turmoil strangely set him free.*

As John, Isa, and I descended from the emphatic heights, talking about a strangely controversial effort to designate 350,000 nearby acres of national park as a wilderness preserve, John stopped, turning around to look at Isa and me with his mouth wide open, pantomiming astonishment. Wondering what could possibly astonish someone as unflappable as John, I looked down the rocky trail.

A young man with no legs was walking toward us. Yep, walking, on his leather-gloved hands, up a trail that sucked the breath out of people with legs. His concentration was so intense that he was unable to acknowledge our presence. I recognized him as the subject of a story I had read online a few months before. Kevin Michael Connolly, born without legs, is, at age twenty-four, a champion skier, a globe-trotting photographer, and, if his website is any indication, a charming smart aleck. He's also the author of a memoir titled *Double Take*.

I've never been quite as awestruck by another person as I was in that moment. Once again, I felt very small, amazed by the community—this time the human community—of which I am a part. So many things, people, and circumstances by which I might be saved.

The things that ignore us save us in the end. They allow us to step out of the endless hall of mirrors we usually inhabit and to find ourselves in a relationship with something outside our fears, fantasies, and projections. This was one of our mother's great gifts: she showed us how we could step outside our defended little selves for a while. She taught us where to find courage when we need it: in this place where we knew ourselves to be small and helpless and yet utterly at home, at least for a few ragged breaths.

24

Barbers, Bison Meat, and the Invisible Hand

OCTOBER 22, 2010

I was back in my shiny new persona as salesperson last week, driving out to all the dude ranches around Bandera in hopes of scaring up a market for the hundreds and hundreds of pounds of bison meat we will soon have for sale. Reaction was generally favorable, despite the fact that I didn't have some basic information at hand, like the prices we'll be charging.

Aside from feeling like a dummy, a phony, and a bat-brained loony, I had fun. First, there's very little that I enjoy more than looking at other people's property. Second, I got to drive down some Hill Country roads I hadn't been on before and go through the Hill Country State Natural Area, a secluded 5,000-plus-acre park dappled with beautiful blooming grasses and gayflowers, stands of hardwoods, and shining creeks. The third fun thing was getting out and meeting people—not a pleasure my usually introverted self would have anticipated. Our pattern when we go to Madroño has been to get there and dig in, not coming out unless we need something really important, like the newspaper or beer or ice cream or antihistamines. Now, for the first time, we're starting to meet our neighbors. We're starting—just barely—to find our way into the community.

I've also been rereading Wendell Berry's *Jayber Crow: The Life Story of Jayber Crow, Barber, of the Port William Membership, as Written by Himself*, in which community is a central concern. (The book has easily reaffirmed its place on my top-ten favorite novels list.) So this week "community" seems to be the theme that wants to beat me over the head until I wake up and pay attention.

As you might guess from the subtitle, *Jayber Crow* concerns a small-town Kentucky barber whose life spans most of the twentieth century. Orphaned at an early age, Jayber is raised by a loving great-aunt and -uncle, who die when he is ten. He is sent to an orphanage and finally, a dozen years later, makes his way back to Port William to become its barber, gravedigger, and church janitor. A philosophical-minded bachelor, Jayber watches the community over the course of several wars and the encroachment of highways and agricultural technology. Although he witnesses and endures great suffering, at the end he can say truthfully that his book is about Heaven because of the profound love the community bears for itself and for its place, both temporal and spatial.

In part, this love manifests itself in Port William's economic life. When Jayber returns to Port William, he finds that the town's previous barber has left, not being able to support his family on his shop's limited income. Jayber is immediately taken by an old friend to see the town banker, who in introducing himself says,

> *I'm glad to know you. I knew your mother's people.*

He offers to loan Jayber the money to buy the old barbershop; Jayber describes the terms of the loan as "fair enough, but very strict in what he would expect of me."

Jayber adds,

> *You will appreciate the tenderness of my situation if I remind you that I had managed to live for years without being known to anybody. And that day two men who knew who and where I had come from had looked at me face-on, as I had not been looked at since I was a child. . . . I felt revealed, as if to buy the shop I had to take off all my clothes.*

Going into business requires him to become a part of the community, to care about its constituent parts in order to make his own way in the world.

I had imagined that this community might make Adam Smith, the patron saint of free-market economics, sneer. It lives within the limits of the land's fertility, repairs what is broken, patches what is torn, and remains deeply suspicious of debt. Its citizens are generous to those in need, recognizing that they cannot prosper individually without prospering corporately. The villain of the novel, Troy Chattam, is an ambitious young farmer who contemptuously rejects the old-fashioned ways of his father-in-law; Troy's mantra is "modernize, mechanize, specialize, grow." He goes into debt to buy new machinery and listens to agribusiness experts who tell him to use every bit of soil on the place: "never let a quarter's worth of equity stand idle." He seems to be a firm believer in the "invisible hand," famously posited by Smith in his magnum opus *The Wealth of Nations*, which supposedly guides markets to produce the highest quality goods for the lowest price to the benefit of both producers and buyers; this is what we used to call the American way. Like that of the city for which he was named, however, Troy's is not a story with a happy ending.

But wait—why in heaven's name is Adam Smith suddenly part of this conversation? Because I, despite my shocking ignorance of economics, just read Adam Gopnik's fascinating article on Smith in the October 18 issue of the *New Yorker*. In it Gopnik argues that Smith's real question

> was not the economist's question, How do we get richer or poorer?, or even the philosopher's question, How should one live? It was the modern question, Darwin's question: How do you find and make order in a world without God?

Gopnik is ostensibly reviewing *Adam Smith: An Enlightened Life*, by Nicholas Phillipson, but he is really using Phillipson's book as a jumping-off point for his own meditations on economics and community. Readers of *The Wealth of Nations* tend to ignore Smith's earlier *The Theory of Moral Sentiments*, but by doing so, according to Gopnik, we "lobotomize our own understanding of modern life, making economics into a stand-alone, statistical quasi-science rather than, as Smith intended, a branch of the humanities." In order for humanity to live in community, Smith posits the necessity of "an impartial observer who lives within us, and whom we invent to judge our actions." Without this imaginative capacity, a market economy can't exist; unless we can put ourselves in the place of our fellows, we can't imagine what they might need. "For Smith, the plain-seeing Scot," writes Gopnik,

> the market may not have been the most elegant instance of human sympathy, but it's the most insistent: everybody has skin in this game.

It can proceed peaceably only because of those moral sentiments, those imaginary internal judges.

Unfortunately, those imaginary internal judges recede into the background when producers band together in order to eliminate competition and control prices; according to Phillipson (via Gopnik), Smith believed that "the market moves toward monopoly; it is the job of the philosopher to define, and of the sovereign state to restore, free play." The market works toward the benefit of all only when it is broadly just—defined (by me) as being in the long-term interests of both producer and consumer. When the scenario Berry imagines in *Jayber Crow* comes to pass—when economic and business practices fray the fabric of community rather than protect it—then we live in epically tragic times, like those of Troy. When we find communities in economic disarray, then, according to the father of free-market economics, imaginations incapable of sympathy are at the root of the problem.

Of course, this is a pretty self-serving position, since we at Madroño are about to go head-to-head with such giants as H-E-B, who can charge much less for bison meat than we can. But I honestly believe that the long-term health of H-E-B depends on a diverse economic ecosystem in which the building of community—which requires a mutually sympathetic imagination—will rest on the flexible backs of small, dynamic businesses. Which maybe, with the help of our local community, we will become.

25

"Sit. Stay. Stay! I Said STAY, Dammit!"

NOVEMBER 5, 2010

Despite the temptation to give myself over to ululations for the natural world in light of the recent midterm elections, I will be brave and strong. In fact, I'll look to our dogs for clues about how to move ahead in confounding times with good cheer, if not always with a lot of grace, and perhaps with only an occasional low moan or two.

In an earlier piece, I considered the change my walking pace has undergone over the years. What has remained constant is the presence of dogs on these rambles. When I'm in Colorado, I usually borrow dogs from my sister or my father. (Walking with my mother's dogs was often a little demoralizing; she worried aloud that bears and mountain lions might attack them, but she never expressed any anxiety for me.) At Madroño, I've walked with a long line of brave and stupid dogs who've both saved me from and almost led me to some gruesome fates.

The first was sweet Daisy, a lovely golden retriever/English setter mix and the mildest of dogs—until she was on the ranch, where she became Trained Assassin Daisy, Scourge of Armadillos! I had never known that armadillos had much to say until I watched Daisy in hot pursuit of one at the north end of the property; speedier than it looked, it made a loud whirring noise, as if it were wearing a propeller beanie. Daisy missed that one, but she got lots of others. We decided that she loved them because they were "crunchy on the outside, chewy on the inside."

One Thanksgiving Day at the ranch, we were all—parents, siblings, children, dogs, friends—walking up the steep hill above the lake when

Daisy proudly came galloping up to us with what she must have thought was an unusually hairy armadillo in her mouth. She was delighted until she dropped it at our feet and found that much of it remained in her mouth. (It was, of course, a porcupine.)

Sweet as she was, she allowed us to pull out many of the hundreds of spines in her snout, under her tongue, in her gums, etc., but the job proved to be too much for us. Even though it was a holiday, we tracked down a laconic vet in Hunt who said he wasn't doing anything but watching football, so sure, bring her on in. When they had gotten Daisy anesthetized and yanked out the remaining spines, Martin said to the vet, "Well, I bet most dogs only make this mistake once, right?" The vet cocked an eyebrow and said, "You'd be surprised." Thank heavens we haven't been surprised since then.

A few years later, we found a black puppy with a broken back leg at the gate who turned out to be Phoebe, our now-blind life-guide. Phoebe has been a wonderful walking companion, although one of her chief virtues—steadiness—may very well stem from the fact that her eyesight was never very good; maybe she just didn't see all those armadillos and porcupines and deer. She did notice snakes, however, and helpfully made little sideways hops to notify me that I should step elsewhere.

But even the admirable Phoebe occasionally caused me dismay. Aside from her tragic and annoying moans whenever I stopped to listen for and look at birds, Phoebe proved to be susceptible to wayward influences like, for example, our next dog, Honey. One day, a couple of months after Daisy died, I was at our neighborhood pharmacy in Austin. A couple of local kids who worked there had brought in a dog they'd found on the downtown hike and bike trail, skittish and covered with fleas. Their mothers had told them to find it another home. I looked and saw a fluff-bomb with an absurdly curling tail who might have had chow and/or golden retriever and/or some mountain dog in her, and maybe a little Ewok too. The kids noticed that I couldn't take my eyes off her and asked, "Do you want her?" "Yes," I said, helplessly smitten. Martin said something else, which I can't repeat here, when I returned home with toothpaste, shampoo, and a new dog, but Honey was irresistible.

She was also, alas, flightier than Phoebe. Once, after the kids and our friend Charles and I had scrambled up a beautiful and nearly inaccessible draw at the ranch, we came upon a herd of aoudads, who were as surprised to see us as we were to see them. Honey got a young aoudad in her sights and went after it, determined to tear its throat out, despite the shrieks and rocks we hurled at her. She backed the youngster into a fence while its mother threatened to eviscerate her with her great curling horns. Charles gallantly gave up his belt to get our darling murderous fluff-bomb under control, as Phoebe valiantly barked encouragement from a safe distance.

Another time, one of my favorite emergency-backup children and I went walking with Phoebe and Honey. We were in the canyon where we had once found a pair of rusted iron bedsteads and a rusted cast-iron Dutch oven, just poking around to see what other inexplicable but suggestive oddities we might find, when we heard a series of distinctively coyotic yips in the dense woods around us. In an instant, the dogs were gone, gone, gone. Despite our most beguiling efforts, Phoebe and Honey yodeled their way up to the top of the draw, and then Dave and I heard something else: snorts. Hogs. The woods were so thick we couldn't see them, but we could hear them. Lots of them. Close by. Oh, great, I thought. How am I going to explain to my best friend that her sweet gangly son was carved up by feral hogs because my idiot dogs went gallivanting off to be eaten by a pack of coyotes? We all made it back to the house safely, but Phoebe's irresponsible behavior still galls me.

And then another time, the dogs and I were out by ourselves when they, officers of ranch security, uncovered a plot by a couple dozen sows and piglets to disrupt our walk. Much barkage. Much squealing. Much inelegant scrambling by Someone to get into a tree and above tusk level. Much hilarity in the kitchen after our return to think about Someone sitting in a scruffy little scrub oak for half an hour wondering if the dogs were still alive and if the pigs were really gone. Phoebe got a really scalding series of lectures for that lapse.

Generally speaking, though, Honey and Phoebe were fine walking companions. When Honey died of cancer a few years ago, we realized that she had been acting as Phoebe's seeing-eye dog, because Phoebe's deteriorating eyesight meant she was quite literally lost without her. Phoebe's ranch rambles have ended, but Chula the Goggle-Eyed Ricochet Hound has become my new companion and is presenting all sorts of interesting challenges.

While she doesn't seem to have Daisy's and Honey's ferocious streak (except, sadly, when it comes to chickens), she has a hair-trigger chase reflex and is speedy enough to catch a deer, as we learned to our amazement a few years ago (fortunately, once she finally cornered it in the angle of a fence, she seemed content just to lie there panting and stare at it), or anything else that roams the ranch. (She's learned to ignore the bison, a fine survival strategy; despite their awkward-appearing bulkiness, bison are plenty quick themselves, and they definitely don't like dogs.) I've started using a shock collar on her, to discourage her from rocketing off after hogs; I heard not too long ago about a woman whose dogs took off after a bunch of hogs, who then turned on the dogs, who then ran back to their mom, who ended up with sixty stitches in her leg from the pursuing porkers. Fortunately, Chula is a total wienie when it comes to pain, and the early results with the shock collar have been promising.

The adventures, clearly, will continue.

26

Faith, Bureaucracy, and Sheep
Thoughts on Changing One's Mind
NOVEMBER 19, 2010

In my last piece, I decided to postpone my public ululations over the recent elections. As I've spent the last week or so in an apparently endless struggle to get the Madroño Ranch bison label approved by the Texas Department of State Health Services, my ululative impulse has caught in my throat. Maybe Republicans and Tea Partiers are right.

I mean, what difference can it possibly make whether the net weight of the package appears on the bottom third of the label (as required), the middle third, or (gasp) even the upper third? And don't get me started on the "approved" list of cuts, a list whose existence we discovered only after we'd submitted the label, and which has driven our obsessively copy-editing family mad with its redundancies and omissions. Our "Boneless hump roast" was not on the list and so was nixed, but we're fine if we say "Bison Roast (Hump)." Generously, the state allows both "Bison for Stew" and "Bison Stew Meat."

It's enough to make me think Very Ungenerous Thoughts about the government's regulatory role in business or about authority in general.

Some of these thoughts are just moans, like the ones our dog Phoebe the Phabulous used to make when she was forced to stop on our walks while I looked at birds. Oh, the personal inconvenience! But the issue of authority has, in fact, been in my thoughts recently, to wit: when does authority cease to be authoritative? What makes us change our minds? What would make me stop being a "liberal" (if that's what I am) and become a Republican, or even join the Tea Party? I'm not talking here about repressive political authority, but rather those internalized authorities to which we bow without really being aware that we've made a choice.

In thinking about my own track record when it comes to mind changing, I've come to the conclusion that it's not primarily a rational process, as we often presume. Rather, it's a supra-rational affair, requiring the willingness and discipline (and perhaps the talent) necessary to learn a new language.

Here's what I mean: I used to think that all Christians were most likely not just fools—an identity St. Paul claimed—but idiots. Jerry Falwell and the Moral Majority began to fill the airwaves when I was about fifteen or sixteen. Not having had much contact with self-professed Christians at that point, my exposure to this most vocal sector of Christians forced me to conclude that I could never be one of them. From what I could infer, they were anti-intellectual, judgmental, and closed-minded. Their rhetoric made me think that Christianity represented everything I had been taught to turn away from. (Especially the "judgmental" part.)

Imagine my chagrin when, after a series of unexpected and absurd events, I came to be enrolled as a student at the Episcopal Theological Seminary of the Southwest (now known simply as the Seminary of the Southwest). My habitual place of study was a nearby coffee shop. As I studied, I made sure that any books that had the words "God," "Church," or "Jesus" (especially "Jesus"—such an embarrassment) on the cover or spine were face down and turned to the wall. I didn't want to be mistaken for one of "them," one of those stupid sheep who followed an anti-intellectual, judgmental, and closed-minded shepherd. Authority. Whatever.

I learned during my years at the seminary—and during my years as a practicing Christian since then—that I had been mistaken in my first ideas about Christianity. I had to change my mind, and, consequently, my self-identity—an anxiety-provoking and disorienting business. This doesn't mean that I like all Christians. Or even most of them. When I started at seminary, knowing nothing, I had expected to find a bunch of Bad Thinking I could counter and correct.

What I discovered instead was that my initial premise was wrong. I found out that practicing a religion is not the same thing as signing a lease, requiring you to follow a bunch of rules or else be kicked out. Rather, I found that practicing a religion is more like wrestling with a new language. There is a grammar to learn, there are rules to follow. But unless you immerse yourself in it, unless you try to speak it yourself with native speakers—even if you have a lousy accent—you will be just another Ugly American, unaware of your own foolishness.

Having become reasonably fluent in Christianity, I'm trying to learn at least something about the other languages around me. As I learn more about Judaism, Islam, Hinduism, and Buddhism, I don't become less fluent in my own language; rather, I understand it more profoundly. I understand its distinctiveness and thus its limitations. I understand something of its fraught interactions with other religions and have learned the uneasy need for shame and humility. I try not to speak slowly and loudly in my own language when speaking to nonnative speakers and hope they will do the same for me. In my limited experience, I've found hospitality, not hostility, whenever we try, in our different tongues, to speak with each other.

And so I wait to hear yet again from the inspector at the meat processing plant about the newest version of our label. I know that he's pleased about the results of the recent election, as are most of my Hill Country neighbors. I'm pushing this metaphor past its limits, but in order to be a good neighbor myself, I may have to have to learn a little bit of a new language. To understand myself better, I may have to be willing to change my mind.

27

Hosts, Guests, and Strangers
Thoughts on Hospitality

DECEMBER 3, 2010

The season of hospitality is upon us, with all its pleasures and burdens. Known in the Christian tradition as Advent, it focuses on the need for preparation, both for the very intimate event of a baby's birth and for the cosmic birth of a new order. One of my favorite images for the season, if I'm remembering rightly, comes from a series of woodcuts made by a northern Renaissance nun. In it, she imagines herself as a housewife, preparing for the coming company of the Child and the Judge by cleaning the house of her heart: dusting, sweeping, washing, polishing. The images refuse any pretensions to profound theology or high art; they are reassuringly earthbound and homey. If you pay attention, you can almost smell the baking bread.

"Hospitality" is one of those words whose meaning has changed over the years. In our current culture, it often refers to an industry directed toward travelers or those in need who are expected to pay for its services. If hospitality isn't a primarily economic exchange, it usually refers to the opening of home and hearth to friends, family, and associates.

In ancient times (or in places that still hew to ancient ways), hospitality wasn't a service or an option; it was a necessity and a moral imperative. Before the development of institutional hospitality (hospitals, hospices, hostels), vulnerable individuals outside of the normal network of social relations—travelers, refugees, the sick, pilgrims, orphans, widows—were able to rely, at least for a while, on a code of hospitality that brought shame to those who were able and refused to engage it. Christine Pohl, professor of Christian social ethics at Asbury Theological Seminary, writes: "In a number of ancient civilizations, hospitality was viewed as a pillar on which all other morality rested: it encompassed 'the good.'"

Curiously, the words "host" and "guest" are closely related etymologically, if they don't actually come from the same source. Even more interestingly, "guest" shares an etymological bed with "enemy," rooted in the notion of "stranger." The idea that any of us might move from providing hospitality to needing it—to and from strangers—gives the word a kind of trinitarian energy that caroms from the poles of host to guest to stranger/enemy until the parts are indistinguishable from the whole. I don't usually feel that charge when I check into a motel, but I think the hospitable artist nun knew that she was a part of that energy, as hostess opening her heart to the Child; as guest and sojourner on the earth; as stranger before the greatest mystery.

One of the reasons I'm thinking about hospitality, aside from the advent of Advent, is that today we'll welcome seven guests, whom we have never met, to Madroño for the weekend. They'll be attending "Deer School," the brainchild of Jesse Griffiths, chef, butcher, and proprietor (with his wife Tamara Mayfield) of the Dai Due supper club and butcher shop. Deer School will include several guided hunts followed by instructions on how to field dress and use the animal from nose to tail, followed by some really fine eating.

While I've been thinking recently about what it means to be a good host (new sheets and shower curtains), I'm also thinking about my role as guest, sojourner, stranger, enemy; after all, they are intimately connected. As Martin has observed: "On Thanksgiving the acts of preparing, serving, and eating become consciously sacramental; the cook(s) giving, the guest(s) receiving, in a spirit of gratitude that can, sadly, be all too rare at other times of the year." As one of the cooks this year, I was less attuned to what I was giving than to what had been given to me: the gorgeous vegetables from local farms, the fresh turkey from our oversubscribed friends Jim and Kay Richardson, and the freshly shot and skinned half hog that unceremoniously appeared on the kitchen counter (and then spent eight hours roasting in a pit) after my brother, his son, our son, and Robert, the redoubtable ranch manager, went hunting early Thursday morning. The astonishing abundance and hospitality of the land was quite literally overwhelming: half a 150-plus-pound sow is a lot of meat.

I'm blundering onto mushy and possibly treacherous literary territory here, I know: Mother Earth nourishing her offspring, big hugs all around. But I'm increasingly grateful for the bounty of the place and hope the same for those who come here seeking community, solitude, rest, refreshment, and, yes, fresh deer meat. We call Madroño Ranch ours by some weird cosmic accident; the more we know it, the more we know that it belongs to itself or to something even broader, wider, more generous. What we hope now is to avoid being the nightmare guest/enemy, the one who comes and overstays his or her welcome within twenty minutes, who demands foods you don't have, strews clothes all over the house, leaves trash and dirty dishes in the guest room, noisily stays up late, assumes you'll do all the laundry, and never says please or thank you. Who seems to think he or she owns the place.

We all know places where that's exactly what has happened; for me, one such place is the stretch of Interstate 35 between San Antonio and Austin, which Martin and I drove last Sunday morning, and which is almost completely lined with outlet malls, chain stores, fast-food franchises, and other such marks of our collective thoughtlessness. Somehow, we've managed to promote the idea, especially in the American West and particularly in Texas, that among the rights accruing to property owners is the right to destroy or devalue their property in the name of short-term economic gain. In fact, destroying property may be seen as the ultimate proof of ownership.

I struggled in an earlier piece ("Made for You and Me: Some Thoughts on Private Property") with the idea of landownership, and I struggle with it still. All land came as a gift at some point. Not literally to its current owner, perhaps, but the land still bears the trace of its giftedness somewhere on that deed. In this season when we prepare for the arrival of guests, giving the gift of hospitality, or head somewhere hoping to be good guests, bringing gifts of thanks, it can be easy to forget that we are also always empty-handed strangers, constantly looking for a wider hospitality than we are ever able to offer or sometimes even to know that we need. We're only a week past Thanksgiving; this is as good a time as any to thank the land that sustains us. Without it, we can never fill a house with the smells of baking bread and roasting meat—or any of the other things that sustain us.

28

Singing in the Dark

DECEMBER 17, 2010

The relentless sunshine of the current weather here in Austin might make those in the Midwest or on the East Coast sigh with envy. A photo on the front page of Tuesday's *New York Times* shows an Ohio man ineffectually fending off the great whorls of snow around him with an umbrella. His head is bent, his shoulders hunched, his attention presumably forced inward. Strangely, as I bask in the sunshine, I'm the one who's a little envious.

Not of the cold, certainly—I start getting chilly when the temperature drops below eighty degrees. But what I see in the picture is someone forced by the world to withdraw his attention from it, to shift his focus inward, even if it's just to check in and notice that he's cold. He won't be able to stay out for long; he must retreat inside.

In one of her typically wonderful blogs, our friend Joy recently wrote an homage to darkness, to the gestational, inward gaze of the season of Advent. The punch line is, of course, that great discipline is required to move inside at this time of year, when a blizzard of parties, shopping, and end-of-year scrambling—or of loneliness and loss—assaults us. Frequently, we just sit out there in the cold, not realizing that we can go inside. Another friend of mine, prone to good works, told me that when she was pregnant and people called asking her to do something, she would look at her waxing belly and say, "Sorry, I'm busy," and then go back to sitting quietly. Even as we attend to the frenetic tempo of this singular season, something beckons us, at least occasionally, to go inside and sit, maybe in the dark.

And what awaits us inside, in the dark? Well, any child can you tell that: scary stuff! *Chupacabras!* Things with too many legs and too many teeth and not enough eyes! With too much hair or not enough, with horns and scales and long dirty nails! The list of monsters gets less imaginative but no less scary as we get older: past humiliations and failures, anxieties about money, relationships, reputation, health, death. All those things wait for us in the dark. (Of course, sometimes they wait for us in broad daylight as well.)

But that's not all that waits there. Wendell Berry, my favorite grumpy sage, has advice on how to get by the monsters:

> *I go among the trees and sit still.*
> *All my stirring becomes quiet*
> *around me like circles on water.*
> *My tasks lie asleep in their places*
> *where I left them, like cattle.*
> *Then what is afraid of me comes*
> *and lives in my sight.*
> *What it fears in me leaves me,*
> *and the fear of me leaves it.*
> *It sings, and I hear its song.*
> *Then what I am afraid of comes.*
> *I live for a while in its sight.*
> *What I fear in it leaves it,*
> *and the fear of it leaves me.*
> *It sings, and I hear its song.*

Those things we fear, according to Berry, have their own songs if we sit still and listen for them. In this particular collection of poems, *A Timbered Choir: The Sabbath Poems, 1979–1997*, the forest is his place of Sunday worship, where he brings his deepest questions and listens to the forest's exhalations, to the words made of branch rustle and river rush and birdsong, iterations of the original Word spoken by God in the beginning. Berry is not alone when what he is afraid of approaches him; he's in the midst of a community he knows intimately.

This kind of trope can dissolve into rank sentimentality and cruelty when those in the midst of the light and bustle use it to admonish those sitting in the sight of what they fear to buck up. But Berry's language in this collection is rooted in an ancient warrant for the practice of sitting in the company of chaos and darkness—when, as God began creating, God shared space with the tohubohu, the formless void, with the darkness, and with the deep. Through them came the words: Let there be. And what came to be was good. It sang.

The fears don't have the last word in the poem: Here's the final verse:

> *After days of labor,*
> *Mute in my consternations,*
> *I hear my song at last,*
> *and I sing it. As we sing,*
> *the day turns, the tree moves.*

Only after he labors and rests from his labors, after he sits quietly and listens to the songs of what fears him and what he himself fears, does Berry hear his own song. Only then is he able to join the singing already in progress, a singing that harmonizes with a wider reality (the turning of the day) and the immediate reality (the moving of the trees).

Whether or not you're observing Advent, the deepening shadows of the season encourage most of us to move inside and prepare ourselves for this inexorable guest, darkness. Some of us will cook, some of us will shop, some of us will wrestle with monsters and despair, some will not pause from our labors or notice anything at all. If possible, go sit quietly among the bare trees. Or sit hospitably at home with whatever invisible reality is leavening within you and tell everyone you're busy. Then go find your community and sing.

29

The Rising Light

JANUARY 14, 2011

Although it's sometimes hard to tell, we're in the season of rising light. Some of us have a confused relationship with this time of year. The prevailing story, at least in Western culture, has a particular purchase on anyone who's lived through a northeastern, midwestern, or Great Plains winter. That story relates the flare of cheer in the Christmas season, followed by a plunge into the long, dark, depressing slog of January, February, and March. People who live in this story yearn for sunlit beaches, skimpy clothing, and drinks with little umbrellas in them, reminding them of what they've temporarily left behind. Anyone with aching snow-shoveling muscles in New England after this week's blizzard will attest to the power of this story of the season. The rising of the light—the lengthening of days—is a promise of kinder times ahead.

Many of us in Central Texas long—perversely, perhaps—for this story to ring true here as well. (I'm wife or mother of some of them.) We yearn for a white Christmas, and when the late December temperature creeps up to the 80 degree mark, we moan, "It's not supposed to be like this! It's supposed to be cold!" Despite the prevailing story that cold and dark are to be dreaded, in Central Texas this is the season to yearn for, the season of dark and (intermittent) cold. For at least some of the year, it's the light and heat, not the cold and dark, that can be downright unpleasant, almost unbearable. I feel that our winter and spring (so compressed they can be conflated) are the equivalent of fall in New England. Tourists come and say, "How beautiful!" but the natives sigh, knowing that what's just ahead will require some toughness to get through. Here it can be a real pleasure to burrow into the dark; the rising light brings with it a whiff of the (probable) scorching to come.

My musing on light has its roots in nonclimatological terrain as well; Martin and I are in a group that's reading and discussing *Genesis: Translation and Commentary*, by Robert Alter. Although there's no particular comment on that most famous of first utterances, Let there be light, I can't help but think about what it might mean that light is the firstborn of creation, at least according to Jews and Christians. This light is distinctive from sunlight and moonlight, which weren't created until the fourth day, and which seem to be subordinate to the aboriginal light of the first day. As God's breath hovered over the waters, over the deep, and the darkness, God spoke, and there was light. And God saw the light. Presumably this means that God had not experienced light before this moment, although virtually everything I just wrote—God, experienced, light, before this moment—should probably be in quotation marks or resting on a tower of footnotes. But according to this story, light is humanity's older sibling, both of them created by that which knew the deep, the dark, the tohubohu before they did in a distinctive way: before the light.

I've also been lurching my way through Marilyn Robinson's elegant new screed *Absence of Mind: The Dispelling of Inwardness from the Modern Myth of the Self*, in which she argues against what she sees as an absurdly reductive definition of the human brain and mind by some, perhaps many, modern scientists, a definition that refuses to take into account what she calls "that haunting I who wakes in the night wondering where time has gone, the I we waken to sharply aware that we have been unfaithful to ourselves, that a life lived otherwise would have acknowledged a yearning more our own than any of the daylit motives whose behests we answer to so diligently." This "haunting I," so profoundly felt, is dismissed by those scientists (or "parascientists," as she calls them) as mere subjectivity or, worse, evidence of the annoyingly persistent and primitive superstition we moderns call religion.

In one of those serendipitous encounters with my subconscious, as I reread Robinson's description of this persistent human sense of haunted-ness, of leasing interior real estate to someone you recognize but don't really know, I read the next sentence completely wrong. She writes: "Our religious traditions give us as the name of God two deeply mysterious words, one deeply mysterious utterance: I AM." Except at first, I read "I AM"—God's own self-definition—as "1 A.M."

I AM often awake at 1 a.m., in the deepest dark of the night, the time when most of us know ourselves to be haunted. If you awaken at 1 a.m. with a dream vibrating in your mind, the dream stays with you in ways that it doesn't when you wake to light. Sometimes you can play with the dream, poke and shape it in ways that make it pop when it encounters daylight. Sometimes at 1 a.m. you can be wide awake and create as complicated a nightmare as any dreaming mind can produce. To stalk the mind at night—at least, for some of us—is to move as close to the realm of tohubohu, of aboriginal chaos, as created beings are able to get, at least without ingesting psychotropic drugs or harrowing the hell of human atrocity.

Despite the categorical confusion it causes, this season may be my favorite, if for no other reason than the blade-bright light of late afternoon, especially as I get to see it from the kitchen window at Madroño. The copper and golden grasses of the pasture in front of the house blaze as the sun drops behind the western hills, each shoot seemingly sharp enough to pierce the chests of the bison passing across it. The bison themselves look like something out of an ancient dream, not the product of my own tiny experiences but arising from some atavistic communal memory.

There are those who might pooh-pooh these moments as fanciful or irrelevant to anything "real." But in this time of rising light, this time between sleep and waking, between the relief of winter and the slog of summer, I'm compelled to remember that light and humanity once inhabited the same chaotic womb, that we rise and fall together. It's a good season, once you've written your thank-you notes, to watch the rising light with gratitude for the family of creation. And with resignation, too: if it's already January 14, August will be here before we can even blink.

30

Shooting Holes in the Constitution
Some Thoughts on Guns and Violence
JANUARY 28, 2011

Recently, like many Americans, I've been thinking about the issue of guns in civil society. The tragic shooting in Tucson certainly focused attention on the topic, as did a story on National Public Radio that identified the United States as the source of most of the guns being used by cartels in the Mexican drug wars, a story that aired days before we visited friends whose ranch is just a few miles from the Rio Grande. But other, more personal circumstances also got me thinking, like the three different episodes of gun violence, or the threat of gun violence, that occurred during the past semester on the college campuses (two thousand miles apart) where two of our children are students. And all this happened before our first bison harvest at Madroño Ranch this past Monday, in which two 1,500-pound animals were felled by single shots from a .270 rifle.

Full disclosure: I don't own a gun myself, although we have a gun safe well stocked with rifles and shotguns at the ranch. (They mostly belong to our son.) My grandfather taught me to shoot with a pellet gun, an activity he oversaw carefully and I enjoyed mightily. I still take pleasure in target practice and found, the one time I tried it, that shooting skeet was a fine way to while away an afternoon. I don't hunt and don't expect that I ever will, although I have no objection to ethical hunting. I've thought that it might be wise to have a pistol when I wander around the ranch, in case one of the dogs riles up a pack of feral hogs and brings them back to me. My fear of shooting my own dog is sharper than my fear of rampaging pigs, however, and I remain pistol-less.

While there's been no change in the number of guns I own, my thinking about guns has changed considerably over the last few years, to wit: I've concluded that there's a difference between urban guns and rural guns. (Yes, yes, hold your applause.) A gun is a necessary tool on a ranch or farm. I'm very grateful that Robert, the ranch's fearsome manager, is an excellent shot. If the bulls we harvested this week felt any pain, it was less than momentary; they were dead quite literally within a couple of seconds.

And then there's the issue of self-defense. A friend recently told me about an encounter he'd had on his remote South Texas ranch with an armed and heavily tattooed non-English-speaking trespasser he suspected of being a member of the fearsome MS-13 gang. My friend didn't have a firearm at hand, but fortunately, after a tense exchange, the trespasser left. "I've never felt so naked," my friend said. I understand: I, too, would have wanted some clothing in that situation.

And yet, and yet . . . we recently saw and thoroughly enjoyed the Coen brothers' adaptation of *True Grit*. That is, Martin saw it; I had my hands over my eyes during several violent scenes. Even so, I loved the movie. At the same time, I made a new connection: embedded in the myth of the American West is the image of the lone gunman, meting out swift and violent justice. No amount of regulation is going to smother the breath from that compelling image.

Don't get me wrong; I'm all for intelligent gun control. I've never felt so naked as the day that a student opened fire on the UT Austin campus a block from the room where our son Tito was in class. But I emphatically would not have felt more clothed if, as a bill passed by the Texas senate in 2009 proposed, his fellow students been permitted to carry concealed handguns. Guns do not belong on campuses. Or in the hands of the mentally ill. Anyone who wants to own a gun has a responsibility to register, and law enforcement agencies should be able to trace every gun to its owner. Anyone who wants to buy an automatic or semiautomatic weapon should have to jump through a lot more hoops than a weekend hunter does. Gun shows should be heavily regulated. But the image of that lone, justice-seeking gunman is more powerful than any regulation. Did I walk out of *True Grit* disgusted by its glorification of violence? Of course not. I loved it, even as I was distressed by some of it. The story is part of my identity as a westerner, as a Texan.

On Wednesday, as I was wrestling with this piece, Martin received a membership solicitation from the NRA. I suspect that the trigger for this unlikely offer must be the fact that he recently purchased from Amazon.com a copy of José Ortega y Gasset's *Meditations on Hunting*, the introduction of which was written by a visiting professor of environmental perception at Dartmouth College—not exactly a rip-roarin' shoot-'em-up. If I'm correct, the NRA's tracking mechanisms qualify as spooky at best, and maybe terrifying, but also revelatory of a mentality that refuses to see any kind of subtlety or gradation of perception.

Here's the opening salvo of that membership solicitation: "Your constitutional right to own a gun is under attack by hundreds of anti-gun politicians, global gun ban diplomats at the U.N., militant anti-hunting extremists, radical billionaires and the freedom-hating Hollywood elite."

The letter consistently associates freedom with gun ownership; restricting gun ownership equals restricting personal freedom. "Remember: the NRA is the one firewall that stands between our Second Amendment rights and those who would take our freedoms away." Freedom, in this view, has nothing to do with national service, with love of country and fellow citizens, with restraint or knowledge or self-discipline.

I visited the NRA website and found it even more appalling than its fear-mongering letter. Of the assault in Tucson, it says:

> Our thoughts and prayers are with the victims of this senseless tragedy, including Representative Gabrielle Giffords, and their families during this difficult time. We join the rest of the country in praying for the quick recovery of those injured.

There was no condemnation of the gunman who perpetrated the senseless tragedy. There was no call for self-examination. There was no exhortation to the faithful to adhere to any code of responsibility or ethics. I found nothing that encouraged gun-owner restraint or training, or an acknowledgment of the enormous social responsibility that comes with owning a gun.

I did find a persistent paranoia that encourages NRA members and sympathizers to view strangers as threatening and potentially aggressive. I did find—even as someone with a sympathetic view of some gun use—a willful and destructive distortion of that figure so many Americans love: Rooster Cogburn, the courageous gunman who takes the law into his own hands and then rides off into the empty landscape. Many of us love Rooster, yes, but his place is in the mythic past, not in the increasingly urban present.

I know and respect—and even love—individual members of the NRA; my grandfather was one of them. I went to its site in hopes of finding something to change my mind about gun control. But I left loathing the rhetoric the NRA has adopted in recent years. (In this regard, I highly recommend Jill Lepore's excellent article "The Commandments," about the way various groups, including the NRA, have sought to interpret the Constitution, in the January 17 issue of the *New Yorker,* and thank our daughter Elizabeth for bringing it to my attention.) To encourage people to think that their fellow citizens are their enemies is surely to unravel the careful work of the Constitution, which recognizes the precarious balance inherent in a federalist system, a balance requiring trust, self-restraint, and mutual good will among its participants. So while calls for legislation are important in curbing American's extravagant gun violence, they aren't enough; we need to call the NRA's violent distortions of the Constitution to account. Maybe guns don't kill people; maybe it's NRA rhetoric that kills people.

31

Meat and Flourishment
Carnivorocity, Take Two

FEBRUARY 11, 2011

Martin's recent piece describing the first slaughter (and I use the word "slaughter" advisedly) in our new endeavor as purveyors of bison meat elicited a comment that urged us to consider the ethical fault line (presumably) running through every conscience, that unsteady place where we find ourselves rationalizing our actions to ourselves or to whatever audience our imaginations conjure up.

Martin tried to make his/our unease clear with the piece's title: "Bloody Hands." So I'm wondering once again about the ethics of carnivorocity, as visible and treacherous a fault line as abortion, euthanasia, gun control, climate change, or cloning: when you stand on one side of the fault line, it's easy to think that the earth itself will justify you when it opens up and swallows the dummies over there, proving that you were on the right side, at which point you can stop worrying all the time, for heaven's sake, and go on your merry way without thinking about the issue ever again.

As usual, diving into the conversations available on the internet just sucked me deeper into the murk. A defense is available for every possible position and offered with wildly varying degrees of civility: meat eaters supporting vegans and trashing vegetarians; meat eaters sneering at any thought of self-restriction; vegetarians and vegans calling meat eaters all sorts of names; vegetarians acknowledging that some meat eating is environmentally acceptable; meat eaters acknowledging that American meat production and consumption is for the most part grotesque. What's a utopian-minded bison rancher to think?

Serendipity, as usual, is my guide. In chasing internet rabbits down their holes, I found a momentary resting place in a review of Maggie Kozel's book *The Color of Atmosphere: One Doctor's Journey In and Out of Medicine*. After describing a flummoxing patient she had as a second-year medical student, Kozel said, "[I] devoured the answers without asking the right questions."

Of course, if you're obsessive the way I am, then you'll immediately begin worrying about what the right questions are, as in, if I'm "right" then others must be "wrong." One of the hallmarks of the debate about meat eating and its impact on the environment or the individual soul is the array of statistics and science that each side has amassed to prove the objective superiority of its argument. I've been persuaded by both sides and neither side, depending on the time of day, what I've just read, the weather, my most recent meal, and/or the health of my family, among other random criteria.

In other words, I don't think science and statistics by themselves allow us to ask the right questions, since apparently convincing evidence can be found to shore up either side. Eating is one of those human activities rich with multiple levels of meaning; expecting questions directed at a specific level to adequately address the full range is a little like expecting a monoculture to support the diversity a polyculture allows. Although science poses some vitally important questions when it examines the issue of meat eating, the nature of its inquiry must ignore other equally pressing but less quantifiable questions, such as, what conditions allow a multispecies community to flourish? Does eating meat (by humans) contribute or detract from our community's flourishment (a word coined by our friend Hugh Fitzsimons of Thunder Heart Bison)?

I hear the howls of protest even before I finish typing this sentence: how do you measure flourishment? Who decides the standards? Invalid! Too subjective! Well, yes. That's what makes this a fault-line issue; it addresses the limits of our humanity and so necessarily includes subjective experience. To be honest, I don't know how to measure flourishment; I suspect you just know it when you see it. And when you see it, you're moved to describe it, knowing that the urge will be frustrated to at least some degree because flourishment, like all fruit, is the result of such a complex interaction of elements in space and time that any description will be incomplete. And of course it's not a steady state; it waxes and wanes as circumstances change and sometimes double back on themselves.

In this context, the question of whether meat eating is ethical can be answered unequivocally: it depends. One of the preconditions for flourishment is a sense of justice, a perspective that includes but also rises above the immediate tit-for-tat concerns of fairness. The scope of justice includes not just humanity but the earth itself—and perhaps the cosmos. It unrolls over the course of history, recognizing that particular injustices sometimes take generations, centuries, or millennia to wither, even with the powerful witness and effort of prophets and their followers. As I said in an earlier piece, it may be that vegetarians and vegans are living forward into a time where justice is more fully realized. At the same time, issues of fairness and justice press at us every moment in this world where the lion and the lamb cannot yet lie down together, where predators are a vital part of an ecosystem that has developed in sync with domesticated animals.

Can meat be produced and consumed in a way that encourages justice and, hence, flourishment? I think it can. There are multiple instances of communities and societies that eat meat and live within that delicate balance that looks to the long-term well-being and dignity of the system as a whole, places like Joel Salatin's Polyface Farm, although there are many, many others. (We'd love to hear some of your favorites.) There are multiple instances of communities and cultures flourishing without eating meat, most notably for the purposes of this piece the Hindu cultures whose vegetarian cuisines I eat with great pleasure. (We'd love to hear some of your favorites.)

Likewise, there are communities and cultures that eat meat without flourishing, including most of the industrialized world, where concern for short-term profits and their consequent incitement of unrestrained appetite smother any hope of flourishment under mountains of animal excrement and anguish. Those places that encourage us (in the industrialized world) to measure the value of food in one way only—cheap is best—smother flourishment. Food is at the center of family, of community, of myth, of life. To reduce its essence to a single component is to denature its multivalent nutritional value.

Back to the ethical fault line, that place we stand uneasily, knowing that we may be swallowed: may those of us who recognize the fault line join hands—bloody or not—across the chasm and help each other seek the firmer footing of justice as our foundation. Flourishment will surely follow.

32

A Field That Don't Yield
Writer's Block and the Language of Community
FEBRUARY 25, 2011

One of the many notable gatherings in which Martin and I participated this past weekend was the opening of my sister Isa Catto Shaw's show at the Harvey/Meadows Gallery in Aspen, Colorado. In a series of watercolors and collages, she took the dark, mute burden of grief over the death of our mother and worked it into beautifully articulate packages, in some ways (perhaps) making that grief more easily borne because it is shared with a community of unknown mourners who see the paintings, with the community of artists from whom she has drawn inspiration, and from the community in which she and her family live. As far as I could tell, the opening was a wonderful success, the gallery full to overflowing as Isa and the ceramicist Doug Casebeer, with whom she shared the show, each spoke movingly about the impetus behind their individual efforts.

Knowing that she had been working like a madman for several months, I was glad (and deeply moved) to see the results of her labors. And aggravated. We've been talking since our mother died about a collaboration of my poetry and Isa's art to be titled "Blessings of a Mother." Isa's done her part, and it's intimidatingly beautiful.

I, on the other hand, have done squat. This doesn't mean I haven't thought obsessively about the project or that I haven't written multiple lists of topics and scraps of lines and stillborn poems. It does mean that I've been willing to be endlessly distracted and grumpy about it. I've developed all sorts of hypotheses about why I'm not writing and what I might do about it, most of them ultimately involving running away from home. My favorite defense against the terrorism of the blank page is to read, figuring that in doing so I'm in the company of someone else who has faced, at least temporarily, the tyranny of That Which Demands Expression And Remains Unexpressed. Plus, if I'm reading, I can't write.

So here's what I'm currently reading to fend off—and perhaps eventually to outsmart—the intimidation tactics of the blank page: *Standing by Words*, a collection of essays by Wendell Berry, in particular the title essay and its assertion that the primary obligation of language is to connect the idiom of the internal self with the multivalent tongues the self encounters in community, both human and otherwise. When language loses that capacity—a loss currently encouraged by the forces of industrial technology—both the self and its community languish in their isolation, succumbing eventually to a fatal disconnection from the web of love and life.

As always, Berry is defiantly unfashionable, insisting on the possibility of "fidelity between words and speakers or words and things or words and acts." He believes that genuine communication is possible, even if its processes are ultimately mysterious and unavailable for dissection by specialists. The life of language is rooted in community and by the precision that life in community necessitates:

> It sounds like this: "How about letting me borrow your tall jack?" Or: "The old hollow beech blew down last night." Or, beginning a story, "Do you remember that time . . .?" I would call this community speech. Its words have the power of pointing to things visible either to eyesight or to memory.

Community speech doesn't imagine abstract futures; rather, it deals with what IS. It creates a walkway between internal, personal systems and external, public systems. Community speech registers the need to include both objective and subjective experience; it deflects the argot of specialists; it recognizes spheres of being beyond its domain. Says Berry:

> If one wishes to promote the life of language, one must promote the life of the community—a discipline many times more trying, difficult, and long than that of linguistics, but having at least the virtue of hopefulness. It escapes the despair always implicit in specializations: the cultivation of discrete parts without respect or responsibility for the whole. . . . [Community speech] is limited by responsibility on

the one hand and by humility on the other, or in Milton's terms, by
magnanimity and devotion.

Although I would argue with Berry's assertion that all specialists are with-
out awareness of their place in the "whole household in which life is lived"
and thereby exclude themselves from the liveliness of community speech,
I hearken to the limits he sets on speech, limits that protect the tender
shoots of hopefulness, a crop that can be distressingly rare in an often
grief-stricken world.

Forgive me. For an essay that aims, in part, to wrestle with ways to express
the specificity and universality of grief, my language is so far distressingly
abstract, a symptom, I suspect, of my current stuckness. I just received a
note from an acquaintance who recently lost her husband to pancreatic
cancer; she wrote that although she and her daughter have prepared for his
death for a year, "it is like the bad dream where you show up for an exam
without having read the book, in your PJs, totally unprepared." I was struck
by the generosity of the image, by her assumption that, though I have not
experienced her particular and devastating sorrow, I could somehow imagi-
natively engage with it, and that we both belonged to the same community,
despite the fact that we've only met twice before.

Writing is usually perceived to be a solitary pursuit, and in a very literal
way it is. I'm trying to remember, however, that when I stare at the blank
page or screen I'm seldom alone. (I'm not referring to the cats who often
take naps behind me on my chair.) Trying to remember: trying to listen
for the cloud of witnesses, the dead and the unborn, that root us in the
past and impel us toward the future. I found Rainer Maria Rilke's *Duino
Elegies* compelling after my mother's death, in part because their language
is so rich and their meaning so elusive, like a whispered conversation from
another plane of being. In the translation by J. B. Leishman and Stephen
Spender, they begin with this lament:

> *Who, if I cried, would hear me among the angelic*
> *orders? And if one of them suddenly*
> *pressed me against his heart, I should fade in the strength of his*
> *stronger existence. For Beauty's nothing*
> *but beginning of Terror we're still just able to bear,*
> *and why we adore it so is because it serenely disdains*

to destroy us. Every angel is terrible.
And so I repress myself, and swallow the call-note
Of depth-dark sobbing.

Although Rilke refuses to call on the angels, they soar in and out of the poems, weaving them together, helping create a complex whole from parts threatening to hurtle toward meaninglessness and isolation.

I'm usually suspicious of angel-talk, but Wendell Berry and my widowed acquaintance and my sister all remind me that I am—we are all—surrounded by angels, by community, even when we don't sense its presence. When we are deaf to its song, we are deaf to our own.

Now if they'd only settle down and write those poems for me. Or at least recommend some nice writer's residency where I could get them started.

33

Lenten Reflections
Dead Trees, Bafflement, and Submission

MARCH 11, 2011

Fittingly, this Ash Wednesday began with a vigorous north wind, the kind that knocks dead branches out of trees and can make you a little leery about walking outdoors. It blew me back to the moment when I first got a glimpse into the meaning of Lent.

I had vaguely thought of "giving something up for Lent" as an opportunity to practice self-discipline and to display a sense of commitment to a "good" life, a sort of spiritual calisthenics that made you feel better, especially when you stopped. The events I recalled weren't, on the surface, particularly interesting or dramatic, but they allowed me to see myself from a previously undiscovered vantage point. For the first time, I could see I was like a tree filled with dead branches that needed some serious pruning in order to keep growing. Observing Lent wasn't a way to prove how strong I was; it was a space offered in which I might look at all my dead branches and wonder how I, with the north wind's help, might clear some of them out, while trusting that I wouldn't get knocked out by falling timber.

A time for submission; no wonder Lent gets a bad rap. Who wants to submit, especially after a look at the roots of the word: "sub-" is from the Latin for "under," and "-mit" is from *mittere*, to send or throw or hurl. To submit to something is to hurl yourself under it—"it" presumably being a force much greater than your itty-bitty self, a force like, say, a speeding F350 pickup. In fact, it might even take some courage to submit to the scouring blast of Lent.

In a recent blog post, Martin considered some of the complexities of being from a particular place, ending with a beautifully expressed desire to be here, rooted in this rocky Hill Country soil. Imagine his exasperation when I said last night that I felt like I needed a vacation. My desire to run away (presumably temporary) probably has several sources, but one of them may be an awareness that the idea of Madroño Ranch is taking on heft and weight, leaving behind the dreamy elasticity of fantasy.

I'm reminded of my reaction to our daughter Elizabeth's first vision test. It had been suggested by her third grade teacher, who had never had a student make so many arithmetic mistakes, especially in copying problems from the chalkboard onto paper. The test results were normal; Elizabeth wasn't nearsighted, just math-impaired. First I mourned that she would never be an astronaut or an engineer or a mathematician, but then I realized that we now knew more about who she really was; she was beginning to take on her own form, independent of my fantasies for her.

In a lovely essay titled "Poetry and Marriage: The Use of Old Forms," Wendell Berry (of course) unearths the kinship between marriage and formal poetry: both begin in "the giving of words," and live out their time standing by those words:

> In marriage as in poetry, the given word implies the acceptance of a form that is never entirely of one's own making. When understood seriously enough, a form is a way of accepting and living within the limits of creaturely life. We live only one life and die only one death. A marriage cannot include everybody, because the reach of responsibility is short. A poem cannot be about everything, for the reach of attention and insight is short.

Choosing a form implies the setting of limits, limits that appear arbitrary from the outside or at the outset, but that can open into generosity and possibility as they are practiced. Even as they limit, these old forms point their practitioners to a way through self-delusion toward truth, through loneliness toward community. Individual failures are certainly possible, but they aren't necessarily arguments against the forms themselves. In fact,

> it may be . . . that form serves us best when it works as an obstruction to baffle us and deflect our intended course. It may be that when we no longer know what to do we have come to our real work and that when we no longer know which way to go we have begun our real

*journey. The mind that is not baffled is not employed. The impeded
stream is the one that sings.*

This past weekend we hosted "Hog School" at the ranch, the second in an
ongoing series of sustainable hunting/butchering/cooking/eating extrava-
ganzas put on by Jesse Griffiths of Austin's Dai Due supper club. I spent
much of the weekend baffled (and not in a good way) by rifle-toting guests
scattered across the property hunting feral hogs, by the seemingly effortless
magic with which chef Morgan Angelone produced gorgeous and delicious
treats from the kitchen (*my* kitchen, mind you, my *philandering* kitchen
purring in someone else's hands), by my own mental contortions.

I finally decided to go for a walk where I was unlikely to be mistaken for
a hog. Marching through the field by the lake and muttering imprecations
against the wind (no birds to watch), the lack of rain (no grass coming up),
and the hunters (no long walks available), I decided to climb to the base of
the cliffs above me and head back to the house by a new route.

Though they can be steep, the Hill Country hills aren't exactly the Alps;
climbing to the base of the cliffs only takes a few minutes and a lot of grabs
at branches to keep from sliding back down in the loose mulch and rocks
that just barely hold the hills up. Once I got into the still-leafless trees, I
began lurching across the perpetually shifting terrain and found that it was
impossible to walk and look at the same time; if I wanted to walk, I had
to watch my feet carefully, and if I wanted to look, I had to stop and make
sure I was balanced before I shifted my gaze. It made for slow going because,
unexpectedly, there was a lot to see that I hadn't noticed from below.

I found a fine moss-covered boulder that allowed me a new vantage
point from which to look down and into the trees and brush I normally
looked up at, a posture that causes the painful condition among birders
known as "warbler neck." I quickly misidentified several sparrows, and with
an un-aching neck, was able to track down some raucous spotted towhees
making rude observations from a clump of yaupons and to lecture them
briefly. Staring at my feet as I staggered across the hillside, I found that
grasses, indeed, were beginning to sprout, despite the drought. Skidding
onto my derriere—it always happens off-roading on these hills—I was able
to observe the first blush of a blooming redbud tree, closely guarded by the
great daggered yucca beside it. And then, as the wind picked up again, the
rich thick smell of honey clogged the air. The source? Tiny yellow blossoms

nestled under agarita spines—tiny and extravagantly generous and impossible to pick without getting pricked. The wind blew my hat off, and, setting off multiple rockslides, I chased it gracelessly down the hill.

Limits: from dust you were made and to dust you shall return. Bafflement: unexpected forms arising, unforeseen paths opening. Submission: throwing the deadwood of the ego into the flames of the Unnamable One. That's a lot to wrestle with during the mere forty days of Lent.

34

Tragic Waste
Thoughts on the S-Word
MARCH 25, 2011

Watching the bats from the kitchen stoop at Madroño Ranch the other
morning was a little like watching my own thoughts. They swooped in
and out of my line of vision, limited by the dawn darkness, more audible
than visible.

Actually, my comparison is disrespectful of the bats; their flight is only
apparently erratic, driven by the ever-changing location of the insects they
were chasing. My thoughts are *actually* erratic. As the promise of light
bloomed into dawn, the bats settled into the bat house, a feat of precision
flying and landing almost like none I've seen, and I noticed the pile of guano
under the house and thought that soon it would be time to collect it and
put it on the compost pile.

And so began my musings on shit and the difference between good shit
and bad shit. My apologies to the bats become ever more profound.

One of our current projects at the ranch is figuring out how to use the
abundant quantities of manure the residents of the Chicken Palace produce.
Currently, it's just collected and dumped onto the compost pile, but we're
working on a plan to get the chickens more fresh greenery to eat, in part
self-fertilized (by the chickens, that is). We're planning to cordon their
pasture off into sections and seed the sections with cover crops, alfalfa,
rye—whatever the season will grow. We'll soon have a rainwater collection
system in place and will be able to irrigate with it (assuming it ever rains
again). Using a portable fence, we'll be able to rotate the chickens from
section to section. We have no idea if this will work, but it seems like a
good idea and a fine, closed-loop use of all that poop. We're also looking

to collect buffalo leavings (summer "interns": consider yourselves warned!) and use them as well.

Perhaps you've noticed that I used all sorts of synonyms for shit in the previous paragraph; one of the few I didn't use is "waste," because in natural systems, or systems that mimic natural systems, shit isn't waste, it's integral and beneficial. Paraphrasing Our Hero Wendell Berry, Michael Pollan notes in *The Omnivore's Dilemma: A Natural History of Four Meals* that industrial agriculture has taken an elegant solution—crops feed animals, whose manure in turn fertilizes crops—and "divide[d] it into two new problems: a fertility problem on the farm . . . and a pollution problem on the feedlot." Concentrated Animal Feeding Operations (CAFOs), the current source of most of America's meat, produce mountains of manure that becomes toxic to the animals and to the communities around them, and the monoculture farming that produces most of America's grains and vegetables doesn't use animals to fertilize the soil, requiring farmers to use chemicals instead. That's the difference between good and bad shit: when something that could be beneficial becomes useless, even toxic, waste.

In fact, I'm beginning to wonder if a community's or even a culture's capacity to endure might not be assessed by how effectively it mimics nature in dealing with its own discharge. I've just been rereading T. C. Boyle's darkly comic *Drop City*, which begins at a northern California commune of the same name in 1970. The commune's stated *raison d'être* is to provide its residents with a place to escape the confines of bourgeois America and get back to the land and basic values by expanding their consciousness with meditation and drugs.

Of course the place is utter chaos, overflowing with the metaphoric excrescences of abusive sexual practices, racism, child neglect, and rampant narcissism, along with literal shit. The septic system is overloaded and the two characters who concern themselves with the problem get no help at all from the community. Eventually, the county government threatens to raze the buildings because the commune constitutes a health hazard. Because they can't deal with their own shit on any level, the residents of Drop City abandon what was once beautiful land and move their chaos to the bush country of Alaska just as summer is waning. When they get there, most of them realize that they need to leave or get their shit together so they don't die.

The problem is that getting your shit together necessitates acknowledging that you are, in fact, going to die. (It's still Lent, after all. You knew we'd get to this.) Ernest Becker, in his Pulitzer Prize–winning *The Denial of Death*, identifies the human dilemma in scatological terms: we are the "god[s] who shit."

> *Look at man* [sic], *the impossible creature! Here nature* . . . [*has*]
> *created an animal who has no defense against full perception of the*
> *external world, an animal completely open to experience.* . . . *He not*
> *only lives in this moment, but expands his inner self to yesterday, his*
> *curiosity to centuries ago, his fears to five billion years from now when*
> *the sun will cool, his hopes to eternity from now. He lives not only on*
> *a tiny territory, not even on an entire planet, but in a galaxy, in a*
> *universe, and in dimensions beyond visible universes. It is appalling,*
> *the burden man bears, the experiential burden.* . . . *Each thing is a*
> *problem and man can shut out nothing. As Maslow has well said, "It*
> *is precisely the god-like in ourselves that we are ambivalent about,*
> *fascinated by and fearful of, motivated to and defensive against. This*
> *is one aspect of the basic human predicament, that we are simultane-*
> *ously worms and gods."* *There it is again: gods with anuses.*

Human civilization, says Becker, is built on this unease, which encourages us to throw our energies into an "immortality project" by which we deny our smelly mortality; those who confront it with none of the filters an immortality project provides wither into mental illness. Becker doesn't attempt to solve this conundrum but rather to set some boundaries within which we can wrestle with it with "the courage to be." He writes in his conclusion:

> *We need the boldest creative myths, not only to urge men on but also*
> *and perhaps especially to help men see the reality of their condition.*
> *We have to be as hard-headed as possible about reality and possibility.*

So it was with interest that I watched the video produced by a Japanese media artist to explain to Japanese children why everyone was so worried about the Fukushima nuclear reactor after it was damaged by the tsunami and earthquake on March 3. The video compares the damaged nuclear reactor to a boy with an upset stomach who needs to poop. So far the boy has just farted—smelly enough for everyone around him—but the video assures us that a team of selfless doctors are doing all they can to prevent Nuclear Boy from pushing out his stinky poop.

The video says that the Fukushima reactor is more like Three Mile Island Boy—who just farted—than like Chernobyl Boy, who not only pooped but had diarrhea that went everywhere, likening nuclear waste to a dirty diaper. My first thought after watching it was that Japanese doctors would be overwhelmed by waves of constipated children, convinced that evacuating their bowels might bring their struggling nation to even deeper depths. My next thought moved me to images in last Sunday's *New York Times* of the city of Chernobyl in its abandoned state and the interview with one of the guardians of "the sarcophagus," the concrete structure built to contain Reactor No. 4, which can't come in contact with water without risking the escape of highly radioactive fumes. Scientists estimate that an area around the reactor the size of Switzerland will remain affected for up to three hundred years. The aftermath of a nuclear meltdown "is a problem that does not exist on a human time frame." The guardian figures that the work he does will be available to his children and grandchildren.

Using my heavily truncated recapitulation of Becker's thought, it seems that proponents of nuclear power (which I have sometimes been) are refusing to be "as hard-headed as possible about reality and possibility," are as unwilling to get our shit together as the drug-addled utopians of Drop City. We are as schizophrenic as the video artist who proposes that we just not poop. A few pages away from the article about Chernobyl was a piece by a Japanese astrophysicist who wrote in reference to the Fukushima reactor crisis:

> *Until a few years ago, power usage in Japan was such that during the summer Obon holidays, when people typically return to their ancestral homes, it would have been possible to meet demand even if all nuclear power plants were turned off. Now, nuclear energy has come to be indispensable for both industry and for our daily lives. Our excessive consumption of energy has somehow become part of our very character; it is something we no longer think twice about.*

Now that I'm trying to tie together all these thematic threads, I have to swoop back to my bat-intensive stoop, to the manure-heavy compost pile in the pasture outside the Chicken Palace. May we humans be as useful as Madroño's bats and chickens as we consider our energy future; may we refuse to resort to the narcissistic chaos of Drop City's residents, who left their spiritual and literal bad shit for someone else to deal with.

35

Dorothea Brooke, Betty Friedan, and Big Ag

APRIL 8, 2011

I'm a lousy housewife, which, in my initial phase of housewifery, is exactly what I aspired to be. Not for me the bourgeois passion for clean baseboards and orderly closets, especially after graduate school in literature in the mid-1980s, in the wake of second-wave feminism. Not for me the fate of the American suburban woman as Betty Friedan described it:

> *freed by science and labor-saving appliances from the drudgery, the dangers of childbirth and the illnesses of her grandmother. She was healthy, beautiful, educated, concerned only about her husband, her children, her home. She had found true feminine fulfillment. As a housewife and mother, she was respected as a full and equal partner to man in his world. She was free to choose automobiles, clothes, appliances, supermarkets; she had everything that women ever dreamed of.*

Nope, I was going to be an independent, defiant, equal-rights-demanding sort of woman who kept her mind on higher things and never, ever got a pedicure—which is why I completely fell in love with Dorothea Brooke, one of the main characters in George Eliot's novel *Middlemarch*: *A Study of Provincial Life*. So complete was my admiration for Dorothea that our younger daughter Thea is named for her.

In rereading *Middlemarch* for the first time in many years, I find that my self-identification with Dorothea's high-minded knuckleheadedness was spot-on. What my younger self missed, of course, was the author's attitude toward it. In the first chapter, Dorothea and her much more practical younger sister Celia are looking through their dead mother's jewelry. Dorothea, fond of renouncing things, at first tells Celia to take all "the trinkets" for herself. Says the narrator: "Celia felt a little hurt. There was a strong assumption of superiority in this Puritanic toleration, hardly less trying to the blond flesh of an unenthusiastic sister than a Puritanic persecution." A few lines later, they find an emerald ring and bracelet they hadn't known about before, and Dorothea's eye is caught by their beauty, "all the while her thought was trying to justify her delight in the colours by merging them in her mystic religious joy." And we're only on page nine of 766; the buds of Dorothea's knuckleheadedness blossom in a leisurely and luxuriant way, flower after flower bursting into a gaudy and most unpuritanical riot in the course of the first 250 pages.

Needless to say, Dorothea doesn't aspire to housewifery (nor, because of her gentle birth, does she much need to), but one of the minor heroes of the novel is, in fact a housewife. Susan Garth is wife to Caleb, a kind and financially inept land surveyor and agent. Before marrying, Susan was a governess, and after marrying she runs the farm, raises their six children, and continues to take in pupils, earning money for her sons' formal educations. She makes her students

> *follow her about in the kitchen with their book or slate. She thought it good for them to see that she could make an excellent lather while she corrected their blunders, "without looking,"—that a woman with her sleeves tucked above her elbows might know all about the Subjunctive Mood or the Torrid Zone—that in short, she might possess "education," and other good things ending in "tion," and worthy to be pronounced emphatically, without being a useless doll.*

Like everyone else in the novel, Mrs. Garth has her weaknesses, but her creator clearly admires her independence, intelligence, hard work, and excellent housewifery skills, which include planning ahead and refusing to let anything, material or emotional, go to waste. When her son begins to snack on the peels from the apple pie she is making, she says, in between pronouncements on grammar: "That apple peel is to be eaten by the pigs, Ben; if you eat it, I must give them your piece of pastry."

One of the most notable differences between Mrs. Garth and Betty Friedan's housewife is that one is an independent producer in a local economy and one is a consumer in a transnational economy. Mrs. Garth's life is the one from which science and labor-saving devices have freed Betty Friedan's housewife, as they free her to choose whatever she liked in consumer goods. I want to make one thing clear: I'm not made of stern enough stuff to lead Mrs. Garth's life, but along with the narrator of *Middlemarch*, I've come to see the unexpected power and vital importance of the place she and her spiritual sisters (many of whom are still around) occupy.

Speaking with an urban farmer friend the other day, I heard about the persistent policy roadblocks in the way of small farmers and the bureaucratic tactics that restrain and even stifle connectivity among local food producers. Although no complaints have ever been raised by customers of this farm in the twenty years of its operation, no sicknesses reported, the assumption of the Texas Department of State Health Services—and apparently of most governmental agencies that deal with food—is that non-factory-produced foods are inherently riskier than factory-produced ones, even though the evidence is overwhelming that the reverse is true. My friend's glum assessment was that the real issue, masked by the apparent anxiety over health concerns, is Big Ag's desire to stomp out competition posed by small, organic farmers and farmers' markets, which have grown at a remarkable pace in the last few years.

In "Feminism, the Body, and the Machine," an essay that infuriated me when I first (mis- or under-)read it years ago, Wendell Berry muses on the responses he got from another essay published in *Harper's*, many of which expressed outrage over his revelation that his wife types his manuscripts after he finishes handwriting them and accused him of exploiting her. He responded that the feminist outrage ignored two possibilities: that marriage can exist as "a state of mutual help," and that households can operates as economies. The marriage and home that he has in mind looks very much like the Garths' and

> *makes around itself a household economy that involves the work of both the wife and the husband, that gives them a measure of economic independence and self-protection, a measure of self-employment, a measure of freedom, as well as a common ground and a common*

satisfaction. Such a household economy may employ the disciplines and skills of housewifery, of carpentry and other trades of building and maintenance, of gardening and other branches of subsistence agriculture. . . . It may even [he says slyly] *involve a "cottage industry" of some kind, such as a small literary enterprise.*

He hastens to add that what he says about this kind of marriage applies to men and women equally, and then calls for "a broader, deeper criticism. . . . The problem is not just the exploitation of women by men. A greater problem is that women and men alike are consenting to an economy that exploits women and men and everything else," particularly as it is practiced by global and "sentimental" capitalism, which operates a lot like sentimental communism: they both demand the sacrifice of "everything small, local, private, personal, natural, good, and beautiful" for the sake of security and happiness for "the many" at some unspecified future time. In freeing transnational corporations from the responsibilities practiced in local economies—knowledge of the needs and capacities of a particular place—our economy produces an astonishing number of products under the condition that consumers "agree to be totally ignorant, totally passive, and totally dependent on distant supplies and self-interested suppliers."

To be honest, I can't really assess Berry's pronouncements. My assumption is that, at least to some extent, he paints with broad strokes and tars good and bad alike. I'm pretty sure that there are big businesses with a profound sense of civic involvement and responsibility. Even so, I take very seriously my farmer friend's assessment that Big Ag is out to crush competition, even if Big Ag would never admit that such is its goal. Even if it's not, the policies Big Ag's political muscle put into place have that effect. If the free market is the natural force we're so often told it is, then, like a natural force, it requires a polyculture for true health, a carefully maintained balance of local, national, and international business. Just as humans can't thrive when they destroy the delicate intricacies of topsoil or the webs of interdependency in particular ecosystems, so businesses—even big transnational businesses—will eventually cease to thrive if they undermine the necessary balance in which local economies can thrive.

Which brings me back to the unlikely power of Mrs. Garth and all those household economies that produce goods and services, those households that are not just centers of consumption, like the one described by Betty

Friedan. These little centers of independence and self-reliance are beacons in the dark described by Wendell Berry and my farmer friend, revolutionaries in a war that most of us barely know is being waged. Who knew that excellent, productive housewifery could be an aspiration for high-minded knuckleheads? If Dorothea Brooke were to appear today, she might very well be a local organic farmer or some other tough-minded local entrepreneur. She might look a lot like Mrs. Garth.

36

The Power of Poetry
Peace, Demons, Sonnets, and Resurrection

APRIL 22, 2011

Something that might seem fragile—a group of words arranged on a page—turns out to be indestructible.

—*Ed Hirsch*

Sometimes—maybe even often—I wonder why in heaven's name it ever seemed like a good idea to open a residency for environmental writers and artists. It can seem like an awfully precious response to the unholy forces in the world, to the seemingly implacable powers that sneer and smear and humiliate, ravage and amputate, and leave sterility in their wake. Surely there are better weapons, ones more powerful and direct, to fight the battle. Let's face it: writers and artists don't get a lot of press as warriors.

To top it off, this is Holy Week, when those demonic powers seem to have won. Today is Good Friday, and the Word is tortured, broken, murdered. Silenced. It's a day that can be particularly horrid for writers, killing any impulse to communicate.

And yet, and yet . . . we spent last weekend at the tenth annual Poetry at Round Top festival, in the rich rolling countryside between Austin and Houston. Just the drive to Round Top presaged a mythic encounter, the possibility of resurrection; despite the extreme drought conditions in Central Texas, patches of courageous bluebonnets and Indian paintbrushes bloomed. Later than usual, apparently aware of the scorching to come, live oaks and pecans unfurled their precious leaves, whose sweet green humidity was instantly thrashed by stiff dry southern winds. Wildfires are blazing across the state: the morning we left, we smelled smoke from the Rock House fire in Marfa, 450 miles away. And yet spring unfurls its banners.

"So what? And, by the way, mythic encounters are so-o-o-o 1970s," says the legion of demons in my head.

"Shut up," I explain, thinking they might be right. It's not as if spring has any choice. What's courageous about doing what you can't help doing?

My little herd of demons kept up its background sneering once we got to Festival Hill, a strikingly beautiful and eccentric campus of older wooden buildings enlivened by lavishly unlikely additions: stone grottos and follies, great tumbling fountains, stone cherubs and goblins and saints, whimsy and careful craftsmanship everywhere.

"Nice," they said. "You're doing a lot to challenge Big Ag and stop carbon emissions by ooh-ing and aah-ing and hanging out with a bunch of poets."

"Shut up AND go away," I said, enunciating carefully.

They thought that was funny.

We all settled down when Ed Hirsch shambled up to the podium. Hirsch is a much-published poet and teacher and author of *How To Read a Poem and Fall in Love with Poetry*, a "surprise best seller" only to those who haven't read it. He's one of those gifted speakers—warm, passionate, wise—who makes you wish that he could keep talking until he has nothing left to say.

He spoke about the power of lyric poetry to "allow the intimacy of strangers," sometimes separated by centuries, even millennia. Lyric poetry, created in solitude, calls wildly unlikely community into being. He recounted his first contact with the power of lyric poetry, when he was electrified reading one of Gerard Manley Hopkins's "terrible sonnets." Hirsch—a Jewish student at Grinnell College in the 1960s—was stunned to find someone—a British Victorian Jesuit priest, long dead—who could describe his feelings of isolation and distress better than he could himself.

Even deeper than the jolt of recognition, the young Hirsch became aware that Hopkins had *made* something from his desolation: "Holy shit!" he remembered thinking. "This thing is a sonnet!" He felt Hopkins's "tremendous generosity to take that isolation" and create something of beauty from its wretched depths "so that I might come along later to be comforted." Poetry in its very structure is hopeful even when it despairs, Hirsch believes, because poets must imagine "a reader on the horizon," someone to whom the poem must be directed, in order to write at all.

Poetry as an act of generosity to strangers, as the creation of intimacy across divides of time and culture: these hospitable acts require courage, especially in a fearful time.

"How convenient for your chicken-hearted, lazy soul," said my loitering demons.

"Don't you slander chickens, you morons," I replied irritably, having forgotten for a minute that they were there.

"Oh, we're cloven by the thrust and parry of your rapier wit," they smirked. "Oh, we're slain!" And they fell all over each other, howling.

"Oh, shut up," I said.

The next morning—Sunday, no less—we sat in the beautiful deconsecrated chapel used for more intimate readings, sunlight pouring through the neo-Gothic windows into the meditatively dim sanctuary. We listened to Chris Leche, a poet who has taught in war zones for the past ten years. She read three of her own poems along with a stunning essay by one of her students who was fighting in Afghanistan. He wrote about his struggle not to stand too long in the soul-destroying acid of hatred, most vividly triggered when he saw a ten-year-old Afghani boy, face filled with rage, stare at him and then pointedly pull a finger across his throat. Even as fury for revenge rose in him, the soldier remembered that this was a child, a child whose soul was already poisoned and dying. His words were like smelling salts to those of us seated in the sanctuary, jolting us into consciousness. This soldier had reached across time and distance and shaken us awake.

After Leche and several others (including our new friend Barbara Ras) read, we watched a documentary titled *Every War Has Two Losers* about the great American poet William Stafford, who was born in 1914, the year in which World War I erupted, and died in 1993. From his youth, he was convicted by the certainty that violence cannot end violence, but only perpetuate it. He was a conscientious objector during World War II and spent the war in camps for conscientious objectors in California and Arkansas. He spent the rest of his life bearing witness to the possibility of peace as positive force, rather than a mere cessation of war. In the introduction to the book of the same title, Stafford's son Kim, also a poet, writes:

> As a child my father somehow arrived at the idea that one does not
> need to fight; nor does one need to run away. Both these actions are
> failures of the imagination. Instead of fighting or running you can
> stand by the oppressed, the frightened, or even "the enemy." You can

witness for connection, even when many around you react with fury, or with fear.

Many contemporary poets influenced by Stafford's willingness to stand in the uneasy role of witness were interviewed in the film, including Robert Bly, Coleman Barks, Naomi Shihab Nye, Maxine Hong Kingston, W. S. Merwin, and Alice Walker. They all pointed to his insistence that we do the hard work of imagining "the enemy"; that we wonder about his family, his childhood, his children; that we imagine what might have led him to consider us as enemy; that we refuse ever to lose sight of his humanity, of his hunger, joy, and pain. The discipline of always imagining the enemy as clearly as he could imagine himself left Stafford, like the spring, unable to do anything but bloom with love of neighbor.

Stafford wrote: "Save the world by torturing one innocent child? Which innocent child?" He wrote:

> *Is there a quiet way, a helpful way, to question what has been won in a war that the victors are still cheering? . . . Or does the winning itself close our questions about it? Might failing to question it make it easier to try war again?*

He wrote: "Keep a journal, and don't assume that your work has to accomplish anything worthy; artists and peace-workers are in it for the long haul, and not to be judged by immediate results."

He wrote and decades later I, like Hirsch first reading Hopkins, was electrified. I felt seen, known. When my demons woke up and started jeering, I asked them politely to come in. I wanted to know (maybe) where they were from. Ha! they said. You wish, they said. Yes, I said. When I'm brave enough, I think I do.

So many courageous poets at this festival, living and dead, bore witness to the glory and depravity of the human condition. Such a community of witnesses. Maybe spring really will come again (even if just barely this year). Maybe Jesus really will rise from the dead. Maybe it's not ridiculous to open a residency for environmental writers and artists, to provide a haven for those whose efforts might electrify others to work for beauty, for harmony, for wholeness. For salvation.

37

Learning to Listen, and Love

MAY 6, 2011

I have a new role model: Steve Nelle, a wildlife biologist with the Natural Resources Conservation Service, an arm of the USDA, in San Angelo. Martin and Madroño Ranch's formidable manager Robert and I went to hear him speak about "Managing Your Hill Country Habitat Effectively" at the spring meeting of the Bandera Canyonlands Alliance in Utopia last week. There was a good turnout of area landowners, ranging from all-thumbs novices like Martin and me to older ranchers whose wide, calloused hands spoke to a lifetime of work with the land.

For those of you with no interest in land management, stick with me; it's not actually my topic, although Nelle gave an excellent presentation on the role of ash juniper (commonly referred to as cedar) in the Hill Country ecology. Cedar is a species that everybody loves to hate because it's so remorselessly successful, often at the expense of other species—sort of the Gordon Gekko of Hill Country flora. People here have Opinions about how to manage cedar, ranging from getting rid of most of it to getting rid of *all* of it.

Nelle spent most of his talk gently lobbing little bombs onto these Opinions, even as his rhetoric defused them. First, he had the authority of thirty-five years of fieldwork, although even as he established his authority, he encouraged us to question it, pointing out that he had spent most of his time in mesquite country, not cedar country. Second, he showed that he knew his audience by noting that one of his principal sources was a local, Eric Lautzenheiser, who has argued that cedar has been unfairly stigmatized; when he brought Lautzenheiser's name up, Nelle had to pause briefly while several in the audience discussed the exact location of the Lautzenheiser family's ranch. Third, he was funny. He quoted H. L. Mencken, who said, "For every complex problem, there is an answer that is simple, neat, and wrong," and when someone asked him how to address a specific issue, he began by saying, "This isn't the right answer; it's just what I'd do." Finally, he acknowledged that there are multiple ways of managing land well; he encouraged each of us to be patient, persistent students of our own land and not to let anyone else tell us what to do with it. He trusted that all of us loved our land and wanted to do the best we could for it. In other words, he expected the best from us.

During the talk I wondered if people might not actually get up and leave, so persistently did Nelle herd up and shoot the sacred cows of cedar control. In fact, as we left, Robert said something like this: Well, hell! He just blew holes in everything I thought I knew! But we agreed that the presentation was ultimately persuasive because of Nelle's disarming willingness to claim little authority for himself, to link his own experience to someone already known to many in the room, and to respect the experience of everyone present. I'm ready to send him to negotiate between our warring political parties in Washington and Austin.

He was the latest and most welcome example of how people of strongly differing opinions might talk to each other, an undervalued skill these days. The religious historian Karen Armstrong recently published a book titled *Twelve Steps to a More Compassionate Life*, structured consciously around the twelve-step program pioneered by Alcoholics Anonymous. With it, she hopes to reclaim what she says is the original and most powerful directive of all the world's great religions, which is to train adherents to become skillful practitioners of the Golden Rule in both its positive and negative formulations: always treat others as you yourself wish to be treated, and do not treat others as you would not like them to treat you. She adds that all these religions "insist that you cannot confine your benevolence to your own group; you must have concern for everybody—even your enemies."

She lays out a program to help us break our addiction to egotism, which causes us to act with thoughtless violence in both private (our thoughts and relationships) and public (our politics and religion) arenas. "We cannot think how we would manage without our pet hatreds and prejudices that give us such a buzz of righteousness," she writes; "like addicts, we have come to depend on the instant rush of energy and delight we feel when we display our cleverness by making an unkind remark and the spurt of triumph when we vanquish an annoying colleague."

To those who would belittle this effort as naive, she responds that the great religions all arose in response to profound violence:

The sages, prophets, and mystics of these traditions did not regard compassion as an impractical dream. They worked as hard to implement it in the difficult circumstances of their times as we work for a cure to cancer today. They were innovative thinkers, ready to use whatever tools lay at hand in order to reorient the human mind, assuage suffering, and pull their societies back from the brink.

They were warriors of nonviolence, working to break the deeply entrenched cycles of violence directed at self, neighbor, and the world—not a job for the faint of heart.

These are the (wildly simplified) steps she suggests for those who would break their addiction to egotism and violence:

1. learn what the world's religions teach about suffering and compassion;
2. look at the expanding rings of your own world and see where suffering is present and compassion is absent;
3. develop compassion for yourself, for if you cannot acknowledge your own pain, you will not be able to acknowledge the pain of others;
4. use the power of art to develop the muscles of empathy;
5. learn to watch yourself mindfully, without judgment, in order to know who you are and to know that you are more than your thoughts about who you are;
6. know that every other being has the same desire to be seen and acknowledged that you do, and to act toward others accordingly;
7. acknowledge the extremely limited horizon of your knowledge, of yourself, of anyone else, or of any particular situation;

8. wonder how you might speak to someone with profoundly differing views from your own, given the fact that you know very little;

9. become aware that you cannot restrict your wonderings to people you know, but that you must extend your hope for wellbeing beyond the bounds of your tribe;

10. become curious about a people you know nothing about;

11. realize the radical commonality between you and those whom you don't know;

12. see that to hate your enemy is to hate yourself, and that to love your enemy is a matter of survival.

I actually don't like this book very much; it calls me out on lots of behaviors I thoroughly enjoy, like the one that calls us away from trying to defeat opponents verbally and exhorts us to enter empathetically into a rival viewpoint. Armstrong points out that we often identify so strongly with our ideas that we feel physically assaulted when they are questioned, criticized, or corrected. Truth becomes an ancillary issue when we are so enmeshed with our ideas that we can't imagine another way of thinking, nor enter imaginatively into a perspective that counters our own. Armstrong exhorts us to listen with "the principle of charity," which requires us to assume that whoever we listen to has as much need to be taken seriously and respectfully as we do.

Well, hell.

While pondering Armstrong's injunction to respond charitably to my fellow humans, I was reminded of the description of Charles Darwin in Adam Gopnik's *Angels and Ages: A Short Book about Darwin, Lincoln, and Modern Life*. Gopnik wrote that even if Darwin got some of the particulars of evolution wrong—which he did—he got them wrong in the right way, because the spirit of his inquiry into the minutiae of biological operations was filled with the kind of reverent curiosity about all living creatures that Armstrong calls us to show about the human community. Gopnik describes Darwin's last publication, an unlikely best seller:

> *The Origin and The Descent of Man are more obviously great books, masterpieces of the human spirit. But if I had to pick up one book to sum up what was great and rich about Charles Darwin, and*

in Victorian science and the Victorian mind more generally . . . it might well be On the Formation of Vegetable Mould, through the Action of Worms. *Limitless patience for measurement . . . an ingenuous interest in the world in all its aspects, a desire to order many things in one picture, a faith that the small will reveal the large. And a gift for storytelling. Darwin makes the first person address never feel strange in this scientific text, because we understand that the author is in a personal relation with his subject, probing, testing, sympathizing, playing the bassoon while the earthworms listen and striking the piano while they cower, and trying in every way to see who they are and where they came from and what they're like—not where they stand in the great chain of being beneath us, but where they belong in the great web of being that surrounds us, and includes us.*

Personally, I can imagine playing a bassoon for earthworms more easily than I can imagine entering imaginatively the minds of the many politicians and cultural commentators whose bloviating makes me seethe. But our survival depends on listening carefully and appreciatively to each other. Steve Nelle will make me think about the particular life and condition of each cedar tree we cut down. Perhaps this mindfulness will extend out toward my own species, though I may have to route it through the earthworms first.

Baby Heather in a swing, date unknown. Catto-Kohout family collection.

With cousin Laura Hobby, early 1960s. Catto-Kohout family collection.

Young Heather, 1963. Catto-Kohout family collection.

Young Heather with a flower, date unknown. Catto-Kohout family collection.

McLean, Virginia,
date unknown.
Catto-Kohout
family collection.

With her mother Jessica Hobby
Catto, Woody Creek, Colorado,
date unknown. Catto-Kohout family
collection.

With mother-in-law Nevea
Donell Kohout and Marti?
Colorado, mid-1980s.
Catto-Kohout family
collection.

With her father, Henry E. Catto, on a rafting trip, Colorado, date unknown.
Catto-Kohout family collection.

'n Paris, ca. 1980.
Catto-Kohout family
ollection.

With Martin, early 1980s.
Catto-Kohout family
collection.

With college roommates Peggy Redfield, Emily Grossman, and Lynne Rowley at her wedding, McLean, Virginia, 1985.

Martin and Heather's wedding, McLean, Virginia, 1985. Catto-Kohout family collection.

On honeymoon in northern England, 1985. Catto-Kohout family collection.

With newborn daughter Elizabeth, Seton Hospital, Austin, 1986.

With son Tito, Washington, DC, ca. 1990.

With children Elizabeth, Tito, and newborn Thea, Seton Hospital, Austin, 1992. Catto-Kohout family collection.

With her sister Isa at Isa's wedding to Daniel Shaw, Woody Creek, Colorado, 2001. Catto-Kohout family collection.

With daughter Elizabeth, Austin, 2003.

With an unknown Elvis
impersonator, Graceland,
Memphis, Tennessee,
2006. Catto-Kohout family
collection.

With daughter
Thea, 2007.

On the porch,
Madroño Ranch,
2011. Catto-Kohout
family collection.

Dai Due Supper Club,
Springdale Farm, Austin,
2011. Catto-Kohout
family collection.

With son Tito,
Barcelona, 2012.

San Antonio, date unknown.
Catto-Kohout family
collection.

t the Poetry at
ound Top festival,
estival Hill, Texas,
014. Catto-
ohout family
llection.

38

Gratuitous Beauty

MAY 20, 2011

Our friend John Burnett recently returned from a trip to Japan, one of a handful of places he'd never been in a long career as a reporter for National Public Radio. As a specialist in the American Southwest and Latin America, he was surprised to find that both Japan and its people utterly enchanted him. When I asked him what had so appealed to him, he thought for a minute and said that "random acts of gratuitous beauty" won his heart, sending me a photo of a gratuitously beautiful manhole cover to explain what he meant.

That phrase rang in my mind: gratuitous beauty. As I left Madroño Ranch the other day, I saw a pair of painted buntings chasing bugs right by a lesser goldfinch perched on a purple thistle as a redwing blackbird sang its cheerily cacophonous song from a nearby walnut tree. On that morning's walk I had spotted birds ranging from the drabbest to the showiest, from Tennessee warblers to yellow warblers, from blue-gray gnatcatchers to indigo buntings, from shy green herons to lark sparrows to summer tanagers—and these were just the beginning of the list. It was just a little show-offy. Gratuitous.

I wondered about the extravagance of this display, especially of the males with their vivid breeding plumage. Surely they become more visible to predators as well as to potential mates as they brighten up? Apparently the trade-off is worth it, evolutionarily speaking. Being bearers of such beauty trumps the risk of being eaten.

Of course, wondering if beauty has evolutionary value isn't very scientific. We take for granted that beauty lies in the subjective, not the objective, realm; beauty is culturally conditioned, notoriously hard to measure or pin down. We tend to think of it as a value-added category, not as a necessity for life, an evolutionary necessity every bit as muscular as the competition for survival of the fittest.

There seems, however, to be a growing body of evidence suggesting that evolutionary success depends on much more than tooth and claw; it also requires cooperation and nurture. Although this may sound like a squishy sentimental left-wing sort of idea that comes out of liberal academia, there's even a conservative who thinks the idea has merit: this week in the *New York Times*, David Brooks reviewed a number of recently published books about the human imperative to collaborate. The most important thing about the research, he says, is this:

> *For decades, people tried to devise a rigorous "scientific" system to analyze behavior that would be divorced from morality. But if cooperation permeates our nature, then so does morality, and there is no escaping ethics, emotion and religion in our quest to understand who we are and how we got this way.*

I would raise Brooks's bet on morality as a critical evolutionary component by claiming that we, individually and as a species, also need beauty in our lives only just slightly less than we need to breathe, eat, sleep, and procreate.

One of the reasons I think this is my consistent experience of finding human-created beauty in the most poverty-stricken and dire of circumstances. In the 1970s, my family lived in El Salvador, and we had the good fortune to travel extensively through Guatemala as well. Even as a young teenager in the iron grip of self-involvement, I was struck by the beauty of the textiles and artwork we encountered in the most poverty-ridden parts of those countries. I still have *huipiles* I bought almost forty years ago and am still enchanted by their colors and intricate designs. If survival were a matter only of competition, what could be the point of this time-consuming and ancient art? What is the point of any art? Why do we go to all that trouble when we could expend our energy in more apparently efficient survival strategies like decimating our enemies?

I think that one of the reasons we value, and even seem to require, beauty in our lives is that we long ago learned that the natural world values beauty, and we all know that ontogeny recapitulates phylogeny. (I don't really understand what that means, but it has the unmistakable ring of authority, doesn't it?) I recently found an engrossing book issued by Trinity University Press: *Moral Ground: Ethical Action for a Planet in Peril*, edited by Kathleen Dean Moore and Michael P. Nelson. It's a collection of essays asserting the moral imperative to protect the corpus of the earth at least as carefully as we would care for any of the technological or financial assets around which we organize our individual and corporate lives. The essays are by poets and scientists, presidents and farmers, professors and religious leaders.

The title of one essay in particular, by Stephen R. Kellert, a professor emeritus at the Yale School of Forestry and Environmental Studies, caught my attention: "For the Love and Beauty of Nature." He contends that modern humans have "lost their bearings as biological beings, as just another animal and species in the firmament of creation." In fact, we often measure our "progress" almost directly by our alienation from our biological roots. This is true even of many of those scientists and activists whose work is environmentally directed, says Kellert; their focus on technological, policy, and econometric issues often further exacerbates this alienation, inadvertently accelerating our rush to destruction.

We preserve what we love. When an empty home burns down, people risk their lives to save old photographs. Of course, some people will try to save objects with monetary value, but in our private lives we often value what is useless in the eyes of the world. We save the things that have meaning for us, that we think are beautiful, the things to which we have intense emotional and spiritual connections. Even if environmentalists implement all of the policy currently deemed necessary to save the world, its preservation would not be assured. We have to love the world in order to preserve it. Without that entirely subjective component in the mix, lovers of technology and objective measurement can save nothing except technology.

Our cultural devaluation of the pivotal role of subjective experience in the flourishing of culture is highly visible right now. What do we choose to cut out of federal, state, and local educational budgets? The first things to go are those that value what we deem to be training in subjectivity, in the appreciation of beauty: the arts. In the move to become more efficient and streamlined, however, we teach our children (and ourselves) to undervalue the most powerful forces that will drive their movement through the economic, technological, public world: love. We will value and save what we love, and we love what we think is beautiful. Do any preservation societies rally when big-box Walmarts get pulled down?

Aldo Leopold, one of the twentieth century's most fervent and judicious conservationists, developed what he called a "land ethic," which he considered to be a moral imperative and not a luxury to be applied only in times of economic well-being:

> *An ethic to supplement and guide the economic relation to the land presupposes the existence of some mental image of the land as a biotic mechanism.* [By this I think he means "a living reality."] *We can be ethical only in relation to something we can see, feel, understand, love, or otherwise have faith in. . . . A thing is right when it tends to preserve the integrity . . . and beauty of the biotic enterprise. It is wrong when it tends otherwise.*

We have ceased to love the natural world because so many of us no longer know it subjectively, emotionally, viscerally. Too many of us don't know its intricacy and beauty, its drama and miraculous precision, its redundant abundance and efficiency. Ontogeny recapitulates phylogeny: when we know—really *know*—the beauty of nature, we know our own beauty and thus will be saved. Teaching our children and reminding ourselves to love what is beautiful in nature is a move toward long-term survival. We love what is beautiful and preserve and nurture what we love. Gratuitous beauty as evolutionary stratagem: that's science I can finally understand.

39

Signs of the Times
Billboards, Property Rights, and the Enlightenment
JUNE 3, 2011

I've noticed on the highways between Austin and Medina a creeping excrescence of billboards. They pop up even in and near Johnson City, so close to the LBJ Ranch, which was the home of Lady Bird Johnson, the force behind the 1965 Highway Beautification Act, which sought to dismantle the fungal proliferation of billboards along scenic American roadsides.

Can you guess that I will never, ever, under any circumstances buy or use anything advertised on these blights on the beauty of the Hill Country?

To be fair, I rely on the signs along interstates indicating the availability of gas stations at particular exits. Indeed, as someone who tends to coast into a station on fumes, I count on those signs. (When I was still driving a Suburban, I once put 42.3 gallons into its 40-gallon tank. Knowing about those two secret extra gallons was dangerous for me. Once, with four kids in the Suburban at the scorching height of an Austin summer, I pushed my luck a little too hard and actually ran out of gas, which was when I discovered that power steering and power brakes won't work if your engine isn't running. This is information you should probably have *before* you're headed toward a busy intersection with a truckload of children.)

And one August I drove through the Great Smoky Mountains of eastern Tennessee and western North Carolina and saw along those spooky, beautiful winding roads a series of enormous public service announcements broadcasting the dangers of meth use and obesity. I was impressed, wondering about the depths of a community horror that announced itself to all passersby. I don't know if those signs actually saved anyone's life, but they most certainly told me something I didn't know about the area through which I was passing.

But now I'm done being fair. I hate, despise, and loathe billboards on rural byways; since their inception they have advertised—indeed, flaunted—not only goods but also the basest, most cynical side of American culture.

The rise of the automobile, particularly in the 1920s, brought on the first wave of the plague. The first responders against it were the ladies who belonged to garden clubs, led by Elizabeth Boyd Lawton, and the Outdoor Advertising Association of America routinely ridiculed them as "the scenic sisters." They were mere women, and wealthy at that. What did they know about the rough-and-tumble necessities of the business world? Why, billboards were just part of the vigorous energy that made America its aggressive, masculine, successful self. Even so, the association worried enough about the clout and persistence of these women to plant spies in their garden clubs.

Most of my information about this battle has come from reading reviews and excerpts of a surprisingly interesting book titled *Buyways: Billboards, Automobiles, and the American Landscape* by Catherine Gudis, a history professor at the University of California, Riverside. She charts the apparently inexorable and very canny tide of the outdoor advertisers, who have been able to read the landscape of American culture and politics even as they flood its roadsides. They ensured that Lady Bird's Beautification Act was full of loopholes, the most significant of which left underfunded a provision calling for compensating landowners required to remove noncompliant billboards erected on their property. Nor did it impose any height restrictions, which helped create the giant, visually invasive "monopoles" with which we're so familiar today. The billboard industry has grown into a hugely lucrative global multimedia force dominated by three companies: Viacom, Lamar Advertising, and Clear Channel.

At the heart of the struggle between anti- and pro-billboarders is the question: who owns the view? If private landowners want to put up a forest of monopoles, who am I to tell them not to? Maybe it's a rancher or a farmer trying to scare up some much-needed cash. I'm sure there are all sorts of compelling reasons for leasing your property to the outdoor advertising industry. It's your right, isn't it?

I'm starting to get impatient with the idea of individual rights as the

trump card, as if there were no further discussion possible after the pro-
nouncement, "It's my right to do X-Y-Z." Don't get me wrong. I'm not for
a moment thinking of throwing out the Bill of Rights. But like any other
historical document, it's reflective of the conflicts and limitations of the
culture from which it emerged, the European Enlightenment. The Enlight-
enment, which, according to the ever-helpful Wikipedia, "broke through
'the sacred circle,' whose dogma had circumscribed thinking," has had an
extraordinarily long and, in my opinion, occasionally unhealthy shelf life.

In an essay titled "Why Should I Inconvenience Myself?" Mary Catherine
Bateson, professor emerita of anthropology and English at George Mason
University, examines the possibility that the scientific discoveries of the
recent past call into question the whole notion of the autonomous individ-
ual and the concomitant ethic based on individual rights. She writes: "These
ideas have been pivotal in Western culture, and yet they support behaviors
that have led us to environmental emergencies that threaten much of life
on Earth." It's time, then, to envision anew what it means to be a person.

I feel sure that Bateson is right because she's providing ballast to an intu-
ition that came to my most unscientific mind years ago: that our selves aren't
things we have, but are rather gifts given to us in the constant interactions
we have with other beings, both human and nonhuman. Says Bateson:

> I have come to believe that the idea of an individual, the idea that
> there is someone separate from relationships, is simply an error. We
> create each other, bring each other into being by being part of the
> same matrix in which the other exists.

If this is so—that my individual self is not something sealed in a Ziploc bag
I got when I was born, but rather a communally created and continually
changing work of art—then that puts the whole idea of individual rights in
a different light. My individual rights can't be asserted against the individual
rights of anyone (or maybe even anything) else because I don't actually have
an individual self. I suspect we in the West tend to think of ourselves as
something we *own* rather than as something we have been given, something
that ties us, in some mysterious way, to its givers.

We occasionally assign rights to what Bateson calls "charismatic mega-
fauna"—some mammals and birds we empathize with—but we don't tend

to hear much about, say, insect rights (especially from Texans overrun with roaches). She adds:

> *We don't generally speak about the rights of plants. What is more se-*
> *rious, perhaps, is that we do not hear about the rights of oceans or*
> *marshes or jungles, which are treated as containers (habitats) for the*
> *species that capture the imagination. Yet arguably these too are living*
> *systems of which the vertebrates that inhabit them are parts. We make*
> *an effort to protect the whales; but if the plankton in the oceans are*
> *destroyed by changes in acidity, the food chain will collapse, not only*
> *for the whales but for other species as well. On this account, rights*
> *may belong more appropriately to systems than to individual species.*

Bateson proposes an ethic built not on an equality-based system of sym-metrical rights but rather on an asymmetrical rhetoric of stewardship or responsibility, which "may extend more easily to entire species or habitats than equality does." In fact, we may have to junk the idea of equality and "claim a certain superiority in order to embrace responsibility as an alternative to irresponsible exploitation. An enlightened anthropocentrism is potentially practical." She recognizes the potential for paternalism and infantilism inherent in this system but also points to the embedded cor-rective in it: when we learn to recognize differences among species and systems, we have the opportunity to learn that humans flourish only when they interact with a wild, profuse array of other systems.

It's time to dismantle those habits of thinking and being that reinforce our self-sufficiency, that pit my rights against my neighbors' rights, whether my neighbors are individual humans or whole ecosystems or future gener-ations, since the distance between us is an illusion. This isn't an easy task, especially for a people who so value independence. (Secession, anyone?) But if we'd rather die than acknowledge our interdependence on the natural world, then we probably will.

I admit it: I've driven away at breakneck speed from my first paragraph, but I'll try to loop back, maybe even try to find a scenic road to go down. I hate the rising tide of those huge monopole billboards, especially near Lady Bird's old stomping grounds, because they represent a way of seeing and using the world that respects nothing but its own illusory self, that values nothing more than short-term economic self-interest over long-term flourishing. They represent a devolutionary force that degrades beauty, which I declared in my last piece (so we know it must be true) to be as necessary to human existence as food, air, and water. It may be personally inconvenient to change those habits that allow us to think that we stand on our own two feet. We may have to stop and ask people for directions and help, maybe rely on or call forth the kindness of strangers. We may have to be imposed on by others. Benjamin Franklin famously said, "Gentlemen, we must all hang together or assuredly we shall all hang separately." I like to think that today Franklin, a quintessential product of the Enlightenment but an iconoclastic and inquisitive intellect, would expand his remark to include not just gentlemen but all people, gentle or not, and maybe all species.

40

Field Notes from Madroño Ranch
Bison and Birds
JULY 1, 2011

This is a bird-and-bison-intensive kitchen sink of an essay; even Martin's most focused editorial ministrations will be of no avail in trying to flush out some kind of narrative thread. To lend it at least an illusion of coherence, I decided to title it "Field Notes from Madroño Ranch."

* * *

Every April the barn swallows and purple martins return to the ranch; the barn swallows tend to congregate at the Lake House, and the purple martins tend to congregate at the Main House. They all inhabit the fabulous mud nests constructed by the swallows: how do they build these elegant constructions with no hands? Under one of the eaves of the Main House there are probably sixty or seventy condo units, many currently filled with fledgling martins and swallows. The business of feeding all these babies keeps the parents very, very busy, swooping their great athletic loops in search of insects.

The swallows have constructed one nest on a tin light fixture on the ceiling of the breezeway outside the Main House front door. Every summer I have to train myself not to turn that light on when I head to the garage or down to the Chicken Palace at night, since it panics the nest's inhabitants. This year's fledglings will probably be gone by the time you read this; they've already learned to fly from and return to the nest, and their three bulky adolescent bodies fill the sturdy little construction to overflowing. Last week, a little late putting the chickens up in the evening, I headed down to the Palace with a flashlight and thought to look up at our nesting guests. Both of the parents were draped across the top, like a too-big feathery lid on a small pot, protecting their babies from night dangers and getting a little rest after chasing mosquitoes all day for their wide-mouthed brood. I know anthropomorphism is out of fashion, but it was a sweet, intimate scene.

* * *

As we near the end of the bison calving season, we've had eight calves on the ground so far and are hoping for two more. Unfortunately, one calf has died, and we don't know why. Robert and Tito (who's working at the ranch until the beginning of the second summer session at UT) noticed something unusual about the calf's head after it was born but couldn't get close enough to see what the anomaly was, and it died within a week of its birth. When we went to the spot where it died, to see if we could find any clues as to the cause of death, nothing was left except for some pelvic bones, a couple of vertebrae, and one tiny hoof. The scavengers had done their job quickly and efficiently.

The other calves seem to be thriving, despite the drought. Like almost all babies, they're awfully cute: biscuit-colored and about fifty to sixty pounds at birth. That sounds big until you see them milling around the pickup with the grownups at cube-feeding time, a ritual that seems particularly important now that there's so little grass. We saw one little guy come out of the melee with a very bloody nose, perhaps from a well-placed kick from a larger relative (even bison have their pecking order). It was a pathetic sight, but he seemed to recover by the following day.

Bison will eat just about any vegetable matter in a drought, unlike their more finicky bovine cousins. Our friend Hugh Fitzsimons of Thunder Heart Bison told me recently that their herd has been eating a lot of mesquite beans and cactus. I'm not sure what ours are eating to keep themselves going; I hope it's cedar, at least as an hors d'oeuvre.

* * *

We've had a steady stream of guests and residents at the ranch recently, several of whom have been enthusiastic bird-watchers, which is a real boon for me. One morning our friend Brian Miller and I went out to see who we could find flitting around. Brian, admitting that he prefers his birds to be showy, particularly hoped to see some painted buntings. It was very windy, which made for a quiet morning, bird-wise, although we got some impressive clattering from a pair of belted kingfishers and an unusually good goggle at a golden-cheeked warbler. As we stood on a little bluff above a creek whose banks are crowded with sycamores, I saw Brian peer at something through his binoculars. It was an indigo bunting so blue—ranging from mountain gentian blue at the head to almost turquoise around the tail—that Brian thought at first that it was a piece of plastic stuck up in the tree. Too blue to be true—sounds like a country song! We definitely got our show.

* * *

The cows we think are still pregnant have that fully stuffed look, especially when they're lying down. The mama who lost her calf now has her yearling nosing at her udder again, so all the mature cows are feeling pretty protective—one of the several things that worried us about releasing the new bull into the herd. We brought him onto the ranch almost a month ago, and he's been acclimating in the retention pen, a high-fenced area that incorporates about thirty acres. T. D., the incumbent bull, has been hanging out by the retention pen gate for weeks, rolling and kicking dust through the fence at the newcomer and then settling his great bulk where the new guy could see him. The cows have been checking him out as well. Bubba and Dixie, the llamas, who are full-time residents of the pens, looked down their long noses at the hulking arrival and kept their distance.

We'd been speculating about what would happen when we finally let the new bull (whom we've tentatively named T. A.) out, which we did last Sunday afternoon. He and T. D. are about the same size, but T. A. seems to be taller at the hump, with a bigger head, although he's slimmer than T. D., who's built like a tank. We envisioned a clash of titans and worried about blood and guts and trampled calves and crazed mama bison and ripped-up fencing; I prudently planted myself on the roof of my car, in case things *really* got out of hand.

Turns out we needn't have worried. T. D. was nowhere in sight when we opened the gate, and the first thing T. A. did after moseying out of the pen was to wander over to some nearby cedar and sycamore saplings and maul them with his horns, just to show them who was boss. Then he set off up the hill, leaving us to follow helplessly in the pickup, wondering how long it would take him to break through the wimpy fencing that separates us from our neighbors. After he abruptly veered off the road and into the underbrush (how can something that big just vanish?), we headed back down for a brief break from the scorching dry heat.

An hour or so later, we found him near the top and managed to direct him back down the hill and into the creek, where the cows finally spotted him. T. D. was lurking in the underbrush above the creek and, to our surprise, made no move to confront him. The new guy kept his tail up and hooked as the cows investigated him, although judging by his sniff-and-grin, chop-licking expression he was clearly pleased to be in the midst of so much shapely feminine flesh.

When T. D. finally emerged, it was clear that there wasn't going to be a showdown: T. A. had so intimidated him that T. D. wouldn't even meet his gaze. Each time the new guy approached, tail up, T. D. walked away. Each time T. A. pawed the dust or rolled, T. D. turned his back. We were all a little embarrassed for him. But breeding season is coming up; maybe the fight is yet to come.

* * *

For Martin's birthday last Saturday, we engaged the expertise of Tink Pinkard, fly-fishing guide and teacher extraordinaire. With unflagging patience, he coaxed us into finally feeling the load of the line as it unfurled over our heads and allowed us to imagine that we were starting to get it. On Sunday morning we quit the creek side to putter around the lake in Tink's doughty (and slightly leaky) johnboat. We actually caught a number of sunfish and a nice little bass, but mostly we caught sight of what a really beautiful cast looks like. Watching Tink with a rod in his hand was like watching a particularly eloquent sign-language speaker when you only know the alphabet; his movements were powerful, fluent, efficient. I want to talk like that.

Now I have another outlet, beyond bird-watching and rowing, for my capacity to hyperfocus. I was hoping that fly-fishing and bird-watching would be less mutually exclusive than rowing and bird-watching, but, alas, my hopes were dashed. Each time I allowed a passing bird to distract me in mid-cast, my line snarled, wrapping around itself, the rod, and, occasionally, me. I briefly worried that I might get so tangled that I would end up casting myself out of the boat and into the water. Many long-time Madroñoites have caught glimpses of The Thing, the enormous . . . what? fish? dinosaur? that occasionally rises from the murky depths of the lake, so I'm determined to stay focused on the casting. At least until the green kingfisher reported by one of the residents shows up again.

41

Silos
My Beef with Freeman Dyson
JULY 15, 2011

I have a bone to pick with Freeman Dyson, professor emeritus at the Institute for Advanced Study in Princeton and generally acknowledged scientific genius. I bet he's really nervous.

On a recent trip to Aspen, I picked up *The Best American Science and Nature Writing 2010*, edited by Dyson, and the latest installment in a wonderful series that began in 2000. In the introduction, Dyson laments that most current science writing appears as brief news items rather than "thoughtful essays" like the ones John McPhee wrote for the *New Yorker*. Apparently magazine editors don't feel that science as science has much reader appeal. Nature writing is much more common; Dyson notes that the book contains twice as many essays about nature as about science. "Nature is now fashionable among readers and publishers of magazines," he grumbles. "Science is unfashionable."

Somewhat later he claims that the essays about nature are "written for nature lovers, not science lovers," because "the quality of the writing is as important as the subject matter." The environmental movement is the product not of science but is rather the "leading secular religion of our age," a replacement for Marxism. "Environmentalism doesn't have much to do with science," he says, although he proudly shares the ethics of the environmental movement. He is hopeful about the future of the Earth because two such committed communities are "working to preserve living space for our fellow creatures."

While his analysis is in some ways perfectly reasonable, I object to the idea that there is an unbreachable demarcation between science and other disciplines rather than a permeable boundary that encourages heavy traffic and frequent discussion about just exactly where that boundary is, particularly between the sciences and the arts. (I include religion in the realm of art for purposes of this essay.)

Subsequent events since I read Dyson's introduction have encouraged me to continue this line of thought. Maggie Fox, CEO of the Climate Protection Action Fund, was the featured speaker at the recent Jessica Catto Leadership Dialogues, a program of the Aspen Center for Environmental Studies. She opened her talk by suggesting that the bar code would be the symbol for this era; technology, media, and advertising have converged in such a way that we are encouraged in all arenas to choose what we already know and prefer and to live in a bubble that reflects our predispositions. She urged us to step out of our silos both inside and outside the environmental community and to refuse to identify too exclusively with what we already know.

The day after this talk I read an article in the *Atlantic Monthly* titled "The Triumph of New-Age Medicine," by David H. Freedman, that investigates the rise—and apparent efficacy—of alternative, or integrative, or holistic medical practices in America. Mainstream medicine has a mixed reaction to this turn of events. Freedman quotes one doctor willing to consider integrative medicine's benefits as saying, "Doctors tend to end up trained in silos of specialization." Those who object to alternative medicine as hokum can be virulently negative about it, despite the opening in recent years of forty-two integrative medical research centers, all of them at major medical institutions like Harvard, Yale, Duke, and the Mayo Clinic. Says one critic,

> *It's cleverly marketed, dangerous quackery. . . . There's only one type of medicine, and that's medicine whose treatments have been proven to work. When something works, it's not all that hard to prove it. These people have been trying to prove their alternative treatments work for years, and they can't do it.*

From there, Freedman takes a look at what constitutes "proof" in mainstream medicine. He interviews a Harvard researcher who claims that many mainstream medical treatments are little better than placebos. Says Freedman,

The vast majority of drugs don't work in as many as 70 percent of patients, according to a study within the pharmaceutical industry. One recent study concluded that 85 percent of new prescription drugs hitting the market are of little or no benefit to patients.

But patients keep buying them, because, according to the researcher, "knowing that you're getting a treatment is a critical part of the ritual of seeing any kind of practitioner."

It appears, then, that effective treatment relies in part on patients' perceptions and expectations, two things that are notoriously resistant to empirical testing. The belief that treatment will be efficacious is frequently augmented by a solid relationship between healer and patient. Freedman says that studies

have even shown that patients still get a beneficial placebo effect when practitioners are honest but optimistic with patients about the placebo—saying something along the lines of "We know of no reason why this should work, yet it seems to work with many patients." Sure enough, it often does.

Freedman also interviewed a neuroscientist at the University of California at Davis who studies the effects of meditation on the brain and who said,

We have to be careful about allowing presumed objective scientific methods to trump all aspects of human experience. Instead, science has to learn to listen in a sophisticated way to what individuals report to us, and to relate those findings to other kinds of knowledge obtained from external measurements.

This, of course, was my takeaway from the article, which deserves to be read in its entirety and not just in my messily truncated version of it.

After reading this article, I attended a concert in the Aspen Music Festival summer series featuring Beethoven's third piano concerto. My father and I sat where we could watch Joyce Yang, the soloist, as she played this beautifully complex and lyrical piece. I'm not able to judge whether it was a flawless performance (it certainly seemed like one), but it was utterly riveting. Her performance took a series of givens, of facts, that any performer of the piece faces: the piano, the musical score, the liturgies required in a concert performance, and technical mastery over all of them. These givens, in combination with Yang's ebullient, unmeasurable, unprovable subjective self, brought forth something beautifully new and of soul-jolting clarity. She was the vehicle of a kind of revelation.

Dyson himself recounted in his own career as a physicist a moment that sounds to me analogous to Yang's performance. A 2009 profile in the *New York Times Magazine* titled "The Civil Heretic" described how he solved a particularly difficult problem given to him by a professor, a subset of a larger problem Einstein had proposed. Dyson had just parted from the brilliant physicist Richard Feynman, with whom he'd been on a road trip through America:

> *Inspired by this and by a mesmerizing sermon on nonviolence that Dyson happened to hear a traveling divinity student deliver in Berkeley, Dyson sat aboard his final Greyhound of the summer, heading East. He had no pencil or paper. He was thinking very hard. On a bumpy stretch of highway, long after dark, somewhere out in the middle of Nebraska, Dyson says, "Suddenly the physics problem became clear."*

The intersection of the givens of the discipline of physics with Dyson's unmeasurable, subjective self brought about something new, a revelation. Perhaps the masters of any discipline are more like each other than they are like the competent workers within their disciplines, the people who move a discipline forward without changing its course.

Which gets me back to my irritation with Dyson's silo-ing off of science writing from nature writing and environmental writing. Of course there are nature/environmental writers whose grasp of science is negligible (like me), whose substitution of sentiment for rigorous thinking is exasperating, whose awareness of the history of nature writing is minimal, or whose identification with a political orthodoxy is absolute. But there are also nature and environmental writers who marry mastery of their craft with their unmeasurable, subjective selves in such a way that something compellingly new arises, something revelatory about the not always entirely overlapping human and natural worlds.

Even as I was reading the new *Best of*, I was also reading *Writing the*

Sacred into the Real, a compilation of essays on beloved places by poet Alison Hawthorne Deming. The quality of her writing is as important as her subject matter, a statement that Dyson would not necessarily intend as a compliment. I'm not sure why he would exclude scientists from the pleasure of reading her essays, which are as much reflections on writing as they are on nature; she is not a scientist but has read and reflected on science, and it informs her observations without being their subject matter. Her subject matter is the ways in which Americans have been shaped by the natural world, even as much of American culture becomes more removed from it and, consequently, careless in its stewardship. Her purpose is to make us look, really *look*, at our surroundings:

> *The human eye does more than see; it stitches the seen and the unseen together, the temporal and the eternal. It wakes me again and again to the astonishment of finding myself in a body moving through a world of beauty and dying and mystery.*

She insists on the power and presence of the invisible in human experience, on the ways in which a deep, focused involvement with nature leads to a glimmer of understanding that surpasses the sum of its parts:

> *For me, the natural world in all its evolutionary splendor is a revelation of the divine—the inviolable matrix of cause and effect that reveals itself to us in what we cannot control or manipulate, no matter how pervasive our meddling. This is the reason that our technological mastery over nature will always remain flawed. The matrix is more complex than our intelligence. We may control a part, but the whole body of nature must incorporate the change, and we are not capable of anticipating how it will do so. We will always be humbled before nature, even as we destroy it. And to diminish nature beyond its capacity to restore itself, as our culture seems perversely bent to do, is to desecrate the sacred force of Earth to which we owe a gentler hand.*

This doesn't sound all that different from what Einstein said about his sense of faith:

A knowledge of the existence of something we cannot penetrate, of the manifestations of the profoundest reason and the most radiant beauty—it is this knowledge and this emotion that constitute the truly religious attitude; in this sense, and in this alone, I am a deeply religious man. . . . Enough for me the mystery of the eternity of life, and the inkling of the marvelous structure of reality, together with the single-hearted endeavor to comprehend a portion, be it ever so tiny, of the reason that manifests itself in nature.

These two masters of distinct disciplines sound very much like each other. Given what I've read of and by Dyson, I don't think he would disagree with me, or them. There seems, however, to be within many disciplines a tendency to defend their boundaries with a tribal fierceness, a tendency that Dyson exhibits in his introduction. I hope that the masters of all disciplines find ways to seek each other out and investigate their common ground rather than defend their own turf—not a bad exercise for the drones, either.

42

Food Science

Mark Bittman, Michael Pollan, and the Old Testament

JULY 29, 2011

When I was in seminary, my Old Testament professor Michael Floyd spent some considerable time and effort trying to disabuse us students of the thought that we were somehow more spiritually advanced than our ancient Israelite ancestors who codified the complicated instructions governing community life set forth primarily in Leviticus. The peculiarities of the purity codes, which propound dietary laws and identify various human conditions as clean or unclean, tend to cause an outbreak of severe neck pain in sophisticated postmoderns due to the angle at which we look down our noses at such ridiculous, primitive thinking.

If you think you aren't governed by purity codes, Michael said, then do this: take a spoon and spit into it, then put the spoon and its contents back into your mouth. Sounds of disgust arose from the class. Why is that such a gross idea? he asked. The spit's not gross when it's in your mouth; why does it become unclean the second it leaves your mouth? He forced us to consider the conditions by which we individually or collectively declare things or states as clean or unclean. He required us to wonder how we had learned these codes. He asked us if different groups had different codes, and how these usually unexamined codes applied to people outside the group.

Michael said (at least, I hope he said; I took his class years ago) that he had concluded that the codes in Leviticus, as strange as they may sound to our ears, are in some ways more humane than the invisible codes that govern contemporary culture(s), because, first, everyone knew explicitly what the codes are; next, everyone became unclean and thus set apart in the course of daily life (menstruation and the emission of semen, for example, caused uncleanliness); finally, there were routine procedures (washing, offering sacrifices) that usually rendered the unclean clean again and reintegrated them into communal life. In the Levitical codes, being unclean isn't the same as being bad or evil or inferior; uncleanness is a necessary component of life, not a judgment.

When codes are unspoken and invisible, however, as they are in most of contemporary America, it becomes much harder to integrate those considered unclean into the community, since there are no explicit mechanisms for doing so, and often no recognition that everyone routinely bears the burden of uncleanness at some point or another. Because mainline American culture doesn't think it has any purity codes, uncleanness can become a permanent status. Think about race, poverty, sexual orientation, foreignness. And lest it sound as if progressives have risen above purity codes, think about political correctness: every group has some version of the clean and unclean, ways of thinking or being that render one impure, ways of segregating those considered unclean. In contrast to the Levitical codes, the invisible contemporary codes condemn those who are unclean as bad, evil, inferior, and offer no way into the community that renders those judgments.

I've smashed Michael's elegant distinctions into an inelegant mass so that I can argue that dietary laws designating clean food from unclean food are alive and kicking today, and that, without realizing it, Americans have cultic feelings about food, giving it the power to determine who/what is clean or unclean, who should be part of or excluded from a particular group. If you think that the passage in Leviticus (11:20–23) that forbids eating four-footed winged insects except if their legs are jointed above the feet is peculiar, then you haven't been paying attention to the weirdness of the current food wars.

Last Sunday's *New York Times* Sunday Review section featured a piece by Mark Bittman with the title "Bad Food? Tax It and Subsidize Vegetables." My first impulse was to agree with him completely. He argues that American dietary choices are, generally speaking, so wretched from a health perspective that government intervention in the form of taxation of soda and perhaps other junk food is warranted—especially since these bad choices add tens, maybe hundreds, of billions of dollars to government spending in health care.

Now, Mark Bittman is a cook, a food writer, and a long-time columnist for the *Times*. In some ways, we're members of the same tribe. I use his cookbooks. I've given his cookbooks to my children. His most recent book is *Food Matters: A Guide to Conscious Eating*. A fake sticker on the cover says: "Lose Weight, Heal the Planet." I really like and agree with Mark Bittman. I don't drink soda; I've never liked it, even as a child. It would cost me nothing if soda were taxed. In other words, there's no reason I shouldn't agree with him completely.

Except that I read many of the 273 comments posted by readers on the *Times* website and realized that he had written about something that has cultic status: the way we choose to eat. This food fight is not just about food. In his article, Bittman writes about the food-self and its relation to everything from quotidian family matters to personal responsibility to government philosophy. How could it not result in a heated discussion, or maybe even fisticuffs?

One particularly articulate negative response wondered if the foods Bittman deemed unhealthy would be taxed in high-end restaurants:

> *And what does the avenging Mr. Bittman propose as taxation penalty for the spiced fresh pork belly on Cafe Boulud's menu? How about the* salade frisee *at Bar Boulud (described by* New York Magazine *as containing "too many fatty pork lardoons"), or the Dunkin Donut-inspired* beignets de morue? *Does he make no mention of the celebration of fat and carbs so many upscale restaurants offer because these items are served to urban "sophisticates" and not the unsophisticated rubes whose lives his proposals would manipulate? Or does the mass production and delivery of affordable, corporately produced comestibles just not sit well with him on principle?*

Food is not just about food; it's about personal and tribal identity. If nutritionists, government policy wonks, chefs, organic farmers, conventional farmers, economists, ecoradicals, or concerned citizens think we're talking about "just" food, then we're going to sound as peculiar to each other as the Levitical laws sound to many contemporary Americans. We will use each other's views to identify each other as unclean without knowing that's what we're doing.

In its most recent issue, *Gastronomica: The Journal of Food and Culture* published an article blandly titled "In Defense of Food Science," a reference to my guru Michael Pollan's most recent book *In Defense of Food: An Eater's*

Manifesto. If you've read Pollan, you know that he consistently pushes back against "food science," by which he means processed foods. If the label on a food makes any health claims or lists more than five ingredients, avoid it, he says. The four authors of this unassuming piece take quiet issue with him. They say that Pollan "makes valid criticisms of the modern food industry and offers some useful recommendations for improving the health and well-being of the population." They are clear and precise about the ways in which they agree with him. They take issue, however, with Pollan's persistent emphasis on organic local foods, especially for "those who live in challenged economic conditions, in areas where the growing season is short, or who have busy working lives."

The authors refer to the gap between science and the arts that physicist and novelist C. P. Snow pointed to fifty years ago in his seminal book *The Two Cultures*, a gap they claim has narrowed somewhat since the book's publication. Food in particular offers a bridge between the disciplines, a "prime opportunity for science, art, craft, and the humanities to engage constructively with each other." The article points to the ways in which food science has offered us incontrovertible (at least to me) advances in understanding about foods. They point to a need for mass-produced, inexpensive, and convenient foods, given the realities of the age.

> *We are not suggesting that a diet should be based entirely on processed foods, but every type of food has a place in a balanced diet. The focus should not be solely on* processed *versus* whole *food, but also on* good-quality *processed food versus* poor-quality *processed food.*

They point out that some foods that we now consider "wholesome" are, in fact, processed: cheese, cream, beer, olive oil, vinegar. They concede that many processed foods are nutritionally null and void but insist that this is not and need not always be the case—that food science can and must be a tool in helping fix our current broken food system.

As someone who has railed against mass-produced processed foods, I'm a little flummoxed to find myself agreeing with them. I've always identified "food science" with the soulless stuff we eat alone without knowing or caring where it came from, the stuff we put in our mouths that has more to do with unconscious identifications than with the conscious pleasures of eating well-prepared food in community. Despite their white coats and hairnets, in other words, I've considered food scientists unclean. Well, well. I'm going to have eat my own words, a heavily processed meal filled with unconscious identifications. In my last piece, I moaned about the tendency among disciplines to demarcate their own turf so emphatically that heavy traffic and frequent discussion about the surprising and fruitful overlaps among them becomes difficult, if not impossible. For my tribe of proponents of local and organic foods, that would mean we would talk to other tribes with particular expertise on food topics—food scientists and conventional grocery store operators, for example. People who eat at fast-food restaurants. People who don't like to cook. People offended by foodies. This may give me a terrible crick in my neck from looking down my nose. But it may also make my invisible purity codes more visible, and thereby begin to offer a way to reintegrate a fragmented and self-reinforcing discussion.

43

Children of Dawn
Sin in the Twenty-First Century

AUGUST 12, 2011

Sin is behovely, but all shall be well and all manner of thing shall be well.—*Julian of Norwich*

Sin is our only hope.—*Barbara Brown Taylor*

The most dangerous of all falsehoods is a slightly distorted truth —*Georg Christoph Lichtenberg*

At dinner the other night I managed to elicit a full-brow furrow from Martin and Thea both. Considering the Kohout talent for growing hair, a full-brow furrow is a fierce and fearsome thing. *Two* furrowed Kohout brows is enough to send the insecure in search of a blankie, a pacifier, and a nice safe closet. I'm glad Lizzie and Tito weren't there, because they might have furrowed as well, presenting far more furrowing than any reasonable person should ever be expected to stand up against.

The cause of dismay was my claim that sin is a useful category by which to examine human affairs. "You can't call people sinners!" said my shocked and furrowed daughter. She was entirely right on one level, of course. We had been talking about the horrifying events in Norway, in which Anders Breivik, a thirty-two-year-old radically conservative Christian (or perhaps "Christian"), killed seventy-seven people, most of them children at a summer camp, many of them related to members of Norway's ruling elite who presumably crafted the weak anti-immigration laws that allowed the recent influx of Muslim immigrants that so unglued the shooter.

History tends to support this maxim: virtually anyone who thinks he's been given the power to condemn his neighbors for what he perceives to be their sins will be at the heart of a tragic, absurd, and/or evil situation. The track record of self-proclaimed prophets is pretty bleak. Thea's well-taken point was, I think, that if I call someone a sinner, I'm at the top of a slope slippery with the blood of innocents. To many, calling someone a sinner implies that you're in a position to judge, somehow not implicated in the fray. If you see sin around you and identify it as such, then somehow you remain outside the fire of judgment. You are rendered innocent so long as someone else is guilty. It seems like a good deal, especially if you're someone inclined to condemn others (like "Christians"). It seems like a very bad deal if you're the sinner or if you have any anxieties about absolutist legal codes.

Even so, sin is a concept we're naive to dismiss, whether or not we identify ourselves as religious. In the broader culture of the United States, there are two gauges by which we measure perceived or actual misconduct: mental health and the legal code. Misconduct is the result either of mental illness or willful disregard for civic order. While these are necessary ways to gauge human misconduct, they don't cover the full range and depth of human experience. To imagine that they do creates a story about the human person and human culture that's missing a bunch of pages in the middle. (I've cribbed this analysis from Barbara Brown Taylor's wonderful book *Speaking of Sin: The Lost Language of Salvation*.)

One of the problems in talking about sin is that it's a word in a technical lexicon. Just as projection is one of those ideas bandied around by people who've never studied Freudian theory or its nuances (like me), sin has spilled over its technical boundaries and thereby become diluted, distorted, and generally misunderstood. As far as I can tell, it's as misunderstood within the Christian community as it is outside of it, in part for the same reason: it's considered to be a subset of either mental health or the legal system and not its own discrete and rich category.

While Anders Breivik probably has mental health issues and clearly broke all kinds of laws, I suspect that there are many other reasonable people besides Thea who would balk at identifying sin as an important component of his story, although it may be that story's most salient component. While breaking laws is often a side effect, sin's primary work is the precarious, discordant elevation of the self above the sturdy, harmonious network of God, self, and neighbor. With that definition in mind, you can be a law-abiding, mentally healthy member of a community and still be a sinner. Indeed, if you're a Christian, you're guaranteed to be one; that's what the story of the Fall is about.

One of the persistent themes in both testaments of the Bible is that God is the only judge of sin because humankind has a severe allergy to identifying sin as sin when it's tied to self. We have a very long history of pointing a finger at our neighbors and saying, "S/he made me eat it." In writing the covenantal community's early history, the biblical writers were uneasy with the idea of kingship. Even when the kings were beloved of God—and most of them were not—the biblical writers point out time and again that human authority is almost ludicrously unable to judge with any regularity what's pleasing to God.

I'm exercised about sin because so many critical misunderstandings of it seem to be spotlighted right now, and I'm trying to figure out how it is that I'm right and they're wrong. Rick Perry, the governor of Texas, is about to declare himself a candidate in the Republican presidential race, having struggled to discern if he's called by God to do so. The backdrop of his declaration was the rally last Saturday in which he and several thousand others prayed for a troubled America. He prayed for the military and political leaders who cannot see the light in the darkness. There was no indication that he thought he might be one of those blind leaders. For all the Bible reading that went on, no mention was made of the fact that in the Bible God never gives the rich and powerful more power when they ask for it. Instead, God regularly undermines them by granting it to the least or youngest in the community.

In a terrific op-ed piece in the *Austin American-Statesman*, Jim Rigby, a local Presbyterian minister, pointed out the absence of several other key biblical passages at the rally, like the passage in which Jesus expresses a clear distaste for public shows of prayer. The common thread among the passages Rigby mentions is an awareness of our steady insistence on seeing sin as something "out there" without any indication that it resides ineradicably "in here" as well.

But there's a problem for those who see sin as residing ineradicably "in here," who believe that we must struggle constantly to set self-interest under the discipline of a higher and more generous law. Reinhold Niebuhr, whom I always seem to read in the deepest, hottest part of summer, calls these "children of light," in opposition to the "children of darkness," the moral cynics who "know no law beyond the self." According to Niebuhr, the problem is that the children of light are dumber than doorknobs. They fail to account for the power of sin in both individual and collective lives, and even within and among themselves. Children of light tend to think that if they reform, correct, educate, convert, clean house, start over, then human affairs will radically improve. Niebuhr says fuggedaboudit: "no matter how wide the perspective which the human mind may reach, how broad the loyalties which the human imagination may conceive, how universal the community which human statecraft may organize, how pure the aspirations of the saintliest idealists may be, there is no level of human moral or social achievement in which there is not some corruption of inordinate self-love."

Niebuhr identified Marxists as children of light whose stupidity allowed their creed to become "the vehicle and instrument of the children of darkness." I believe that Perry and his followers are also children of light. Their creed is that eliminating homosexuality and abortion, giving free rein to business, and insisting on Christianity's primacy will renew America, a creed as naive as Marxism and as easily made into the tool of moral cynics. Of course, as a self-confessed utopian, I'm a child of light as well. I'm looking for admission to another group, made up of what I'll call children of dawn. They know the power of sin, they work to name it in themselves and in the world, and their despair or anger at knowing that they can't conquer it by themselves is overridden by hope and generosity. I think of St. Paul, that proud Pharisee, who opened the doors of Christianity to the uncircumcised and the eaters of unclean foods and invited them to come in, sit down, and eat. More recently, I think of people like, say, Nelson Mandela, but children of dawn don't tend to be particularly visible until you bump into them in the darkness. The hospice nurses who helped us through my mother's death were children of dawn. The friend who tells you a hard truth with great love. The artist who brings new beauty into the world. The teacher who gives his students his best work and requires that they return it with interest. The attorney who works on death row. The director of a no-kill animal shelter who cooks Thanksgiving dinner for all the creatures in her care. The soldier who struggles to treat the enemy with respect.

It's a long list, thank goodness, and unrestricted by any creed or class. There's no litmus test for joining it, other than the willingness to do the wretchedly hard work of forgiving each other, ourselves, and the world again and again and again. Most of us would rather sleep in than be children of dawn. But when we wake up and acknowledge sin's destructive power at work within each individual, corporation, and nation (even and especially the ones we love); when we approach each other with the profound humility that this knowledge engenders; when we move ahead in good faith knowing that we may be wrong and need to change course, this is when the power of sin begins to loosen its grip. Furrow all you want, but that's why I think sin is behovely, and the acknowledgment of sin is our only hope.

44

A Furry Flurry of Fully Furrowed Brows
My Beef with Freeman Dyson, Part II
AUGUST 26, 2011

My previous piece revealed the furry fury of the fully furrowed Kohout brow, especially when a flurry of furry brows furrow in unison. I'm a Kohout by marriage, not birth, so perhaps I do not wield the full power of the brow, but I'm no slouch, either.

The source of my current furrow fest is this: a month after taking on Freeman Dyson—and clearly knocking him out—I'm still struggling with his assertion in the introductory essay of *The Best American Science and Nature Writing 2010* that environmentalism has "replaced Marxism as the leading secular religion of our age," and that it "doesn't have much to do with science." Although he says he's hopeful about the future because of the environmental movement, it's hard to ignore the comparison with Marxism, which by most standards was a dismal failure when put into practice, however exalted its intentions in theory.

I agree with the assessment that environmentalism is a secular religion; what annoys me is the implication that scientists sit on a higher rung of the ladder of knowledge than environmentalists, who are somehow contaminated by their quasi-religious fervor and therefore need to be quarantined on a lower rung. Scientific ways of knowing trump religious ways of knowing.

I also got an email from a friend of mine, a formidable public theologian, who reminded me that the natural world is no replacement for the most amply understood Christian God. He wrote: "I do have a theological quibble (probably more than a quibble) with your view that nature in some way reveals God. If it does, I'm not sure I like this god very much." As Robert, our redoubtable ranch manager, is prone to say: well, hell. I'm aggravated by the implication that an abstracted theological way of knowing trumps experience of and reverence for nature.

So where's a huffy environmentalist Christian (or sometime Christian) supposed to stand on the ladder of knowledge, especially if she's wearing a skirt? Well, any eight-year-old with playground experience can answer that one: get off the ladder and go play somewhere else.

I'm setting up an opposition that's perhaps unreasonable: from what I've read, Dyson honors the mystery and gravity of the natural world, as I know my theologian friend does. But I can't quite shake the feeling that two of the *magisteria* of human knowledge—science and religion—tend to regard the natural world as a mere springboard to a more important kind of knowledge: science seeks to control nature and its processes, Christianity to transcend them. Environmentalism at its best requires that we seek understanding of the endlessly changing framework into which we as a species have been born, and that we work for the short- and long-term flourishing of both framework and species. Environmentalism demands a recognition of limits. I think it can be a vital safeguard for both science and Christianity for just that reason.

In his book *Forbidden Knowledge: From Prometheus to Pornography*, Roger Shattuck, late professor of modern languages and literature at Boston University, examines the vexed borderlands between constructive and destructive human knowledge, first in myth and literature, then in the case histories of the atomic bomb, the human genome project, and the Marquis de Sade. In a chapter titled "Knowledge Exploding: Science and Technology," he examines the boundary between pure and applied science and wonders if there really is one. Science operates on the assumption that scientists can safely move between two distinct realms, but Shattuck concludes that there is a lawless and often unacknowledged no-man's-land between the two:

> *The knowledge that our many sciences discover is not forbidden in and of itself. But the human agents who pursue that knowledge have never been able to stand apart from or control or prevent its application to our lives.*

Scientists, Shattuck believes, are often unable to move cautiously when they enter the realm of forbidden knowledge.

Freeman Dyson, who later came to work with most of the scientists involved in the Manhattan Project and who now heartily disapproves of nuclear weaponry, said this in 1980:

> *I felt it myself, the glitter of nuclear weapons. It is irresistible if you come to them as a scientist. To feel it's there in your hands. To release the energy that fuels the stars. To tell it do your bidding. And to perform these miracles, to lift a million tons of rock into the sky, it is something that gives people an illusion of illimitable power, and it is in some ways responsible for all our troubles, I would say, this what you might call "technical arrogance" that overcomes people when they see what they can do with their minds.*

And yet in his book *The Scientist as Rebel*, published in 2006, Dyson writes: "Science flourishes best when it uses all the tools at hand, unconstrained by preconceived notions about what science ought to be. Every time we introduce a new tool, it always leads to new and unexpected discoveries, because Nature's imagination is richer than ours." "New and unexpected," however, does not necessarily lead to flourishment for all. Dyson's prediction that we can technologize our way out of the depredations of excessive carbon emissions has a hollow ring for those of us anxious about the lawless borderlands around forbidden knowledge.

Environmentalism at its best can provide science with a prophetic voice, a voice that looks back to a time of equilibrium and harmony within a community, assesses present troubles in light of that ideal, and outlines the consequences of continued disequilibrium. (At its worst, of course, it just sounds condemnatory. There are plenty of stiff-necked literalists in the environmental movement.) In these times when technological advances come so quickly that it's hard to know what their long-term effects might be, environmentalists can act in the way an ethics panel in a hospital might act, looking to a wider context for particular cases than the science (or business) at hand. Given scientists' track record of falling in love with the glitter of their tools, the prophets of the environmental world can provide them with a corrective slap.

At the other end of my furrow, environmentalism can provide Christianity with what Old Testament scholar Ellen Davis calls "a wholesome materiality." (Or it can if the scientists in the movement don't look down their noses at the part of environmentalism that draws its power from the subjective realms of art and religion.) Within Christianity is a powerful riptide pulling its followers away from the material world, a tide that runs through misreadings of scripture as well as tradition. In her wonderful (really!) book *Scripture, Culture, and Agriculture: An Agrarian Reading of the Bible*, Davis proposes that the Bible takes the health of the earth very, very seriously. When Israel remembers both its covenant with God and its place within the intricately interconnected creation of Genesis 1, then the land drips with milk and honey and everyone is fed. When Israel forgets its covenant and its place, its sin results in devastation of the land. This devastation is not a poetic image; it's meant quite literally. Thunders the prophet Jeremiah:

> *I have seen the earth, and here, [it is] wilderness and waste;*
> *And [I look] to the heavens—and their light is gone.*
> *I have seen the mountains, and here, they are wavering,*
> *And all the hills palpitate.*
> *I have seen, and here, there is no human being,*
> *And all the birds of the heavens have fled.*
> *I have seen, and here, the garden-land is now the wasteland,*
> *And all its cities are pulled down,*
> *Because of YHWH, because of his hot anger.*

The well-being of the earth is inseparable from human behavior. If we remember that we are meant to be stewards of all the creation (including humans) in a way befitting us as the images of a creative, just, and merciful God, then all will be well. When we forget who we are, our forgetting is made miserably visible on the face of creation, like Dorian Gray's portrait. Our forgetting is not merely a matter of personal misbehavior, as many Christians seem to think; we forget the enormous scope of creation and delicate balances within which we have our being. In trying to stand on top of creation, we often crush it.

I agree with my theologian friend that it's dangerous to assume that you can observe the natural world and thereby know the full nature of God. In some ways, that would be like thinking you can reliably deduce knowledge of parents through the behavior and character of their children. Yet the mark of the parent is inevitably found on the child (in this case, both human and nonhuman creation): expunging God from the operations of nature that are distasteful or terrifying to human sensibilities (by, for example, killing all alpha predators despite their vital place in the biotic community) is as troubling to me as the insistence of some scientists on wandering in the borderlands without a map. Environmentalists in the scientific world can help restore human awareness of the "wholesome materiality" of creation, to look for the intricate and hidden relationships that bind us to one another and make us family—or neighbors, in the salutary command that we love God, neighbor, and self without separation.

Now that I've cleared that up, I declare that the era of furrowing is officially over.

45

Re-Wilding the Monocultural Self

SEPTEMBER 30, 2011

While reading the recently published *Rambunctious Garden: Saving Nature in a Post-Wild World*, by Emma Marris, I found myself simultaneously cheering and exclaiming with a steely squint: Hey! Real conservationists can't think this! You're just giving ammunition for them to lob back at us. Slippery slope turns to avalanche turns into apocalypse! Who the heck do you think you are?

Now that I've finished the book, I've decided to go back to applauding Marris for her cheerful heterodoxy and passionately commonsensical approach to conservation issues in the brave new world of the twenty-first century. I began reading with no problems. In the first chapter she says,

> Nature is almost everywhere. But wherever it is, there is one thing it is not: pristine. In 2011 there is no pristine wilderness on planet Earth. . . . [Humans are] running the whole Earth, whether we admit it or not. To run it consciously and effectively, we must admit our role and even embrace it. We must temper our romantic notions of untrammeled wilderness and find room next to it for the more nuanced notion of a global, half-wild rambunctious garden, tended to by us.

So far so good. Recent climate change and the cascade of new realities resulting from it are clear to virtually every scientist and conservation-minded person on the planet. (Insert punchline about Texans and Rick Perry here.) She explains that environmental sciences, especially in the United States, use a baseline, a reference point that, in formulating conservation goals, tends to assume an ideal time of pristine, stable wilderness to which nature itself yearns to return, hearkening to a time before the destabilizing pressures of human occupancy. We fouled nature up, so it's our ethical duty to restore it to its original, Edenic state.

But then she makes things really messy. From what point do we date human occupancy for the sake of conservation goals? And where? Many scientists assume that the time before the arrival of Europeans to the Americas is the time to which we must reset the clock. This is the baseline that many conservation-minded Americans (like me) also assume, most likely unquestioningly (like me). (One of the reasons I call myself a utopian—i.e., not a realist—is my hope, expressed in an earlier piece, that human stewardship, particularly by ranchers, might at some point not be the worst thing that ever happened to the Earth.) First of all, religious fundamentalists aren't the only ones to believe that the Garden of Eden existed as a historical reality. The idea that there has ever been a stable, self-perpetuating ecosystem is problematic:

> We are a short-lived species with a notoriously bad grasp of timescales longer than a few of our own generations. But from the point of view of a geologist or a paleontologist, ecosystems are in a constant dance, as their components compete, react, evolve, migrate, and form new communities. Geologic upheaval, evolution, climactic cycles, fire, storms, and population dynamics see to it that nature is always changing.

Nor do scientists always know what any particular ecosystem actually looked like at any pre-baseline time. Nor does the Edenic model take into account the fact that many native peoples had purposeful management systems before the arrival of Europeans. Finally, this baseline is also increasingly impossible to achieve, either through restoration or management practices, because the pressures of climate change and population growth have made turning back the clock about as feasible as stuffing a sixteen-year-old boy into the shoes he wore when he was eight. It isn't going to happen, especially if he didn't actually have any shoes when he was eight.

The pristine wilderness toward which so many conservationists aspire is, in fact, an American construction that came into being along with

Yellowstone National Park and the science of the nineteenth century, which saw nature as essentially balanced, static, unchanging in its equilibrium. Contemporary environmental sciences clearly demonstrate that the natural world—before human "interference"—never stood still for long. Some of the most revered natural phenomena—old growth forests, for example—can be the result of climactic anomalies, like long wet spells that interrupted wildfires cycles. And what do we do about issues like the mountain goats at Yellowstone, which are now beloved by tourists, but were introduced from several hundred miles away in the 1940s for hunting purposes?

Well, I can cope with the reality that the Wizard of Oz is actually working levers behind a curtain, even as I'd like to be able to ignore him. But one of the unexpected revelations of that unveiling really hooked me under the ribs: the chapter titled "Learning to Love Exotic Species." I have often moaned and groaned about the nonnative fauna—the fallow, axis, and sika deer, the feral hogs, and the various other oddities—that wander through Madroño Ranch and compete for food with the natives, especially in this drought time. I'm also a member of an advisory board to the Lady Bird Johnson Wildflower Center, the mission of which is "to increase the sustainable use and conservation of native wildflowers, plants and landscapes." I recently sat in on an excellent and nuanced presentation on invasive species by Damon Waitt, the director of the center's Native Plant Information Network. I know as surely as I know that north is up and south is down that natives are good and that invasives are bad. But Marris upends the poles and says, think again. Nonnatives can be not only not malevolent but actively useful. While some exotic species (a term she prefers to "invasives") are "rowdy nuisances" that need active and emphatic controlling, there are far more "shy foreigners" who work for the good of their new ecosystems. In fact, there are human-managed—that is, artificial—landscapes filled with exotic species that outperform their "natural" cousins, if performance is measured by biodiversity and provisions of services to all inhabitants and not just humans.

This is when I began to ask the "just who does she think she is" question with my arms akimbo, which is when I realized it wasn't my scientific, based-on-facts knowledge that was being challenged (it doesn't take much); rather, it was my own self-identity as a conservation-minded layperson. I was adhering to an orthodoxy I hadn't realized I subscribed to. I learned at my mother's knee that any orthodoxy's tires need a good kicking before you buy. I had climbed into this orthodoxy (a Prius, naturally) without doing so and found that I might be stuck on the side of the road with a flat.

In Marris's rambunctious garden, however, the side of the road might not be a bad place to be stuck. If it were managed for biodiversity, for beauty, and as a part of a much larger ecosystem—as a stop for migratory butterflies, for example—a stranded motorist might enjoy the wait for help. We're so used to thinking of "nature" as something outsized and grand and hard to get to that we frequently forget that it's quite literally underfoot or falling on our sleeves as we walk along a city sidewalk. While it's not entirely within our control, there are more ways for human beings to engage in a fruitful relationship with nature than we currently allow ourselves to imagine.

Marris's call for biodiversity everywhere—in industrial sites, apparent wastelands, backyards, hybrid ecosystems developed for economic gain—made me realize that unexamined orthodoxy often leads to monoculture, be it agricultural, social, political, intellectual, or spiritual. In industrial agriculture, monocultures rely heavily on pesticides, ridding crops of insects that in a healthy polyculture can be absorbed into the system (sometimes requiring intensive human labor). In the national discussion about immigration, there seems to be a sector demanding social monoculture, using terms that sound very much like the prejudice in environmental circles against "invasive" species. The extremes in both political parties are demanding that their candidates spray any bipartisan thoughts with herbicide. When she first messed with my assumptions, I mentally doused Marris's proposals, hoping the threat to my preconceptions would go away. Despite the huge short-term returns of monoculture (in my case, the sure knowledge that I was right), the reality of radically diminished liveliness looms just past the identical crop rows. Re-wilding monocultures of the mind, the heart, and the land—acknowledging that there is no single solution to any complex problem—sounds like a critical strategy in the face of what sometimes feels like a threatening future. According to Marris, it's our duty to manage nature, but it's a duty leading to pleasure, beauty, and liveliness. As she urges, "Let the rambunctious gardening begin."

46

Edsels and the Enlightenment:
The Downside of Corporate Personhood
OCTOBER 14, 2011

A headline in Monday's *Austin American-Statesman* reported that the Texas senate is poised for a political shift as four veteran conservative Republican senators step down before the 2012 election cycle. According to the article, those seats could easily go to even more conservative candidates. Beyond these four, the state's new voting districts, created by an already conservative legislature, could usher in an even more heavily conservative supermajority. Rick Perry may end up looking like the Mitt Romney of Texas Republicans by next year, excoriated for any political impulse that aspires to a collective social goal as opposed to individual taxpayer rights.

George Will, whose elegant prose I enjoy when its content doesn't irritate me, pointed toward the reason I find protection of individual rights a necessary component of, but insufficient basis for, the existence of government—a protection that Texans already promote aggressively. In a recent column, Will writes that liberalism's project is

> *to dilute the concept of individualism, thereby refuting the individual's zone of sovereignty. . . . Such an agenda's premise is that individualism is a chimera, that any individual's achievements should be considered entirely derivative from society, so that the achievements need not be treated as belonging to the individual.*

Anticipating the argument that corporations, especially through the power of advertising, have too much sway over a gormless public, Will notes that John Kenneth Galbraith first articulated that case in 1958, even as "Ford's marketers were failing to make a demand for Edsels." The public, Will implies, can take care of itself.

Finally, Will denounces liberalism's penchant for "confident social engineering" in favor of conservatism's insistence on "government humility in the face of society's creative complexity."

Moving backward, as is my wont, the idea that liberals are the only social engineers in the political arena strikes me as curious. All laws and regulations, not just liberal ones, seek to shape society to a particular end; refusing to regulate has social consequences as profound as regulating. The idea that there was some Edenic time of self-balancing governments and economies sounds almost quaint—Newtonian thinking in a post-Einsteinian universe.

Quaint, if it weren't disingenuous. Among the "individuals" that Will is loath to regulate is the corporation, a stance that, to a point, makes perfectly good sense and has a fine American pedigree. Why should individuals lose their constitutional rights when they band together in a common enterprise? It's a reasonable question, but Will's reply assumes a static definition of both individualism and corporations. The concept of an individual to whom particular rights accrued developed in a historical context of monarchies and established churches, whose comforts and quarrels were prone to break the backs of the faceless majority that lay beyond their own intimate circles. That the Enlightenment pried apart individual human worth and dignity from wealth and social status is its crowning glory. That its definition of "individual human" was grossly reductive is an ongoing misfortune, imprisoning those deemed less than fully human in a continuing serfdom, unworthy of the full panoply of rights.

As a nation, we have, most of us, slowly come to see those prison bars and to see that we tossed not only races, genders, and legitimate ways of being, but also whole species and ecosystems into an airless, putrid place. Politically and culturally, Americans have more fully taken in the view of a society based on universal individual rights for which Enlightenment philosophy cleared the way. Yet we continue to distort its essential insight—that every individual has an equal right to the pursuit of happiness—when the legal fiction granting personhood to corporate structures becomes destructive of the very individualism it purports to uphold. Indeed, today's transnational corporations bear a suspicious resemblance to the great, lumbering bureaucracies (monarchies, established churches) whose primary goal was self-preservation and against which the French and American revolutions were fought.

The *New Yorker* recently ran a story about Don Colcord, the owner of the Apothecary Shoppe in Nucla, Colorado. Colcord prefers to be called a druggist, whom he defines as "the guy who repairs your watch and glasses. A pharmacist is the guy who works at Walmart." Colcord repairs a lot of things besides watches and glasses, from chronic medical conditions to broken hearts. His is the only pharmacy for an area of 4,000 square miles, an area with no hospital. Much of Nucla's population lives well below the poverty level. Until recently, there were a few other independent drug stores in the area, but the combined pressures exerted by insurance companies, big chains, and mail-order pharmacies when Medicare Part D came into effect in 2006 forced them to close—along with more than 500 other independent rural pharmacies nationwide that couldn't order at the volume level of big chains. In order to keep his Apothecary Shoppe running, Colcord has had to spend his own savings at several critical times.

There's a lot Nucla lacks, but in its druggist it has someone who sees the humanity of every person he serves, from illegal immigrants to NRA members to the four transgendered people (none of whom live in Nucla) for whom he compounds medicine. He treats them all, whether or not they have the money to pay him. The generosity of his spirit is something that infuses the community and makes its way back to him: a drifter, an older man, settled in the neighboring town and, mistrusting doctors, relied on Colcord's expertise in treating his high blood pressure and other ailments, one of which was chronic loneliness. When he neared death fifteen or so years later, it was Colcord who stayed with him, arranged for hospice care, organized a funeral mass for him, and went through his effects. He found that in his will the old drifter had left him $300,000—coincidentally, almost exactly enough money to cover the outstanding debts run up by customers who had been unable to pay.

As an individual and a businessman Colcord enacts a kind of sovereignty (the trait Will so admires) that becomes less likely when transnational corporations are defined as persons. When Walmart, to choose a convenient demon, is considered an individual with rights, the kind of sovereignty Walmart practices is based on profit. Let me hasten to say that I have nothing against profitable businesses; I rely on them in virtually every arena of my life. But the culture that arises from these supersized "individuals" is one in which generosity of spirit and empathy become secondary—and often undermine—the reign of the profit of the few. A society governed by the values of enormous corporations must despise the apparently inefficient operations of a business like the Apothecary Shoppe.

As the heroes and villains of the Enlightenment sought to uncover the treasure buried in every individual (especially white male ones), cultures arose reflecting the shared values of those individuals, from Ben Franklin to Robespierre, from the American Revolution to the Reign of Terror. Sovereignty in and of itself is to be deplored if it leads to tyranny. When the values that drive successful transnational corporations predominate, the culture that arises among those "persons" is not value-neutral or necessarily benign, as so many business fundamentalists—so many of them in the Texas Republican Party—seem to believe.

47

Field Notes from Inside My Head
Connecting Art and Commerce
NOVEMBER 11, 2011

Point One: When we attended the Alliance of Artists Communities conference in Chicago several weeks ago, I found myself eagerly awaiting the start of a session titled "Earned Revenue and Artist Residencies."

Point Two: The other day, as Martin and I drove past the parking lot of the Kerrville Tractor Supply Company, which is always stacked with neat piles of gates, troughs, feeders, and such, I looked carefully to see if there was any nifty bit of equipment that we needed but hadn't thought of.

I understood at that moment that someone must have performed a brain transplant on me in the dark of the night. Here are the kinds of sessions I would have expected to look forward to at the conference: "Why We Need More Poets"; "Why Food Should Be the Center of Every Residency Experience"; "Why All Residents Should Be Required to Stare at Bugs and Birds for Three Hours a Day"; "Remedial Programs for Residents Who Don't Like Chickens." Here are the kinds of stores I normally eye with pleasure: book stores, kitchen supply stores, stores with great selections of cowboy boots. Earned revenue? Farm equipment? Huh?

Points Three through Five or Maybe Seven: Recently I've read a number of interesting articles in the *New York Times*, some of them in the business section (more evidence of a brain transplant), about such issues as the transformative power of excellent design in the public places of poverty-stricken communities; the involvement of the Danish government in the redesign of unsightly power towers in rural Denmark; the surge of young entrepreneurs (examples: the practitioners of "Gandhian innovation" in India, the Unreasonable Institute) who see that for-profit business and social justice are not at odds with each other; and the powerful but unfocused energy of the Occupy Wall Street protests. Also, the proposed Christo project over the Arkansas River in Colorado, which has environmentalists, government agencies, and artists tussling over how, if, and why the project should proceed.

What has linked these disparate subjects in my mind is a sense that we are witnessing a radical shift in thinking about the nature of commerce. In my lifetime, business has been a stand-alone subject, like medicine or law. As an academic discipline, it has been completely separated from the humanities. There may be writing requirements for business majors, but they're usually specified as such. Studio art for business majors? History? Philosophy? I haven't seen them cross-listed in any departments I've studied in. Business has been cordoned off and cordoned itself off.

One of the reasons I enjoyed the session on "Earned Revenue and Artist Residencies" was its underlying assumption that there is a fruitful overlap between the arts and business beyond the mere sale of art objects. Most of us attending the session represented residency programs, ranging from very urban to very rural, from huge to tiny, from brand-new to venerable. Given the roller coaster of the economy and the shrinking of foundation funding, there's a real sense of energy around the question of how residency programs might become more, or even fully, self-sustaining financially. What for-profit goods and services might residency programs provide, especially when they charge artists nominal or no fees for their residencies? The arts are so automatically relegated to the nonprofit world that the question frequently doesn't even arise.

One of the participants in the discussion runs an organic farm outside Toronto and is able to provide space for artists and make a comfortable enough living between farming and renting space on her farm for work-shops and events. An emerging program in Ajo, Arizona, is planning to use some of its space—an old public elementary school—as a motel that will feed its paying guests excellent local and organic food (they'll have their own garden), making use of the cafeteria kitchen already in place. In fact, the twining of food and its place in the production of art was a persistent subtheme of the conference.

All of this led me to wonder how Madroño Ranch could more closely unite the business of the ranch with the mission of the residency program, which was why the Tractor Supply inventory suddenly looked so interesting. What on the ranch could supply the artists in their work? And how could the artists contribute to the functioning of the ranch? How might the art and writing produced at Madroño waft beyond the perimeter fencing and generate appetites for new business and beauty in the community around us?

Wondering in a vague way about Nice Big Questions is one of my favorite pastimes, which is why I was so pleased to find the very concrete story about power lines in Denmark. The rapid growth of wind and solar energy production in Europe has led to the need for much larger power poles, which are undeniably unsightly. Even as people understand the need for them, no one—especially in rural communities—wants them spoiling the views. (These nasty things are going up all over the Texas Hill Country, every bit as blighting as huge billboards.) To help mitigate the NIMBY response to the power poles, the Danish government commissioned a contest among design companies to see who might come up with a less intrusive structure than the starkly utilitarian poles. While I can't say that the winning design is anything I'd want on my own property, the very fact of the contest pointed to a way of thinking that's foreign not just because it's Danish: aesthetics matter, even when it comes to the most practical of issues.

Of course, the most practical of questions behind the most practical of issues is: what will it cost? How are the costs justified? Most of points three through six I watched in the fields inside my head related to those questions. In Denmark there seemed to be a shadow bottom line floating just below the financial one: can we make what we build beautiful? Can it be a pleasure (or at least not a blight) to the community? The piece on well-designed public spaces in poverty-stricken areas noted that the addition of bright color to housing projects, or of new stairs to replace a steep, eroding dirt walkway in a slum, injected a sense of hope, order, and civic pride where it had been sorely lacking.

In these instances, government has pointed to the need to consider more than one bottom line when spending money. Many young entrepreneurs (this is a very interesting generation coming up) are aware that there isn't necessarily a conflict between the need to make a living for themselves and making the world at large more livable. They operate with the assumption that there is more than one bottom line; their business must succeed financially. But they measure success not just in income to the company but measurable usefulness to the community in which they work. One of the impetuses behind the Occupy Wall Street movement, I think, is the (so far unarticulated) recognition that businesses, especially financial institutions and transnational corporations, have hewed to a single bottom line: short-term profit for shareholders.

Obviously, a company needs to be financially profitable, but I think there is a sense that many of these shadow bottom lines need to be as visible and material as the financial ones in order to judge a business as truly successful. Does a business add to or detract from the beauty, health, social coherence, and ecological systems of the community in which it operates? A business may offer a lot of low-paying jobs and operate profitably but still get an F-minus in the beauty, health, social coherence, and ecological factors. Is it a successful business? The Leadership in Energy and Environmental Design (LEED) certification program is at least a template for how such bottom lines might be developed.

Maybe businesses—especially big ones—could offer residency programs for artists and environmental scientists, recognizing that the costs of such a program are as necessary to operations as paying for the lights. Maybe business and the arts (liberal and otherwise) can develop a new relationship, one that is more than just a charitable donation at the end of a financially solvent year. Maybe the arts are as important to business success (especially in a climate-changed world) as steel is to bridge-building. Maybe I'm standing out in one of the pastures of my mind, mooing to myself. And maybe there are some restless young business-oriented people ready to figure out how we might bring these shadow bottom lines clearly and boldly into view.

48

Angels in the Dark

DECEMBER 9, 2011

Jesus said to them . . . "But in those days, after that suffering, the sun will be darkened and the moon will not give its light, and the stars will be falling from heaven, and the powers in the heavens will be shaken."

—*Mark 13:24–25*

These were among the words that greeted the Christian New Year a couple of Sundays ago, the beginning of the Advent season. Well, dang, commented some of us who meet after the 9:00 a.m. service at All Saints' Episcopal Church to discuss the readings. We might as well fold up our tents and go home if *this* is what the season's bringing.

By the end of the discussion, we surprised ourselves by agreeing that there's something oddly reassuring about the passage in which these verses are embedded, despite the Episcopalian squeamishness often evoked by the apocalyptic Jesus. All this talk about judgment and suffering is fine coming from John the Baptist—what can you expect from someone who eats locusts? When Jesus talks about judgment and end times, however, I get linear, literal, and cross. The world didn't end. Jesus was wrong. Untrustworthy. Oh, forget it. I'll just sit here alone in the dark.

But eventually I have to note the quotation marks around the darkness-coming passage, which means that Jesus is not just throwing wild predictions around. He's quoting scripture, from the times when other prophets saw God's people careening off toward the wilderness without so much as a water bottle. The world did not come to an end after Isaiah used this imagery eight centuries before Jesus used it, something Jesus probably noticed. Nor did it come to an end after Ezekiel or Joel used it in the interim centuries. It was (and is) poetic language used to jolt people out of their open-eyed, daylight sleepwalking. Wake up! There *is* darkness around and within us, but it's not what we think it is. There is light as well, and it too is often not what we think it is.

In Ciudad Juárez, Mexico's most violent border city, angels have taken to landing at crime scenes, at busy intersections, even on the International Bridge. They stand about ten feet tall, with wide feathered wings, and carry signs that say things like "Murderers, Believe and Repent." The fact that these angels are actually teenaged members of Salmo 100 (Psalm 100), a tiny evangelical church, doesn't make them any less impressive; in fact, I think it makes them even more so. Frustrated with the lethal violence that flays their city and with the flabby ineffectiveness of public policy, these young people persuaded the city to donate old office curtains that they turned into robes, raised money for makeup and feathers, and began their work of shocking people awake—particularly those who continue to perpetrate and permit the demonic activities that so plague the city. Their performances are beautiful and dangerous: they stand without speaking, without means of defense, in places where they are very likely to encounter the demonic forces unraveling their world.

They have seen the sun and the moon cease to give light, seen the stars fall from the sky. They have seen the signs that their world is charged with darkness, but they have chosen an energy source beyond the darkness.

Most of us have seen the skies go dark at one time or another; most of us have had times when it seemed that the world is going to end. What our little discussion group decided that Jesus was saying was that there *are* times when the skies go dark and the world seems torn from its course. These times are unavoidable. But don't think that darkness defines the whole nature of reality, or you'll pull from a limited energy source, see from a restricted field of vision. Sometimes it takes darkness to remind you that there is light, and that you want to see it.

It's easy to think about the darkness simplistically. I do it myself, noting the physical and spiritual relief that the presolstice days bring from the scorching Texas sun. I've noted that most things, including us, need darkness in which to grow. But I also hearken to Wendell Berry's pithy distillation of the full power of the dark:

To go in the dark with a light is to know the light.
To know dark, go dark. Go without sight,
and find that the dark, too, blooms and sings
and is traveled by dark feet and wings.

Most of us—used to light, to a particular, merely visual way of seeing—have definitions of darkness that are inadequate to its full reality. Although there is blooming in the darkness, there are also things fully worthy of terror. Because we can't see in the darkness the way we're used to seeing in the light, we often have trouble discerning what blooms from what bites. And sometimes it's the same thing.

In his book *The Blessing: A Memoir*, the poet Gregory Orr recounts the stunning journey of his life into the darkness, beginning when, at the age of twelve, he killed his brother in a hunting accident. His brilliant, erratic, meth-addicted physician father and his depressed mother, who died in surgery a couple of years later, were not able to help lead him through the dark, in which he lived persistently until he returned to the upstate New York village he called home after a shocking experience with Mississippi state police in a civil rights protest in 1965. When he got back, he found that many of the people he'd known all his life wouldn't speak to him because of his civil rights work. The darkness he'd lived in deepened; he wore the mark of Cain.

At the end of the summer, before he left to go back to college, one of his high school English teachers invited him on a drive. She took him to the property of a sculptor who had died earlier that year. Ignoring the "No Trespassing" sign on a barbed wire fence, they climbed into a field filled with metal figures, suggestive of but not restricted by human form. He and his teacher wandered for an hour through the field. Thought Orr:

these were soldiers of art. They brought no mayhem—only a longing to rise up and stand inside meaning as a man might stand in armor. There would be no violent struggles here. This was a field of blessing. A field where the mortal and fallen rose up, transformed. . . . Here in this field, arrayed in long lines, was an army of art. This army was engaged in a war against the nothingness and indifference of the universe. It wasn't the kind of war history fought, where timing

was everything and the clocks ran on blood. This was a war outside
of time. It was a war where you didn't fight, or march, or do violence
to anyone. . . . Somewhere in this field was a rendering of each agony
and exultation [the sculptor] had ever felt. And I could feel them, too.
I knew that somewhere in this field Cain stood; somewhere else, his
slain brother.

Our discussion group came to an equivalent conclusion about the disturb-
ing, apocalyptic words of Jesus. (At least, I think we did.) He was offering
his soon-to-be-tested disciples consolation: do not think that the coming
darkness is all there is. His advice to them: stay awake. Stay awake to the
angels that land in front of you, insisting that there is a way toward meaning.
Stay awake to the power behind love, beauty, forgiveness, and mercy that
moves in the dark and beyond it. Do not let the darkness consign you to
indifference or despair. Stay awake.

49

A Father's Legacy

JANUARY 13, 2012

Heather's father Henry E. Catto Jr. died on December 18, 2011. The following is an adaptation of remarks she delivered at his memorial service at St. Mark's Episcopal Church in San Antonio on January 7.

My friend Mimi Swartz wrote a wonderful piece in the November 2010 issue of *Texas Monthly* about the lovely and sometimes exasperating process of getting to know her father after her mother died. Pic Swartz had been one of my father's dearest friends since before Mimi and I were born, but I read her piece with more than just the prurient pleasure of reading about someone you already know in excellent prose. She very accurately described a process I recognized in my relationship with my own father but hadn't thought about yet. My mother, like Mimi's, was the switchboard operator through whom most family information was routed. When she died, I was faced with what appeared to be a daunting task: getting to know my then-seventy-nine-year-old father without a mediator.

I don't mean for a minute to suggest that he was somehow absent from my life. He drew silly cartoons on my lunch bags when I was in grade school, perhaps to make up for the fact that no one would trade lunches with me—my mother was an early adopter of what was then called "health food," and the other kids utterly scorned my lunches. He scared the shorts off all his children (and his wife) when we made our yearly summer drive from San Antonio (where we lived at the time) to Aspen, Colorado, over a then-unpaved Independence Pass: he loved to pretend to lose control of the station wagon and hear us shriek with pleasure at our narrow escape. (My mother's shrieking may not have been pleasure-based.)

Through my teenage and college years, he impressed on me the importance of being prompt (although I'm not, particularly). The sight of him sitting in a grumpy heap of plaid bathrobe at the bottom of the stairs late at night was one I learned actively to avoid. He also taught me the importance of looking up the meaning of words I didn't know. One day he wrote me a note for school: "Please excuse Heather's absence from school yesterday. She was malingering." When I didn't ask him what malingering was, he suggested that I look it up. After I did so and shrieked, "DAD-dy!" he wrote another: "Please excuse Heather's absence from school yesterday. She was goldbricking." Not yet having learned my lesson, I had to shriek one more time before I received a satisfactory note; my love of dictionaries has continued to this day.

He drove me to Massachusetts from our home in northern Virginia for my freshman year of college at his own alma mater, pointing out places he had known and loved as we got nearer Williamstown. As we approached my dorm, he suddenly spluttered in outrage at the discovery that an architecturally unfortunate library had replaced his beautiful old frat house. Aggravated as he was, he refocused his attentions to carry my station wagonload of stuff to the third-floor room and cried before he drove away, even as he continued muttering imprecations against willful artistic ugliness, an issue that vexed him all his life.

I also knew that he could be an unusually good sport. Political discussions, of course, were always central to our family's common life, and my mother, who was a Democrat and always up for an argument, never let a political proclamation from my father drive by without pulling it over and checking its registration. She taught her children well, which means that it's likely his whole family voted him out of a job he loved in 1992, when President Clinton came in. I never heard a word of recrimination. He didn't stop trying to show me the true Republican light, however much he felt its glow in the past years had dimmed. In fact, in the end I was forced to admit that he might have some points worth considering.

I already knew these things about my father when my mother died: that he was funny, a stickler for precision in language, an advocate for order and beauty in the arts, and usually a very good sport. That's not a bad list to start with, or even to finish up with. What I've learned about him in the last two years without my mother has surprised me and left me very grateful, despite the cost of the knowing.

Most of you who knew him have probably noted that I haven't yet mentioned what might be my father's most salient characteristic: his charm, which, having swum in all my life, I had ceased to notice. When I did notice it, I often thought of his charm as an accessory, a frill. Charm just wasn't Serious. It wasn't Deep. It was Frivolous.

In the past two years, Dad and I spent a considerable amount of time at the M. D. Anderson Cancer Center, where I watched him "oozing charm from every pore." What I came to realize after a while was that his charm was not directed just to the people who might be useful to him. It oozed all over the place in a cheerfully undisciplined flow. Cashiers in the cafeteria, janitors, doctors, volunteers, nurses, all laughed at his jokes, smiled at his suspenders and bow ties, graciously tolerated his corrections of their grammar, and responded to his courtly interest in them so that lightness and buoyancy tended to bob up where he was. I began to notice it in other places we went as well, this capacity to disarm people from all walks of life, people who might easily have dismissed him as a stuffy, inflexible elitist.

This is the backdrop against which I made my most unexpected discovery about my father: he had a capacity to ask genuinely for pardon when he had offended and to forgive when offended against. I have come to see his charm as an outward and visible sign of a deep humility, a bloom that became particularly noticeable to me after my mother died. It was something I had completely overlooked—and perhaps something he hadn't known about himself and which may have sprung from the sharp compassion that can emerge from grief.

In the last two years we had many, many opportunities to ask each other's pardon. Although he had a pair of very expensive hearing aids, he rarely wore them, preferring to accuse me of mumbling and requiring me to repeat myself with frequency, followed by exhortations not to yell. One morning I was driving him somewhere and just lost my temper when told to stop mumbling and yelling yet again. "Maybe," I said with some asperity, "you ought to consider apologizing to me for making me repeat myself over and over again when you could just put in your damn hearing aids." He raised an eyebrow and said, "But it's so much easier to blame you"—and then, just before I pulled over and throttled him, he truly apologized . . . although he did not put in his hearing aids.

We spent a lot of our time together arguing. We argued about his driving. We argued about his tendency to schedule or reschedule his medical appointments without telling anyone else about them. We argued about what he considered my tendency to worry and fuss. We argued about the need for nurses. We argued about the need for new kitchen appliances. We argued about moving the TV in his room to a place where he could actually see and hear it. Arguing with my father was not a novel experience. What began to follow the arguments was. Almost inevitably, I would get a call a few minutes after an argument, or a request for my presence, followed by a genuine apology, which in turn, allowed the same to be called forth from me. I learned that the moments of annoyance were never the last word. I learned to respect and be led by a depth of sweetness that I had previously judged to be frivolous. I learned how to love him all the way down because he showed me how to do it.

Learning to see the deep roots of his charm—which sprang from a genuine desire for peace at global and personal levels—I have come to see that my father was one of the blessed peacemakers Jesus called the children of God. That, in his own struggle with grief, he could reveal himself as this child of blessing was his greatest gift and example to me. Blessed are the peacemakers. Blessed is Henry Catto, with or without his hearing aids.

50

Submission Guidelines

MAY 25, 2012

The cliff swallows have returned to Madroño Ranch. They've expanded their housing development under the western eave of the Main House to several eastern eaves, one of which we can see from inside the house. We watched them build their nests, swooping down to the creek in droves and hovering, beating their wings like oversized butterflies, then soaring back to the house, landing under the eave with grace and precision, using their tails as props as they constructed—with no hands!—their elegant gourd-shaped mud nests.

Then we watched their babies poke their heads out of the nests' mouths, opening their own mouths for food, their ever-busy, ever-graceful parents helping rid the air of the countless blood-hungry insects the recent rains have brought. I now know that the insides of these nests are also carefully padded with grass, having found a fallen nest on the porch last Tuesday morning. Also in the fallen nest were five tiny, almost featherless hatchlings, dead, and one eggshell, still improbably intact; it was so fragile that it disintegrated as I tried to pick it up. They hadn't had time to crush their first homes before their second home crashed to the floor. The disoriented parents flew back and forth, but as I sat on the porch that morning it seemed they'd submitted to the new reality and moved on.

The swallows are a nuisance; they leave a significant mess under their nests. But I love them for their athleticism and the magical moment in mornings and evenings when they fly in mesmerizing patterns from nest to air and back and out and back again. If you sit on the kitchen stoop or stand in the driveway, you can feel as if you are the nucleus of an atom, part of something coherent and powerful, as if their trajectories were weaving some kind of electrically charged nest around you. And then you go back inside and they seem to do their chittering, beautiful work without you just fine. You weren't the center after all, as pleasing as the illusion was.

One day during our recent trip to Big Bend National Park, we left the cool, dry air of the Chisos Basin and drove down to the Hot Springs Historic District by the Rio Grande. As we drove through the relentless desert, with not a tree to be seen, I realized that the innumerable yellow splotches I was seeing weren't blooms from the recent rain but yuccas killed by the drought. How, I wondered, could there be a drought in the desert? The air-conditioned car suddenly felt as fragile as an eggshell.

By the time we got to the historic district, it was 95 degrees and humid, and the idea of sitting in the hot springs had lost much of its appeal; besides, they were closed due to the rains. It wasn't quite a wash, though; we got to see the post office/store and barracks-style rooms built by J. O. Langford, a Mississippian who moved there sight unseen as a homesteader in 1909, with his pregnant wife and eighteen-month-old daughter, planning to turn the hot springs into a business. He had heard about them as he was seeking a cure for malaria in the high, dry air of Alpine, Texas. Several people had already tried to claim the place through the Homestead Act of 1862, though none had been able to meet the requirements, which included a minimum of three years residence on the property. A West Texas old-timer is reputed to have discouraged Langford: "Nothing down there but rattlesnakes and bandit Mexicans. And it's too far away—that damned country promises more and gives less than any other place I saw." It was an eleven-day journey from Alpine, the nearest town (now about a three-hour drive). The Langfords held out until 1912 and left, not returning until 1927. In 1942 Langford sold the property for inclusion in the new Big Bend National Park.

What were they *thinking*? Floods, drought, implacable sun, virtually no trees, snakes, bandits, two young children, loneliness as relentless as the sun. And yet they made some kind of living—enough to build the post office/store, the modest set of rooms for visitors, and a bathhouse (now gone) at the springs.

The next day we drove to the other end of the park to Lajitas, one of the weirdest places I've ever been. The road to Lajitas winds through an even fiercer landscape than the one to the hot springs, if that's possible—the soil toasted a lunar white, virtually nothing growing. We went through Terlin-

gua, the dusty former quicksilver mining center, now the self-proclaimed
Chili Capital of the World. Another ten miles toward great looming cliffs
and we found ourselves in what could have been the set of an old western,
but for the lush grass at the golf resort.

Although Lajitas has been a modestly populated and popular river cross-
ing for centuries, it didn't get weird until the 1970s, when a Houston
businessman bought and poured $100 million into it, building an airstrip
for small jets, an eighteen-hole golf course, ninety-two luxury hotel rooms,
and an upscale restaurant. Not surprisingly, the place went bankrupt, but
another optimistic Texas businessman bought it for $13.5 million or there-
abouts. When we were there a few weeks ago, admittedly the beginning of
the low summer season, the place was virtually empty. The cliffs continued
to loom, and despite obviously steady watering, the golf course was begin-
ning to turn brown under the imperious sun. The high in Lajitas yesterday
was 104 degrees. What are they *thinking*?

On the one hand, I admire the moxie of these people who go into the
vast West Texas landscape thinking they will somehow outsmart it, or at
least wrest a modest living from it. On the other, I've become aware of
the necessity in every life for submission to some other force. In Big Bend
country, most people would find that force pretty hard to ignore. To quote
Flannery O'Connor, "to the hard of hearing you shout, and for the blind
you draw large and startling figures."

In recent months I've found that the power of Love is as startling as the
force of nature. When I found that my life was as fragile as a nestling's egg,
disintegrating as I tried to pick up its shattered pieces, something appeared,
an unexpected padding, to help me into a new life. The realities of death and
illness, grief and anger—the possibility that this new home will fall—never
stop looming. But over time the steady swooping kindnesses have built an
improbable nest in which I have been, for now (and what else is there?),
protected.

Despite years of thinking and reading and analyzing, I've been over-
whelmed by the steadiness of Love's flow, as powerful as the wind and water
eroding the West Texas vastness and almost as impersonal, a force that needs
an outlet, that seeks to move where it is not. I've stood in the midst of the
swallows' enfolding flight and seen that it continues when I step out of it.

It's almost harder to submit to Love because it *is* personal. If I were to try
to return gift for gift, prayer for prayer, I would run out of time long before

finishing. (Also, I would have to learn how to knit, equally unlikely.) I get why those ornery people think they can vanquish the forces of nature— Texans have fashioned themselves as the most stubborn of the stubborn. For a while I drove myself crazy when I tried and failed to respond individually to every kindness. What was I *thinking*? I've discovered recently that people I don't know are praying for me. How can I possibly pay that back? I can't. What can I do instead? Say uncle. Throw up my hands. Submit, give thanks as often as possible, bring some beauty into the world.

And be cautious about buying West Texas real estate in the expectation of a quick return.

51

Take Me to the River

JUNE 8, 2012

Last week I started rowing again after an eight-month hiatus. It has been pure pleasure, despite the inevitable price of blisters on my baby-soft hands. First, the pleasure of seeing my friends at the dock, including the ducks and C. J. the chocolate Lab, who howled and wagged when he saw me; next, the pleasure of reestablishing a relationship with a boat in the water, negotiating the jostling demands of wind, current, oars, river geography, swans, kayakers, and my own stiff body; finally, the pleasure of being on the river itself, of seeing what has changed and what remains the same. The water changes quite literally with each breath; despite the dams, it's still a living river. Trees and boulders have grown or fallen. Purple martins have replaced cormorants. And yet something persists, apparently unmoved by the passage of time. I've missed being on the river.

In the meantime, I was seeing another river, or at least imagining it. Martin has just finished reading Wendell Berry's novel *Jayber Crow* aloud to me, also pure pleasure. As have my rowing muscles, my reading-to-myself muscles have atrophied, and Martin reads with accents tailored to the characters and inflections appropriate to the plot. We've read like this for about a year now, usually at bedtime. Sometimes we can't help but sneak-read in the daytime, wanting to be swept downstream by the whorls and eddies of words, characters, and plot like river-rafting thrill seekers.

One of the main characters of *Jayber Crow* is the river that runs through the valley in which the story is set. Jayber, the narrator of the novel and the barber of Port William, Kentucky, is a river watcher as well. Late in his life and in the novel he asks:

How many hours have I spent watching the reflections on the water? When the air is still, then so is the surface of the water. Then it holds a perfectly silent image of the world that seems not to exist in this world. Where, I have asked myself, is this reflection? It is not on the top of the water, for if there is a little current the river can slide frictionlessly and freely beneath the reflection and the reflection does not move. Nor can you think of it as resting on the bottom of the air. The reflection itself seems a plane of no substance, neither water nor air. It rests, I think, upon quietness. Things may rise from the water or fall from the air, and, without touching the reflection, break it. It disappears. Without going anywhere, it disappears.

For Jayber, the reflection is an image, so to speak, of the divine, of how divinity *is* in this world and how it thwarts any logic that would fix that divinity in one place or locate it. It rests on a condition rather than a location, on a "how" rather than a "where." How can this condition be in the world? In quietness, says Jayber—a quietness that I think is born when the worlds outside and inside a person are married together. The natural world always carries its own quietness as it moves through time, but we humans need to practice marriage to know this quietness.

Honestly, I'm not sure what I'm trying to say by pulling marriage into this already multitentacled discussion, but having just made it to the other side of our twenty-seventh wedding anniversary, and given the national discussion on what makes a marriage, I've been thinking. (Those three words always fill Martin with foreboding.) If you take Jewish and Christian scripture seriously, marriage is that process by which two people become one flesh. This process requires rending; each must leave his or her parents and cling to the other in order to become one flesh. After this rending and clinging, they stand before each other naked and are not ashamed.

As a youngster I thought that becoming one flesh was merely a reference to sexual congress, the least generative and generous level of meaning in this most profound of texts. As an older-ster, I know that becoming one flesh can include sexual encounter but that the two are very distinct realities. Becoming one flesh may, in fact, begin with the self, with learning to bridge the slippery banks of individual consciousness and the physical body, so often at odds with each other. I've come to see cancer as an icon of this struggle, our stuttering inability to conjugate the distinctive languages of consciousness and its endless mysteries and of body and its appetitive requirements. To live as one flesh in the river of the self seems to require an awareness of the reflection that Jayber noticed, the reflection that rests on quietness—a sort of third party that allows the hands of consciousness and bodiness to hold each other, to mingle and flow into the river between them. Of course, to live as one flesh within a single body—to be married to yourself, and thus whole—is a work that flows as endlessly as a river, but that allows those glancing moments of standing naked and unashamed.

To include someone else in the work to become one flesh . . . well. It requires an endless series of rendings and cleavings from the past, from what has been, to create something new, the way a river changes every day and yet is still the same river. Sex *can* be a sign of one-fleshness, but is just as likely to be a hindrance. Only when that third party of quietness, that generous generative flow between the banks of two bodies that reflects something beyond itself—only when the three are present can there be one flesh. When the possibility of being one flesh reveals itself—within the self, within the couple—that body begins to grow, including within itself children, friends, strangers, enemies, the world itself. The capacity for stepping off the banks of the self into the river, beckoning those on the other side to join in, might manifest itself just a few times in a person's life, or never, or every day. A few people barely towel off before they jump back in, married to the whole world and all that's in it, no time for messing with clothes or shame.

So practicing marriage is not the same as being married. One training ground I've found for the practice of marriage has been reading aloud. It's something children know immediately, that a story read or told aloud is an opportunity for teller and listener to jump into a river of words and ride them together, making a net of meaning that holds them even when they scramble up their different banks at the end of the story. That's why the practice of reading scripture aloud is so important; it allows people to jump together off the banks and into its great narrative flow.

It's been instructive to be a child again as Martin reads aloud and I listen, creating for us a net of meaning through both rough and placid rides. Even if we spend the day ignoring the other across the bank, or throwing rocks, we climb together into that river of words, emerging refreshed (or sometimes asleep) or even naked, when one of us is moved to tears or left helpless by laughter.

That's why, with so many figurative rivers running, I'm happy to be back on (if not in) a literal river: yet another chance to practice marriage.

52

Bonfires in the Soul

JUNE 29, 2012

Last week, as Martin and I flew into Denver on our way to the Aspen Summer Words literary festival, we could see giant billows of smoke from the High Park fire outside Fort Collins, about sixty-five miles to the north. The fire has burnt more than 100 square miles over the last several weeks and, as of this writing, is still not completely contained. We met a cabbie who said philosophically that Mother Nature would have her way and that people who lived in fire hot spots should expect to get burned out. We talked about people who build houses in hurricane zones or on fault lines and concluded that human beings could be a little slow on the uptake.

At the festival, we had the great pleasure of meeting Luis Urrea, one of the keynote speakers, and his wonderful wife Cindy. In a session with Chip Blake, editor of *Orion Magazine*, Luis recounted meeting a group of *curanderas* in Mexico several years ago. They immediately sensed that he was accompanied by the spirit of a Sioux warrior, although they were puzzled by the word "Sioux," which they hadn't encountered before. Luis was puzzled as well. Not long before he had been in the company of a Sioux shaman who told him that he was sending a warrior spirit with him for protection, but Luis had understood this in a metaphorical way. The *curanderas* assured him there was nothing metaphorical about it.

When they found out he was a writer, they were disappointed. They had seen that he was a communicator of some sort, but they told him that he was really a healer. Sorry, he said; if I could cure people, I would, but I can't. You've just been lazy, they told him, but if you won't do that hard work, we guess your writing can work to heal the spirits of those who did not die in peace. Don't be lazy now, they said. There is work to be done.

Sick souls rely on art, on works of beauty, to lead them into health and peace. Art, they told him, cures by lighting bonfires in the soul, in souls that were filled with deadwood before they died, deadwood that holds them back even after death. This is not metaphorical—get to work. And he did, writing books that depict the ways of thoughtless devastation and grace. His own soul having been kindled, his work is like a taper that readers can use (or not) to light their own souls on fire for the work of justice, beauty, and harmony.

But how does lighting that flame cure a soul? As a culture, Americans tend to focus more on curing disease in bodies, and for most of us, putting ourselves into the care of the medical profession is an act of faith whether we call it that or not. I go to a doctor, and if I trust her, I do what she tells me to do and take the drugs she tells me to take, even if I have no idea how those drugs work. I also look for a doctor who sees beyond the complex systems of the body to the unique conformation of my very particular life, sometimes called the soul, who helps patients as they walk through the fire that comes with confronting pain and mortality.

In Christianity, curing souls—traditionally the work of priests—involved discerning the movement of the Spirit within a life. This process is now more commonly called spiritual direction. As is the case with other religious traditions, the Christian discernment process calls followers to maturity through the Three Ways of purgation, illumination, and union. Purgation is often associated with dust and ashes, with desert and fire, with wandering lost in the wilderness, with penitence. T. S. Eliot ends his great aria of the Three Ways—confusingly called *Four Quartets*—with the conviction that, even in union, the fires of purgation are present, though transformed:

> *A condition of complete simplicity*
> *(Costing not less than everything)*
> *And all shall be well and*
> *All manner of thing shall be well*
> *When the tongues of flame are in-folded*
> *Into the crowned knot of fire*
> *And the fire and the rose are one.*

According to Urrea's *curanderas*, the care of the body, the cure of the soul, and art are intimately interrelated. Many physicians will not wish to have their work compared to *curanderismo*, the work of folk healers who use herbs, water, mud, and esoteric knowledge to effect their cures—and I understand why. If I had a child with a serious medical condition, we'd go straight to a medical doctor, not to a shaman. And yet Western science seems to be realizing the need to see the human body as more than the sum of its physically constituent parts, to tend to the fractured realities of psyche, mind, genetic inheritance, environment, and time and place in history, the unique friction that some of us call the soul (though naming it feels reductive). We are beginning to acknowledge support groups, meditation, Eastern medical practices, massage, hospice care, and more as legitimate tools in the medical kit, even though Western metrics cannot easily measure their efficacy. We are starting to see that curing bodies is sometimes inextricable from caring for souls. *Curanderismo* has worked with this humbling understanding for centuries, even millennia. The controlled burning of deadwood in the soul—the tinder-dry fuel of fear, pain, and isolation—is not new work to the best of medical doctors. They still try to help if those flames begin to burn out of control.

Given the actual fires roaring through Colorado right now, it seems silly to claim for anyone besides firefighters the distinction of pulling people through fires. But there are people who pull us through fires that are metaphorical and utterly real and destructive. But artists, like firefighters and physicians, walk people through fires, whatever their source, and fire is, after all, a vital component in the maintenance of any healthy ecosystem. I love the idea of bonfires in the soul. It's just the kind of image toward which I'm likely to gravitate. It's beautiful. Poetic. Religious under- and overtones. Words that can drift in and out of my head like smoke, eventually leaving nothing behind. If taken seriously—more than literally—they're a call to get moving. There's work to be done.

53

Spring Creed

AUGUST 11, 2012

*In the endless heat of late summer, sometimes it's hard to remember
that Texas can be a cool and beautiful place—but it can, as we hope
this poem will remind you.*

The lake's complacent waters bloom before
the glamorous, unhurried progress of
the snake that makes its musing way toward
the bank on which I stand. My soul's
geography does not resist its presence
on this luminous cool morning—in fact,
invites it in to join the doe that barks
a warning to her fawn, the turkey yodeling
for a mate, the feathered migrants, tender leaves,
the crackling, stretching meadow grasses.
This gracious equilibrium,
where everything belongs,
where pressure between worlds is equalized
and I can hear and see them both, arrives
without annunciation, invitation, effort.
Even in the yearly banishment
from paradise, when a bleached sky buzzes
with the sucking Texas heat, when every

blessed thing apparently has spines
or fangs or concentrated venom—even
then my arid heart dehisces and allows,
at times, the snake its place stretched out and sunning
on white limestone ledges, admits the
sibilant pronouncement that all is well,
which usually goes unheard.

Only now, at fifty, do I register
interior terrain materially,
see that mine is littered with capricious
wreckage of tornadoes; feel the pre-storm
suffocating calm that makes it hard
to breathe; inhale at night the jasmine
and its drifting ache; or move through shining
winter briskness where every chore's a pleasure.
Now I scan horizons and prepare
for seasons newly gleaned, knowing they will
drench and parch, delight and wrench, approach
and pass. Snakes have always lived here, always will.
I see them sometimes now and sometimes watch
their agitating grace without a lurching
of my heart, but here is the kingdom
of the coiled presence. Here abide the mark
and potency of flood and flaming sky.
I am their host and guest; they don't belong to me.

They are not mine, but are. This is not a metaphor,
but is: language bearing loads past bearing.
Every body is a word exhaled toward violence
and beauty; every body vibrates in
reception, a veil through which the wind
between the worlds whirls. At this intersection
grow fruits of silence, stillness, from the soil
of singleness, where snake and lake and sky
on either side of self's divide sing in unison.

54

Microbiomes and Individual Identity
Alexander Pope and the Archbishop of Canterbury

OCTOBER 19, 2012

I learned a startling fact the other day while listening to Fresh Air's Terry Gross interviewing Dr. Nathan Wolfe, author of *The Viral Storm*, a disconcerting account of his research into pandemics like avian flu and AIDS that leap from animals to humans. Although the interview contained plenty of startling information, the statement that made me jump out of my skin was this:

> *If we were to count the number of cells between the top of your head and the socks on your feet, we would find that 90 percent of those cells are not human cells. Ninety percent of those cells belong to various microorganisms that exist, primarily in your gut and on your skin but also in many, many parts of your body. There's tons and tons of microbes out there.*

The vast majority of these inner-space invaders are vitally necessary to our health. In a story about the Human Microbiome Project in the *New York Times*, one Stanford microbiologist described individual humans as being like coral, "an assemblage of life-forms living together." Another microbiologist commented that from the standpoint of an individual microbiome, the "I" could be considered "mostly packaging." So if 90 percent of "me" is actually not "me" at all, who am I? I feel as if my nice empty 100-percent-paid-for house suddenly belongs almost entirely to an unknown corporation, the enormous staff of which has moved in and begun leaving its clothes and coffee mugs all over the place. How am I supposed to relax in a predicament like this, where my "house" is no longer mine? Where's my place in this mess?

Right in the middle, according to the eighteenth-century British poet Alexander Pope: in between God and beasts, on "this isthmus of a middle state / A being darkly wise and rudely great. . . . Created half to rise, and half to fall; / Great lord of all things, yet a prey to all; / Sole judge of Truth, in endless Error hurl'd: / The glory, jest, and riddle of the world!" Right in the middle of the mess.

I recently reread Pope's *An Essay on Man*, published in 1734, and was struck by two things: I was a really bad reader in grad school and, despite the dyspepsia caused by ingesting hundreds of heroic couplets in a row, I found him to be a humane and delicate thinker. I first read his *Essay* just as the trend of blaming all modern injustices on Enlightenment philosophies was gathering momentum. In rereading it, I fully expected to find evidence of thought-crimes against women, people of color, and the environment, and I came back to it ready to haul Pope and his entire extended family to prison and lock them up until they could see just where colonialism got us. What I found instead was an overwhelming sense of awe for the complexities of the natural world and a deep humility in the face of humanity's capacity to see these complexities only partially, imperfectly, and at times buffoonishly. To scientists he says with asperity:

> Go wond'rous creature! Mount where science guides,
> Go, measure earth, weigh air, and state the tides;
> Instruct the planets in what orbs to run,
>
> Correct old Time, and regulate the Sun. . . .
> Superior beings [angels], when of late they saw
> A mortal man unfold all Nature's law,
> Admir'd such wisdom in an earthly shape,
> And shew'd a NEWTON as we shew an Ape. . . .
> Trace Science then, with Modesty thy guide.

What Pope wants is to put human giftedness in its place, which is in every way reliant on and secondary to what he calls Eternal Wisdom. He wants to give us a place from which to view ourselves, especially when we think we're masters of the universe. We can't know who we are unless we also know where we are. Of course, Pope the poet could himself be accused of overreaching in making his immodest pronouncements, but he nips that accusation in the bud by placing his perspective firmly on the earth with his fellows. In the poem's introduction, he pokes fun at John Milton's *Paradise Lost*, published seventy years earlier, with its lofty, near-heretical goal to "justify the ways of God to men" from the wings of the Holy Spirit. Nope, Pope knows his place, and it's right in the middle of what he calls the "vast chain of being," headed by God, that links all things to each other. One of the loveliest passages:

> *Look round our World; behold the chain of Love*
> *Combining all below and all above. . . .*
> *See Matter . . . with various Life endu'd,*
> *Press to one center still, the gen'ral Good.*
> *See dying vegetables life sustain,*
> *See life dissolving vegetate again:*
> *All forms that perish other forms supply*
> *(By turns we catch the vital breath and die)*
> *Like bubbles in the sea of Matter born,*
> *They rise, they break, and to that sea return.*
> *Nothing is foreign: Parts relate to whole;*
> *One all-extending, all-preserving Soul*
> *Connects each being, greatest with the least;*
> *Made Beast in aid of Man, and Man of Beast;*
> *All serv'd, all serving! Nothing stands alone;*
> *The chain holds on, and where it ends, unknown.*

With their wide, inclusive vision of the workings of nature, these could be Wendell Berry's words. (In fact, Berry much admires Pope's *Essay*.) We have been given a singular place in this great chain, and our work is to learn, through careful observation of the natural world, how to become a blessing to it, to our fellows, and to ourselves. Pope places the primal disruption of the Fall not in Eve's disobedience but in the violence—beginning with Cain and Abel—that we inflict on one another both individually and corporately. Not a bad vision for one of the Dead White Guys of whom I was so suspicious in school.

Despite its plasticity, however, the great chain, as Pope envisions it, is quite fragile—alarmingly so: "The least confusion but in one, not all / That system only, but the whole must fall." One little thing out of place, and the whole shebang comes tumbling down. It's hard to imagine living abundantly in such a universe, hard not to imagine a creeping paralysis arising out of fear of disruption, like someone with a slipping disc in her spine, afraid each thoughtless move might bring on a core collapse. Despite its beauty and humility, there's a caged, claustrophobic quality in Pope's place for us—one that might never have discovered that each one of us is quite literally a world, perhaps a galaxy, in and of ourselves, as the mappers of the Human Microbiome Project suggest.

In a recent lecture, Rowan Williams, the Archbishop of Canterbury, gave another account of where it is that human beings have a place. He talks about the need to distinguish between being an individual—someone identifiable by the facts about him and the center of his own universe—and being a person, a "more frustrating, more elusive, and yet more adequate" way of describing who and where we are.

Primary to a definition of personhood is the reality that each one of us exists at the center of a vast network of relationships, "the point where the lines cross." That point is never static: every encounter with every person, every creature, every historical reality, every memory, every word—indeed, with every moment—provides an opportunity for reconfiguring those intersecting lines. At any given time, a person is the sum total of her myriad, shifting relationships, irreducible to one thing or to a list of attributes. Something about the human person is fundamentally mysterious and inaccessible. For Christians, this messy, elusive intersection of relationships is where the revelatory work of God has its place.

Williams asserts that because "each of us has a presence or a meaning in someone else's existence," a sense of personhood is impossible outside of relationship. When I think of myself as an individual, I am the center of the facts about me. When I consider myself as a person, as constituted by an ever-changing intersection of relationships, I must acknowledge my presence in other people's lives and other people's presences in my own. I can't extricate myself from this web and stand alone, withdrawing from the world. Knowing that I'm fundamentally mysterious even to myself, a creation of these innumerable, ever-accruing intersections, I must acknowledge that this messy, sacred bundle exists within every person and that we are environments for each other. We're in some way located outside of ourselves, a situation that calls for a very different social order than one based on the rights of discrete individuals, an order that devolves into competing, isolated, uncooperative selves.

Pope, the literary king of the British Enlightenment, articulated a profound shift in understanding of humanity's place; he saw an interconnectedness, a democratic necessity for each link in the chain, where before, whole groups—whole races and nations—were accounted as disposable. From thinkers like Pope came the Founding Fathers of the United States and their insistence on the natural rights of its (white male) citizens. In order to function as it should, this chain of interconnectedness that Pope saw and that the Founding Fathers used as the struts and joists of a new political system had to rest not only on personal rights: it needed one more thing.

> For Forms of Government let fools contest;
> Whate'er is best administer'd is best:
> For Modes of Faith, let graceless zealots fight;
> His can't be wrong whose life is in the right:
> In Faith and Hope the world will disagree,
> But all Mankind's concern is Charity:
> All must be false that thwart this One great End,
> And all of God, that bless Mankind or mend.

Without the cushioning of generosity, the assertion of one's rights can become a mere excuse to claim supremacy over another, the chain shatters, and the discrete links become disposable. It's arguable that we're in the midst of this shattering, and I find Williams's elastic and eccentric network a compelling place to set up housekeeping. His call is to look at our individual selves and find, as in a different sense did Nathan Wolfe, that they're not really "ours" at all.

55

Jellyfish and Revelation

DECEMBER 15, 2012

Once again, it's the time of year when we ponder endings and beginnings, when we hunker down for the long nights, wonder where this year has disappeared to, and devise all sorts of convoluted theories about what is to come. Despite the endless recycling of "The Little Drummer Boy" in nearly every commercial space, this time of year also seems to have a peculiar kind of gravity, a pressure on the heart and lungs, a sense of urgency that has nothing to do with shopping lists or end-of-year numbers and everything to do with preparing for something final. But what?

I'm more than usually preoccupied with end-times because a discussion group I've been part of is focusing on *Revelations: Visions, Prophecies, and Politics in the Book of Revelation*, by Elaine Pagels. In it, Pagels examines the cultural and political landscapes out of which John of Patmos's Book of Revelation (the final book of the Christian Bible) arose, and then follows the surprising twists in the history of its interpretation until it became the emphatic omega on the list of officially sanctioned writings that became the New Testament in the latter half of the fourth century CE. She gives the reader a glimpse into the other books of revelation—Jewish, Greek, Roman, Egyptian, Christian—that were written at more or less the same time as John's, books that claim to be "revelations" of a reality that is usually hidden from humanity. While some, like John of Patmos, focus on the end of the world, many do not; they claim, rather, to reveal divine secrets through, as one historian put it, "visions, dreams, and other paranormal states of consciousness."

The genre of revelation is often associated with high drama and vivid weirdness, writing with dragons and angels, backlit with blinding lights or drenched in palpable darkness: revelation as conflict. Yet Pagels cites one book titled *Thunder, Perfect Mind* whose images seek to unify rather than to divide and to find completeness—the divine—in pollution and purity both:

> *I was sent forth from the power,*
> *And I have come to those who reflect upon me,*
> *And I have been found among those who seek me . . .*
> *Do not be ignorant of me anywhere or any time. Be on your guard!*
> *Do not be ignorant of me.*
> *For I am the first and the last.*
> *I am the honored one and the scorned one.*
> *I am the whore and the holy one.*
> *I am the wife and the virgin . . .*
> *I am the barren one and many are her sons.*
> *I am she whose wedding is great, and I have not taken a husband.*
> *I am the midwife and she who does not bear.*
> *I am the solace of my labor pains.*
> *I am the bride and the bridegroom, and it is my husband who*
>   *begot me.*

The whole of the book—the part that still exists, that is—glows with power of a very different sort than John's revelation does. Although it is not a Jewish or Christian work—most probably, it is a hymn to the Egyptian goddess Isis—many of its images harmonize beautifully with biblical language:

> *Hear me in gentleness, and learn of me in roughness.*
> *I am she who cries out,*
> *and I am cast forth upon the face of the earth.*
> *I prepare the bread and my mind within.*
> *I am the knowledge of my name.*

That we learn wisdom in precisely the moments that seem most inimical to it—times of tribulation and violence, of incomprehension and confusion—seems to be the book's central teaching. The repetition of "I am" throughout the text suggests familiarity with the Jewish/Christian awareness of the power of naming. Who am I? Who am I not? What is my name and who named me? How I am in conversation with that which is not me, with the One who named me?

In John's compelling depiction, conversation requires the drawing of very stern lines: there are those whom you converse with and those whom you destroy. Once evil is destroyed, the purified remnant enters the glorious New Jerusalem. I have very mixed feelings about this stern line. I know that evil has some people in such a stranglehold that trying to address them seems hopeless, ridiculous, and lethal; people who shoot children, for instance. How would you talk to someone who could do such a thing?

Thunder, Perfect Mind sets forth a very different conversational strategy: no one is excluded. Purity is an illusion, utterly contrary to the divine self-identity. *Thunder, Perfect Mind* resonates in my heart and mind, an antidote to John's fiercely tribal, exclusionary, accusatory language. And yet it leaves me wanting as well (although less), wanting the street-language translation for a conversation that took place somewhere in the stratosphere. Is there another idiom in which the intersection between the mortal and the divine can be spoken, one that doesn't involve violence, secret codes, hallucinations, and abstractions? Of course I think the answer is yes: revelation does not necessarily require a one-time blast from beyond; faithfulness to daily interactions can work the same ground.

I read in a recent *New York Times Magazine* article about a Japanese scientist, Shin Kubota, whose work with tiny jellyfish that age backward—nicknamed "immortal jellyfish"—seems to tap into some of these questions from a completely different direction. Despite the fact that *Turritopsis dohrnii* is about the size of "a trimmed pinkie fingernail," and despite the fact that it has no brain, no heart, and that it eats out of its anus, its genetic overlap with the human genome is unnervingly significant (insert punch line here). "*Turritopsis* application for human beings is the most wonderful dream of mankind," Kubota told the *Times* reporter:

> *Once we determine how the jellyfish rejuvenates itself, we should achieve very great things. My opinion is that we will evolve and become immortal ourselves.*

Every day for at least three hours a day for the past fifteen years, Kubota has tended to his menagerie of jellyfish, the only captive population in the world. It is "grueling, tedious work," requiring daily water changes, observation under a microscope, and feeding, which can require cutting up nearly invisible dried brine shrimp eggs that sometimes need to be cut up with two needles under a microscope.

> *The work causes Kubota to growl and cluck his tongue. "Eat by your-selves!" he yells at one medusa. "You're not a baby!" Then he laughs heartily.*

When he travels to conferences, the petri dishes come with him in a cooler. There are no days off. He is faithful to his tiny, mysterious dependents.

Five years ago, however, he had what he vaguely refers to as "a scare," a period in which he aged "a lifetime" in one year: "It was astonishing for me. I had become old." Today the hair that was white has turned black again, his energy as exuberant as a middle schooler's. As a consequence of the scare, Kubota started a second career as a singer and songwriter and is now something of a celebrity, "the Japanese equivalent of Bill Nye the Science Guy." He sings about the beauty of his jellyfish and about the natural world, work he now considers the crux of his work. Before humankind can apply what we learn from *Turritopsis* to ourselves, we must first come to love nature; otherwise, we'll misuse our knowledge. "We're very strange animals," he said.

> *We're so clever and civilized, but our hearts are very primitive. If our hearts weren't primitive, there wouldn't be wars. I'm worried that we will apply the science too early, like we did with the atomic bomb.*

He considers his science as having a limited value in his campaign to teach love:

> *"We must love plants—without plants we cannot live. We must love bacteria—without decomposition our bodies can't go back to the earth. If everyone learns to love living organisms, there will be no crime. No murder. No suicide. Spiritual change is needed. And the most simple way to achieve this is song. Biology is specialized," he said, bringing his palms within inches of each other. "But songs?" He spreads his hands far apart, as if to indicate the size of the world.*

Something about Kubota's obsessive fidelity and tenderness allow him access to the same conversations that John of Patmos and the author of *Thunder, Perfect Mind* had (and have) with eternal order. The theatrical volume of famous revelations drowns out the ones that happen quietly over time as a result of the minute, open-hearted engagements to which we're invited in each minute of our lives: do we converse with the creature in front of us, open to something as solid to as ourselves, containing vigor and disease, song and dissonance, grace and clumsiness? Or do we remain stubbornly monolingual? Kubota looks, as surely as does John of Patmos, for a time when every tear will be wiped away, when death will be no more, nor mourning nor crying nor pain, and he looks for this arrival in a conversation that includes tedium and frustration. Can there be any doubt that something new and beautiful will be born?

56

The Cliff of the Unknown
Desire, Tolerance, and Identity

MARCH 29, 2013

The secret history of sex is not a story of fulfilled desires; it's a story of expectations dropped off the cliff of the unknown.

—*Nathan Heller*

This is not an essay about sex, but this sentence stayed with me long after I read it. It's from a review in the *New Yorker* of Andrew Solomon's *Far From the Tree: Parents, Children, and the Search for Identity*, in which Solomon examines the stresses placed on a family's vertical identity—the one that flows through the generations—when a child presents the logjam of a horizontal identity, an identity outside of parental experience. Among the horizontal identities that Solomon investigated over ten years in more than three hundred families are dwarfism, deafness, autism, children of rape, severe multiple disability, and transgenderism. How, the book asks, do parents come to love children they never expected?

This is not an essay about horizontal identity or parenting, either. But it is about desires and the unknown, about the gap between what we feel within ourselves and what happens outside ourselves—the sinkholes that can suddenly open up, evaporating what appeared to be solid, or what was solid and then was just gone. About what can and cannot be named.

During this Lenten season, our church has hosted a weekly series on "Art and the Other," i.e., those individuals or groups who present us with logjams in the flow of our own identities. The series examines how art can be a bridge between "us" and "them," or at least a gesture in "their" direction. At one gathering, after viewing a film-in-progress on the importance of interfaith dialogue, we tried to identify just whom we, as an Episcopalian congregation, see as "the other." We were pleased to note that we were fine with Muslims, Jews, Buddhists, Hindus, atheists, Jainists, Wiccans, and macrobiotists; we agreed that no group has a monopoly on enlightenment or salvation. But our generosity dried up when we considered those groups we view as intolerant and insistent on the supremacy of their own creeds. In our refusal to tolerate intolerance, we wondered, were we in fact mirroring it? How do you engage with a rejection of engagement? And the question that really stayed with me: When you step off the cliff of desire—which you do every time you hope to make any kind of contact with someone else—imagining some kind of fulfillment, how do you respond to a wholly unexpected reply, or none at all?

Or perhaps that wasn't the question, which seems to slither away every time I try to focus on it. In the discussion, we seemed to be framing the question as an issue of tolerance, but as the lovelorn Henrik laments in Stephen Sondheim's *A Little Night Music*, "it's intolerable/being tolerated." And so it is. According to Dictionary.com, the verb *to tolerate* can mean "to endure or resist the action of (a drug, poison, etc.)" or "to allow the existence, presence, practice, or act of without prohibition or hindrance, or contradiction; permit." To tolerate someone or something, then, seems to point to an engagement that can leave the tolerant one comfortably unchanged or unchallenged. Tolerance is often counted as a virtue in the midst of the sinkholes that open up between individuals or groups, when it is merely a pause to catch your breath in the arduous, open-ended journey of communication.

Part of the problem with posing the question is the notion of individual identity as a rock we stand on, a location with well-defined boundaries like a modern nation-state that need to be defended from encroachment. One definition of identity that I love comes from Lewis Hyde's *The Gift: Creativity and the Artist in the Modern World*, from which I've quoted before. Hyde is writing more specifically of ego, which is not perhaps the same thing as identity, but there are significant overlaps. This is a lengthy quote, but more than worth the space:

> *I find it useful to think of the ego complex as a thing that keeps expanding, not as something to be overcome or done away with. An ego has formed and hardened by the time most of us reach adolescence,*

but it is small, an ego-of-one. Then, if we fall in love, for example, the constellation of identity expands, and the ego-of-one becomes the ego-of-two. The young lover, often to his own amazement, finds himself saying "we" instead of "me." Each of us identifies with a wider and wider community, coming eventually to think and act with a group-ego . . . which speaks with the "we" of kings and wise old people. Of course, the larger it becomes, the less it feels like what we usually mean by ego. . . . In all of this we could substitute "body" for "ego." Aborigines commonly refer to their own clan as "my body," just as our marriage ceremony speaks of becoming "one flesh." Again, the body can be enlarged beyond the private skin, and in its final expansion there is no body at all. When we are in the spirit of the gift we love to feel the body open outward. The ego's firmness has its virtues, but at some point we seek the slow dilation, to use [a] term of Whitman's, in which the ego enjoys a widening give-and-take with the world and is finally abandoned in ripeness.

At the core of any great religion is some person or group whose heart has broken open to admit the world, whose boundaries have grown permeable, whose ripeness is a fragrance that fills the space around it like the nard with which Mary of Bethany anointed Jesus' feet in the week before his death. Religion is not the only self-breaker and heart-opener, of course; there are many containers that help us to bear great beauty and great suffering—art, nature, family, and friends among them. The self that seeks mere tolerance of its neighbors in the light of this paradigm has elected a diet of crumbs and water instead of the extravagant feast set before it.

Often, however, we do choose crumbs and water. We choose to walk away from the urgent desire for congress and from the cliff of the unknown. Yet sometimes the choice is made for us, when we long for connection and find nothing. What then?

In his most recent book, *Healing the Heart of Democracy: The Courage to Create a Politics Worthy of the Human Spirit*, Parker J. Palmer names democracy at its root level as one of the containers that help us to bear the great beauty and suffering of history in such a way that our hearts break open rather than merely breaking into a million irretrievable pieces.

This is not an essay about a political system. But I do want to try to describe the sinkhole—the no-ego's land—between desire for communication and fulfillment. Palmer calls this place the "tragic gap," tragic not just because it's heartbreaking but because, in the classical sense, it's an inescapable feature of the human psychic landscape:

> *On one side of that gap, we see the hard realities of the world, realities that can crush our spirits and defeat our hopes. On the other side of that gap, we see real-world possibilities, life as we know it could be because we have seen it that way. . . . Possibilities of this sort are not wishful dreams or fantasies: they are alternative realities that we have witnessed in our own lives.*

In this gap we can sink into corrosive cynicism or fritter away our energy on irrelevant idealism, but another way offers itself, one that allows "the slow dilation" of the boundaries between self and neighbor, self and world, self and self, the boundaries that prevent the cliff-side communion we so long for. Palmer calls us to a complex and open-ended faithfulness, in which I would incorporate two questions adapted from Krista Tippett to help direct us toward the habit of conversation and away from monologue: what troubles me about my own position? What in my would-be partner's position makes me curious?

In the end, I think this is an essay about hope, despite the feelings of frustration and helplessness that spurred it. It's not about the hope that seeks magically to rearrange present reality. Rather, it's a testament to the small acts of great love that pepper everyday life and that step forth despite the absence of an obvious place to step onto, the way many parents step into the slow dilation of identity that embraces a situation or a child they would have done anything to avoid. It's a testament to anyone who steps off the cliff of ego, willing to land in an unfamiliar place, willing to endure the possibility of a heart broken open. In a world in which conversations seem crucified between shouting and silence, sometimes a quiet question is enough.

57

Poetry and the Pelvic Bowl

MAY 3, 2013

Some say you're lucky
If nothing shatters it.

But then you wouldn't
Understand poems or songs,
You'd never know
Beauty comes from loss.

It's deep inside every person:
A tear tinier
Than a pearl or thorn.

It's one of the places
The beloved is born.

April was National Poetry Month, which might or might not be a silly thing, but it has prodded me into thinking about poetry and my erratic relationship with it. When I received my two degrees in English, I was emphatically a fiction person. Poetry made me anxious because I could never figure out how to read it or what it was supposed to mean. My poetry textbooks from college and grad school are studded with frantic and useless annotations: cross-references to other poems by the same author, details about textual corruptions or variations, or underlinings directed by the professor that have no meaning for me now. Only rarely did I mark something just because I liked it, and then I worried about having made such a bold declaration.

What if it didn't mean what I thought it meant? What if someone discovered that I just didn't get it?

I still have no idea what many poems mean, but I more often read poetry than fiction now. I use poetry when I teach and pray. I even read it just for fun. I sometimes write the kind of poetry that gave me brain freeze twenty-five years ago. How did this sea change come about? It began, I think, when I went to seminary and was forced to confront the Bible, a book I had never read and suspected that I wouldn't like and feared would make me stupid. (I still wonder who was on the committee that admitted me: Groucho Marx?) At first the familiar structure of the classroom allowed me to keep it at arm's length. Memorize, analyze, parse, criticize. What do you do with a God who smites and punishes and condemns? Who needs his ego massaged with praise all the time? And yet I couldn't help noticing that many of the psalms, the Song of Solomon, and the Jesus who considered the lilies all addressed a force they considered entirely trustworthy, entirely beautiful, the genesis and end of all desire. I could not see what they saw when I read with a lens of suspicion. And, despite my distrust, I wanted to see what they saw.

I began reading aloud, in groups, slowly and repetitively. It was sometimes helpful to have literary and historical information to draw on, but I was more often hobbled when I came to passages like this from the Letter to the Hebrews:

Indeed, the word of God is living and active, sharper than any two-edged sword, piercing until it divides soul from spirit, joints from marrow; it is able to judge the thoughts and intentions of the heart. And before him no creature is hidden, but all are naked and laid bare to the eyes of the one to whom we must render an account.

It was beautiful. I knew that it was somehow true. I had no idea what it meant. Yet over and over, I found myself run through by the language of scripture, knowing I had been wounded but unable to bind or even find the wound. In the company of similarly riven souls, however, I started finding another way, not so much to read as to be read. Instead of seeking experience—that giddy adrenaline ride of a narrative—I found a place from which to see my own experience, my self in relation to a much greater whole. I was like a one-eyed creature that had been given another eye; reality began to acquire a previously unsuspected dimension.

The April issue of *The Sun* contains an interview with Philip Shepherd, a British writer and actor, whose career has led him explore the implications of the little-known fact that human beings have two brains, one in the head and one in the gut. This is not a fanciful or metaphorical claim. Nuerogastroenterology, a new medical field, studies the web of neurons lining the gastrointestinal tract that send signals to the body independent of the cranial brain. Shepherd is not a medical professional but uses the research in the field to examine the cultural and philosophical implications of this "pelvic brain." Says Shepherd:

> *Our culture doesn't recognize that hub in the belly, and most of us don't trust it enough to come to rest there. Our story insists that our thinking occurs exclusively in the head. And so we are stuck in the cranium, unable to open the door to the body and join its thinking. The best we can do is put our ear to the imaginary wall separating us from it and "listen to the body," a phrase that means well but actually keeps us in the head, gathering information from the outside. The body is you. We are missing the experience of our own being.*

The intelligence of the pelvic brain is not rational, conscious, analytical, or abstract; rather, it arises in the way an enormous flock of starlings alters its course like a single organism. Well, you might say, I'm not a flock of starlings. But we all have an astonishing sensitivity—a sensational sensitivity—to our perpetually changing environments, astonishing in its almost invisible routineness and its capacity to integrate multiple levels of information. It's an intelligence we often take for granted or don't acknowledge as intelligence at all, but it allows you to negotiate your way through space, to remember passages of music, to understand arithmetical relationships, to love or know joy. Our task is not to privilege one brain over the other but to learn to coordinate them, according to Shepherd. He uses a lovely analogy to illustrate what this coordination looks like: the astronauts who took the first photos of the earth from outer space brought them back to earth, giving us a new perspective on our planet's fragility. We responded with environmental initiatives. We were sensitized.

Culturally speaking, though, Shepherd says that those of us who inhabit the "first world" are like astronauts who are stuck in orbit around the head, unable to descend back home to the belly, where the gathered information can be integrated and sensitize us to the great complex flow of the world we inhabit:

> *Our culture has a tacit assumption that if we can just gather enough information on ourselves and the world, it will add up to a whole. But when you stand back and look at something, there is always something hidden from you. The integration of multiple perspectives into a whole can happen only when, like the astronaut bringing the photo back to earth, we bring this information back to the pelvic bowl, back to the ground of our being, back to the integrating genius of the female consciousness. The pelvic bowl is the original beggar's bowl: it receives the gifts of the world—the male perspective—and integrates them. As you bring ideas down to the belly and let them settle there, they sensitize you to who you are and give birth to insight. Our task is to learn to trust that process.*

The belly brain as begging bowl, receiving the gifts of the world. In some Buddhist traditions, monks are mendicants who own nothing but their robes and their begging bowls, in which they receive offerings of food or other gifts from the lay community. These gifts are not considered alms but rather are part of an exchange in which the community supports the monks physically and the monks support the community spiritually. So quite literally, every human being carries a begging bowl to the world, an intelligence that establishes itself in emptiness, in poverty, in suffering, in sensitivity, in loss. Without that bowl, we have no place for the works arising from the cranial brain to incubate and mature before they enter the world. Without cross-pollination from the pelvic brain, the fruits of the cranial brain are stunted and distorted, rooted in the illusion that we are separate from the natural world and thereby at odds with it. Aligning the two intelligences gives us the opportunity to see holistically, with the depth of binary vision.

Given my initial take on the Bible, it seems poetically just that it should lead me to a less literal, more personally demanding way of reading, one that required some self-knowledge before I could make any sense of it. Like scripture, good poetry is a gift in the begging bowl, pressing the reader to claim hunger and absence before the equally great gifts of abundance and presence come to view. In his wrenchingly beautiful volume of poetry, *Concerning the Book That Is the Body of the Beloved* (from which the poems at the beginning and end of this piece are taken), Gregory Orr looks at the world with at least two eyes, that trinitarian third eye of the heart figuring somewhere in this body of stern and tender wisdom. I don't mind that I don't understand it all; reading it, I find that I have been seen, known, understood.

I guess I'm fine with National Poetry Month.

The beloved has gone away.
Always, this is the case.
Each moment turns on its hinge
And loss is there, loss
Announcing itself as absence.

But that's because we're looking
Backward, looking in the wrong
Direction: so desperately clinging
To a last glimpse of the beloved,
As if loss itself is what we loved.

And all the time the beloved
Is coming toward us, is arriving
Out of the future, eager to greet us.

58

A Tale of Two Kitties
Thinking About Predators and Cancer
AUGUST 10, 2013

We lost one of our cats recently. Mr. Allnut (named for Humphrey Bogart's character in *The African Queen*) asked to go out at about four one morning a few weeks ago, and I let him go. He never came back, and a week or so later, a neighbor confirmed Mr. Allnut's fate—met, we all agreed, at the business end of a coyote.

We live in central Austin, but a very steep and heavily wooded ten-acre draw cuts through our quiet neighborhood. The terrain is so treacherous it's hard to explore, even with the permission of the friendly neighbor who owns it, which means it's easy to forget that the nightlife is literally quite wild in our back yard. We used to hear the coyotes occasionally years ago when sirens sounded at dusk or dawn, but they've apparently learned to sing under their breath. They're still here.

I loved Mr. Allnut. He looked like a stuffed animal, with his regular markings and crossed blue eyes, and he behaved like one too. He suffered being cuddled and cooed over with a resigned limpness and clawless stoicism. And I still miss his sister Adelaide, and Spike with the light bulb at the end of her tail, and Kerbey and Skitter and Widget. They were cats of regular habits who just disappeared over the course of the years. I learn a lot slower than the coyotes and must finally acknowledge that we always live in the midst of predators.

Apparently a lot of us are deluded into thinking that large predators are restricted to "wilder" places than cities and suburbs. One multiyear study in Chicago surprised the wildlife biologist conducting it; he found that the city's coyote population was much larger than expected and that urban coyotes lived longer and are much more active at night than their rural siblings. They live not just in green spaces but also in apartment districts and industrial parks. Because they learn very quickly to avoid traps, it's hard to get an accurate number, but the author of the Chicago study thought there could be up to two thousand coyotes there—a much denser population than would cover a rural area of equal size. It's likely that this study applies to most major metropolitan cities, including, of course, Austin. (In fact, former Madroño Ranch resident Melissa Gaskill wrote a piece on the city's coyotes for the *Austin Chronicle* back in 2008, and coincidentally a story headlined "Tensions over Coyote Trapping Split Austin Neighborhood" ran just this morning in the *Austin American-Statesman*.)

Predator. It's a compelling word, derived from the Latin meaning to plunder or to rob, so to call something a predator is to freight it with moral judgment. As far as I can tell (which isn't far because I lost the magnifying glass to our edition of the compact *Oxford English Dictionary*), the word referred only to human behavior until it made a zoological leap in 1907. I wonder if that leap helped give steam to the notion in land management circles that rubbing out entire species was not only a reasonable stratagem but a righteous crusade. Predators rob and steal and, therefore, must be punished. Destroyed.

The Wolves and Moose of Isle Royale project is the longest continuous study of the predator-prey system in the world, spanning more than fifty years of observation on this frigid island on the Michigan side of Lake Superior. The scientists involved have concluded that to designate wolves simply as dangerous nuisances to be eradicated is to miss the hard and necessary work they do; the apex predators are vital to their complex ecosystems, despite the fear they inspire and the losses they cause. In other words, as Aldo Leopold wrote in his essay "Thinking Like a Mountain": "too much safety" from wolves, and presumably other apex predators, "seems to yield only danger in the long run." Because we often don't take into account the needs of the mountain or all the other participants in a predator-prey cycle, we ranchers or hunters or businessmen end up poking ourselves (or our grandchildren) in the eye. The length of the Isle Royale study has brought academic rigor and complexity to Leopold's beautiful musings and has showed the scientists how much they still have to learn: "Navigating that complexity without hubris will be a great challenge."

So you can probably connect the dots so far: despite the loss of Mr. Allnut and his compadres, I can't entirely condemn the responsible coyote, who was just doing his job. He's also probably eaten many, many rats and provided other services I don't know about. A righteous campaign for coyote extinction would be understandable but could also be very ill-advised.

Now I'm going to make a crabwise move. At about the same time Mr. Allnut disappeared, we lost our beloved ranch cat Callie. Despite the fact that she was mostly white like Mr. Allnut, she managed for the eight or nine years she lived at Madroño to stay clear of coyotes, raccoons, foxes, bobcats, hawks, eagles, owls, and the occasional mountain lion. She was also immensely talkative and sociable, always accompanying us to visit the chickens and occasionally eating out of the feed buckets right alongside them. I frequently scrambled her an egg, a privilege she just as frequently lost each time I found her counter-surfing yet again. She spent many, many hours on my lap, drooling and kneading, shedding and purring. She was a good mouser and all-around excellent creature.

After she was diagnosed with skin cancer on her nose and ears, ranch manager Robert Can-This-Really-Be-In-My-Job-Description Selement smeared the affected parts with sunblock as often as possible, but of course she licked it right off. The cancer began quite literally to eat her nose and upper lip. We balanced our distress at her appearance with her comfort as long as we could bear. She's now buried by the shed, near her empty food bowl, her grave awaiting a marker as colorful and lively as she was. It's very hard not to think of cancer as another kind of predator, not to think: Eradicate. Kill. That's what predators deserve.

In her thought-provoking *Illness as Metaphor and AIDS and Its Metaphors*, Susan Sontag examines the language we use to describe some diseases and the use of disease as metaphor in nonmedical arenas. A three-time cancer patient herself (she died of leukemia in 2004), she wanted to release cancer patients from the invisible but real shackles language slaps on them. Cancer, in her view, is "in the service of a simplistic view of the world that can turn paranoid," encouraging radically reductive thinking and action. She particularly objects to the images of war, pollution, military or alien invasion, and genocide that cluster around cancer as a metaphor because they inevitably become confused with the individual cancer patient who becomes a loser by dying, a toxic dump site by being diagnosed, an invaded country, a helpless victim of ruthless overlords. Having cancer is a complex issue in and of itself without having to bear the burdensome, accusatory implications of the metaphors surrounding it.

As a language nerd, I wonder how to name to my own metastatic cancer because my words shape the choices I make in treatment and the rest of my life. While I can see why declaring war on cancer seems appropriate, I've come to find the analogy misleading at best, self-eradicating at worst. This cancer is as integrally a part of me as the coyote in my backyard, as the wolves, as any predator is a part of its distinctive ecosystem. Like a coyote, my cancer quickly learns to avoid the traps we set for it. While I don't want to be eaten, I also don't want to declare war on myself. Perhaps we'll find some intimate connection we don't know about yet between the loss of apex predators and the rise of cancer. Perhaps cancer provides some kind of service in this world of ours that has been so rapidly rearranged in the last century, when we began to use the word "predator" to describe nonhuman behavior and then went to war. Perhaps we need a new metaphor that allows us to live consciously and respectfully and curiously with the world around us and within us, navigating that complexity without hubris—and without metaphors of violence and condemnation.

59

This and Not That

SEPTEMBER 6, 2013

Last Sunday Martin and I attended a dharma teaching at Green Gulch Farm, on the western flanks of Mount Tamalpais, above Muir Beach. It was the kind of morning for which this part of California is famous: foggy and cool with sudden glittering glimpses of ocean or mountain that as quickly disappear back into the magician's hand. After scurrying down the eucalyptus-buttressed driveway, we arrived at the temple late and at the wrong door. The temple was packed and listening to the robed priest read a children's story to perhaps twenty well-behaved but wiggly children. Once the children were sent off to their own separate programming, the priest began his teaching in earnest, an hour-long disquisition on the relationship between labor (it was Labor Day weekend, after all) and Zen practice. He read two poems by W. B. Yeats, one by Patrick Kavanagh, and referenced Shakespeare and Northrop Frye. I would bet that his radio is usually set on the local NPR station, and that he was looking forward, as I was, to reading the Sunday *New York Times* that afternoon.

When we got to the *Times*-reading phase of our own Sunday liturgy, I read a beautiful essay in the book review titled "Articles of Faith" by Dara Horn, in which she muses on the easy confluence of contemporary Jewish fiction, even if it's overtly nonreligious, with ancient questions of faith. She contrasts this Jewish feast with the slim pickings on the post-Christian literary table: "Whither the Flannery O'Connors of yesteryear? Marilynne Robinson can't do this all by herself!" Because Judaism is a faith based on the concept of preserving memory, she asserts a peculiar affinity between Judaism and fiction writing, "a mystical and irrational belief in a type of memory no neurologist would recognize, a phenomenon both uncanny and eternal," a conviction that "time can be stopped, that somewhere, whether on our notebooks . . . or our spirits, everything is perfectly preserved and recorded, ready to return to life." The essay ends with a call to listen to and create the stories that give a deep anchorage in history and a shapely hope to our personal and communal lives, even as the anchorage has made clear the murderous powers in which we swim.

All right, I thought, I guess I'm Buddhist *and* Jewish today. Does that mean I'm not a Christian? Oh, dear. And on a Sunday.

Being in California, particularly in Point Reyes Station, leaves me a little disoriented, especially since I come from a state that has ignored virtually every vote I've cast in the past twenty years. Martin and I are in like-minded company here: virtually every voice loudly proclaims with gusto the gospel of sustainable and local. We've driven north to Bodega Bay and south to Mill Valley and in fifty miles passed not one fast-food joint. Cattle are vital to the local economy and yet are grazed and raised humanely on federal lands. Signs supporting the Marin Agricultural Land Trust—which protects about half of Marin County's agricultural land from development—appear in almost every eatery with monotonous, almost sinister, regularity: could you end up in Tomales Bay wearing sustainably produced, free-trade cement shoes if you try to run a restaurant without supporting MALT?

Could I as easily be a Buddhist or a Jew as a Christian? A northern Californian as a Texan? The answer is probably yes, but I'm not. At some point in asserting an identity, in describing your part in the created order—something most Americans and maybe most post-Enlightenment people feel compelled to do—some sifting is necessary: *this* and not *that*. So I'm wondering why or how I'm a Christian. (Figuring out why or how I'm a Texan is probably too complicated an issue to tackle here.) The Nicene Creed seems as good a place to start as any. It's quite possible that the mere mention of those words—Nicene Creed—will start the sifting process in some readers: here's my stop! It certainly would have stopped me twenty years ago.

I used to hate the creed, and I hated it even before I started going to church. How could you not hate something that required you to believe a dozen impossible things before breakfast? And not just impossible but downright unethical and sometimes just plain silly? The bit about the Spirit proceeding from the Father and the Son always makes me think about opening a collapsible telescope. When we first started going to church, not so many years ago, saying the creed could ruin the whole service for me by starting an avalanche of arguments in my head that must have been audible at least to the people sitting next to me.

After years of saying and hating it, I began to say it with a few grudging assents. I was eventually surprised that immediately after the agitating "Father Almighty," God's next attribute was surprisingly democratic: maker. I've known lots of makers: hat-makers, bread-makers, policy-makers, cheese-makers (this is the home of Cowgirl Creamery, after all), and homemakers. Okay, I could say "maker." I came to appreciate that creation included things both seen and unseen. Whether I believed it or not, I loved the effect of the introduction to Jesus: "eternally begotten of the Father, God from God, Light from Light, true God from true God, begotten not made, of one being with the Father." I didn't know what it meant (still don't), but it was like entering a dense fog with a deep gong sounding, and it was followed by the bright iambic rhythm of "through him all things were made." Okay. I could say that.

I can now say almost all of the creed, even the Father Almighty part. I've had a father. I'm married to a father. I'm the mother of someone I hope will be a father someday. I know a lot of fathers and with all my heart I believe— *credo*—in the power and tenderness and explosive energy that seems to be bundled with fatherhood and that is, at least in a post-Jungian world, no longer the exclusive domain of men. I can also say what kind of fatherhood I don't believe in, to which I emphatically do not give my heart. Nor do I imagine that calling God "Father" can possibly limit what I understand God to be, what the prophets and saints imagined and imagine and will imagine God to be. If in a moment of Christmas amazement I address the infant Jesus as "Sweet Potato," as I have addressed each of my children, I don't really expect a creedal formula to arise, but I glimpse the power that binds God and creation. I can say that with all my heart.

It's taken some time to sift through these things, to say *this* and not *that*. I remember a discussion at the Seton Cove in Austin when Patty Speier, the director, listened to a bunch of us talk about which tenets of the creed we thought we could toss out while still calling ourselves Christian. (One older woman in the group, Roman Catholic from long before her birth, listened to our passionate discussion with quiet amusement.) God the Father, of course, was thrown out immediately. Only son—on the trash heap. (No one had any objection to sitting in the reverberant fog of God from God,

Light from Light, etc.) Virgin birth—are you kidding? Finally Patty asked us what we couldn't throw out and stunned us into silence. I eventually answered that question by writing my own creed, which I have to change nearly every time I go back to it. I don't actually say it, but it helps guide my steps when I pick my way across the capital-C Creed, showing me where to balance—here and not there—on the rocks that are tippy. It goes something like this:

> *I believe in one living God,*
> *author, judge, faithful lover,*
> *unseen, usually unheard.*
> *I believe in Jesus Christ, the flowering vine,*
> *who was born in danger of Mary*
> *and unexpectedly loved by Joseph;*
> *who walked in beauty through a world*
> *rent by greed and grief;*
> *who healed and mourned, who taught and raged;*
> *who sang the old songs and spoke nonsense, sometimes;*
> *who called hidden truths to the surface;*
> *who forced a crisis in those who met him.*
> *He died in agony—deserted, betrayed, true.*
> *He rose and bloomed somehow, beckoning*
> *everyone in time and space to join him.*
> *And most of all I believe in the Spirit, who binds*
> *with luminous swaddling the Creator, the Beckoner,*
> *and all that is, has been, will be.*
> *I believe they are the source of all just anger, all quiet courage,*
> *all patient love, all improbable forgiveness.*
> *I believe this mostly at night, in poems and music,*
> *and when I don't think too hard.*
> *I believe this whenever friends and strangers gather for a meal.*
> *I believe this as I can, which is sometimes not at all,*
> *but I know I must believe or wither.*

My identity as a Christian (and perhaps as a Texan) has taken—and continues to take—a series of unexpected turns. Many of the paths on which I have found myself peter out, but some of them allow me to move ahead.

Since Martin and I are in this beautiful place to hike, I can't help but imagine this process as walking in a wild place with a map that is useful in a general sort of way—you know what direction you're headed in, where significant landmarks are in relation to each other—but less helpful when it comes to the specifics of navigation. The trail becomes fainter the farther you go, more like a deer trail, and suddenly you find yourself walking in high shrubs or reeds or thick understory. Several paths, equally well trodden, present themselves to you. You take one, puffing through the scratchy gorse, wishing you'd worn long pants, and swatting at mosquitoes. The trail becomes available only to those walkers with four feet. You swear and head back, hoping you're actually on the main trail. You are, but it divides again, and all of a sudden the trail is nothing but thick impassable mud. You hear running water and know from the map that the trail is supposed to be near a creek. So you take off through the chaparral or whatever this damn stuff is and tear your shorts on a branch in an annoyingly conspicuous place. You feel *sure* that a trail will appear somewhere if you just get a little higher up. And all of a sudden, your partner now muttering unattractive observations about your sense of direction, you glimpse the quiet shining lake. You're still not sure where the trail is, but the lake is right there.

60

The Unsteady Rock
Descartes, Salamanders, and the Nicene Creed

SEPTEMBER 27, 2013

In my last piece, I compared saying the Nicene Creed to stepping on unsteady stones across a creek, stepping *here* and not *there*, meaning *this* and not *that* in an effort not to end up with wet feet and an unsayable creed. One of the tippiest stones for me is the word *believe*, which for a long time I understood as a sort of thought bubble in the brain in which the creed could be said and remain unspotted from the world. Upon this rock I now place a salamander.

A story in Monday's *Austin American-Statesman* reported on the multimillion-dollar battle being waged in two Central Texas counties over who will protect the Georgetown salamander and its cousin, the Salado salamander, local authorities or the US Fish and Wildlife Service. It's a story that I suspect will cause some eye rolling among developers, conservationists, scientists, laymen, liberals, and conservatives alike. But here's the thing: these embryo-like creatures, which live in caves and springs in declining numbers, are bellwethers of water quality for the region. Their skin is so thin their beating hearts are visible, and they absorb any toxins in the water directly into their bodies. Their declining numbers in the face of new development in both counties can be attributed and weighed and argued, but the last word is that our well-being and theirs are inextricably entangled. No one in the story seems to be arguing about that.

On my tippy rock, next to the salamander, I now place a book, *The Spell of the Sensuous: Perception and Language in a More-Than-Human World*, by David Abram, a philosopher, cultural ecologist, and sleight-of-hand magician. This beautiful work is in part about learning to locate ourselves outside ourselves in order, quite literally, to understand ourselves: we cannot separate what we stand on—the Earth in all its history and destiny—from who we are and how we know it. Without this understanding, we cease to know anything, or indeed to be fully human. Yes, yes—I'm off the rock and in the creek. But Abram writes about these contorted philosophical topics with a lyric and embodied clarity, eschewing abstract language. His topic— how we know what we know—has become a signpost on this uneven path toward believing.

As a philosopher, Abram is a phenomenologist, someone who studies human consciousness, particularly as it focuses on direct experience. How do we know that we know something? Descartes famously sought certainty as the baseline for knowledge. When you experienced something through your senses, how could you be sure you weren't dreaming or mad? What could you stand on to say anything with certainty? Descartes found certainty inside his mind—he thought, therefore he was—and effectively drew a line in the sand between the subjective, autonomous mind and the objective, inert world of things. Descartes was no atheist; he acknowledged that without God there could be no confidence in the reality of the external world. But Descartes's pronouncement released God to become an idea, cloven from creation, while the primacy of scientific method and mathematical truth became almost inescapable over the next centuries. After Descartes, anyone saying "I believe" more likely believed in a second-tier proposition as it stacked up against scientific rationalism, one that was merely subjective and consequently of little use in the real, objective worlds of science, commerce, and politics.

Abram rejects this split between what we know and how we know it, and he does it by taking us out of our Cartesian heads and back into our sensing bodies. Despite the power and information that the scientific revolution has brought us, we cannot separate our daily lives—even those spent in laboratories—from the ambiguous, preconceptual ground of sensory experience. Writes Abram, "The fluid realm of direct experience has come to be seen as a secondary, derivative dimension, a mere consequence of events unfolding in the 'realer' world of quantifiable and measurable scientific 'facts,'" facts which descend from some impersonal, objective dimension like *putti* from heaven." Abram does not question the accomplishments of science and technology. He does, however, want to uncover how a blinkered commitment to their processes has left us blind to the subjective, sensuous, sentient life of bodies—all bodies, animal, vegetable, mineral—and the great breathing body of the Earth. To be deaf to the lively ancient and ongoing conversations of the Earth is to be cut off from our own humanity because the perceiver and the perceived are made of the same stuff.

So imagine that you're sitting outside, watching your cat stalk a lizard climbing a sunflower as a blue jay heckles from a nearby tree. Where is all this happening? Inside your mind? There's a reliable solidity to this tableau, no matter what Descartes says. Or is it happening "out there," with no participation from you, the observer? Abram points to another place, what he and other philosophers call the life-world, the world we don't pay much attention to; the one where the kitchen radio is on and the mail is being delivered and the dogs are sniffing something foul and widgets are being made. This is a collective rather than private space, ever shifting and open-ended and containing the unceasing activity of its innumerable inhabitants. The point of entry into this life-world is the sentient body of each inhabitant. When I watch the cat-drama, perception doesn't happen just in me or just in the participants; rather, it occurs in the crucible of this communal space, belonging to it and not its individual participants. In this view, the air is no longer empty but bursting with relationship. Nor does perception occur without the literal ground we stand on, which from its depths shapes the life-world in which we dwell. When we elevate ourselves into some objective realm of fact, we're unable to participate in or even hear the ongoing conversations with the created world that ensure our own full humanity.

Back to my unsteady rock, on which I now place a small gong. Knowing even less about gong design than I do about philosophy, I imagine it looking something like an atom, its dense nuclear heart the place the clapper hits, its reverberations spreading outward, gaining power. I put it on the rock to remind myself of one of the images that first drew me to take seriously the possibility of a Christian life. In *A Testament of Devotion*, Thomas R. Kelly, a mid-twentieth-century Quaker mystic, writes of his own faith journey not as an ascent toward belief but as a descent into the Light:

> *There is a way of ordering our mental life on more than one level at once. On one level we may be thinking, discussing, seeing, calculating, meeting all the demands of external affairs. But deep within, behind the scenes, at a profound level, we may also be in prayer*

and adoration, song and worship and a gentle receptiveness to divine breathings. . . . Between the two levels is fruitful interplay, but ever the accent must be on the deeper level, where the soul ever dwells in the presence of the Holy One. For the religious man [sic] *is bringing all affairs of the first level down into the Light.*

Kelly does not leave the Earth behind in his God-ordered life but digs deeper into it, perhaps alluding to the literal fire that burns at its center. Wikipedia tells me that the Earth's hyper-hot inner core, which was liquid for its first couple of billions of years, has been solid for the second couple of billion, although it is surrounded by the turbulent viscosity of the equally hot outer core. When I say—or preferably sing—the creed, I imagine voices sinking into the light beneath the Earth's skin, mingling with the wild subsonic frequencies sounding at the core, and then reverberating back into our haunted air and beyond, audible to those listening for them.

So I believe. And when I say "I," I also must say *we* since "I" can't be entirely separated from the Body extending through time and space that says it. We believe in the disagreeing fellowship around the necessary salamander, whose name, *Eurycea naufragia*, means "remnant," and thus sneaks a prophetic note into the conversation. We believe in God's love for creation, so profound that the Body of God can never be disengaged from it. We believe that when humanity separates itself from the Body of God, it ceases to be fully human and commits atrocities both willfully and ignorantly. We believe in the gravity of all created things, whose resonance pulls them down toward the singing Light and which carries its cadences back to the surface.

Sometimes it takes me a long time to get across that creek, what with trying not to step on salamanders, knock over gongs, and such.

61

Mind the Gap
Ghosts, Trees, and Goodbye to a River

OCTOBER 18, 2013

There's a 5,000-pound ghost hovering over Austin's Lady Bird Lake, the remains of a thirty-five-foot cedar elm painted white and hoisted onto a shaft sunk into the water. Titled *Thirst*, this collaborative project memorializes the estimated 301 million trees in Texas that have died in the current drought.

It's a haunting sight, this desiccated tree with its roots hovering just above the water that would have kept it alive. Looking at it and its reflection in the water, I couldn't help but wonder about ghosts, who seem to reside in that gap between sustenance and death. When you can't see the space that *Thirst* creates, the space between the roots reaching for the water and the water itself, it's easy to forget that it exists when the roots are underground as well; that gap, that amazing gap across which roots somehow get the nutrients they need to grow—or don't. The floating tree gives room to investigate that ghost-thick space in more-than-literal ways as well, a seasonally appropriate exploration as Halloween rolls its perky little way across our neighborhood.

When Martin and I were in California last month, we went hiking through the area of the Mount Vision fire, which burned 12,000 acres of the Point Reyes National Seashore in 1995. Hundreds of charred trees—most of them Bishop pines—still stood in testament to the devastation of the fire, riding like gray ghosts on the backs of the hills galloping into the ocean.

Despite the reminder they provided of pain and loss, I was struck by their place in the busy landscape. Woodpeckers, warblers, chickadees, hawks, and coyly hidden singers flew in and around the old ghosts, nesting, feeding, resting. Some of the dead trees had melted into mulch, providing cribs for numerous other species. I read later that Bishop pine cones, which grow in tight thick clusters on the parent pine's branches, won't release and open except with intense heat.

Something about the scene reminded me of an afternoon I spent years ago walking through a predominantly Mexican cemetery on the west side of San Antonio, probably about this time of year, just before the Day of the Dead. Families were picnicking among the grave markers, many of which bore photos of the dead. Many of the dead were long gone and couldn't possibly have known in life some of the generations gathered there, and yet there were balloons and fresh flowers and toddlers all bouncing through the scene. It was the first time I had seen this intentional, comfortable coexistence of the living and the dead, a reaching across the gap that usually separates them, and something lively was released.

It's easy to romanticize that gap, to say that it's just a Ouija board's journey from one side to the other, or to deny that any interpenetration across it is possible. One thing I know about the gap is that it's often delivered in a placenta of suffering.

Martin and I also just finished reading *Goodbye to a River* by John Graves, who died on July 31 of this year. Born in 1920 and raised in the Fort Worth area, Graves left Texas as a young man and returned in 1957 to take care of his ill father. In November of that year, when he heard that the Brazos River, the site of many adventures in his youth, was to be dammed, he decided to canoe and camp along the part of the river that he had known the best, between Possum Kingdom Lake and Lake Whitney, a trip of two hundred or so miles that took about three weeks. He wrote not only about his adventures with "the passenger," the dachshund pup that accompanied him, but also about the history of the river and its people. Graves had no patience for the myth of the noble "Anglo-Ams" (as he called the white settlers) who ousted the savage native Americans; his respect for the Comanche nation ("The People") and other indigenous tribes was unfashionable at the time. His respect for the river and its environs was equally unusual at a time when the natural world shared the same degraded status as the Native American.

At the same time, Graves was respectful of the Anglo-Ams whom he called "the old ones." He had a particular fondness for Charles Goodnight, one of the namesakes of the famed Goodnight-Loving Trail, whose ranch Graves passed on his journey. Graves wrote of Goodnight, "He was a tough and bright and honorable man in tough not usually honorable times, and had respect and a kind of love for the Indians even when he fought them," which was often. Graves tells a tale so haunting about Goodnight and The People that I think it must float, almost visible, around that bend of the Brazos, whether it happened or not.

Many years after the buffalo herds—and the Comanche way of life—had been effectively extinguished, a group of reservation Comanches rode their "gaunt ponies" to see Goodnight. Goodnight and his wife had rounded up the last stragglers of the southern bison herd, the seedbed from which the current Texas state herd has grown. Goodnight knew some of the older men; he had fought them and then gone to visit them on the reservation in Oklahoma to reminisce. They had come to ask him to give them a buffalo bull, to which, according to Graves, the crusty old rancher responded, "Hell, no."

They may or may not have asked again, but in the end, after camping patiently for several days in his yard and on his porch, much to the amusement of Goodnight's curious cowhands, the Comanches left with a bull, Goodnight "maybe deriving a sour satisfaction from thinking about the trouble they'd have getting it back to Oklahoma."

But they didn't take it to Oklahoma.

> *They ran it before them and killed it with arrows and lances in the old way, the way of the arrogant centuries. They sat on their horses and looked down at it for a while, sadly, and in silence, and then left it there dead and rode away, and Old Man Goodnight watched them go, sadly too.*

Graves watched ghosts all the way down the river, recalling tales of "the old ones" and their children, tales of murderous feuds and crude bravery and epic misuse of the land. Reflecting on the bloody, violent stories, he wrote facetiously:

> *Were there, you ask, no edifying events along the Brazos? . . . Didn't sober, useful, decent people build for themselves sober, useful decent lives, and lead us, soberly, usefully, decently up through the years to that cultural peak upon which we now find ourselves standing?*

Well, yes, he says, but "neither a land nor a people ever starts over clean." Both land and people inherit what has come before. Both leap over the amazing gap that separates one moment from the next and yet binds them together. A people's progenitors "stand behind its elbow, and not only the sober gentle ones. Most of all, maybe, the old hairy direct primitives whose dialect lingers in its mouth, whose murderous legend tones its dreams, whose oversimple thinking infects its attitudes toward bombs and foreigners and rockets to the moon."

Because he was willing to engage with ghosts—especially the hairy, scary, foul-mouthed ones—John Graves's voice is still audible somewhere in the gap between the floating tree and the river, through the interstices that link the living and the dead. Within those interstices, something lively is released—though released in the fires of suffering. No wonder we don't like ghosts. But, oddly, they can tie us to a place, a history, and to each other, so long as we have time to tell their stories in that space between the river and the roots. It's those interstices that allow for the development of unexpected and fruitful connections.

62

Repairing the World
Beatles, Alaskan Mountain Goats, and Asiatic Cheetahs
NOVEMBER 8, 2013

At the annual conference of the Alliance of Artists Communities, which we attended in San Jose, California, two weeks ago, I had the good fortune to attend a session with Joshua Wolf Shenk, author of *Lincoln's Melancholy: How Depression Challenged a President and Fueled His Greatness*. He is currently finishing another book titled *Powers of Two: Finding the Essence of Innovation in Creative Pairs*, and at the conference he talked about this work in progress.

According to Shenk, the traditional paradigm of the lone genius has recently been countered by a more nuanced story of the complex network out of which genius emerges. While he doesn't deny the existence of either the loner or the network, he asserts that a very specific electricity arises from creative pairs: think John Lennon and Paul McCartney, Georges Balanchine and Suzanne Farrell, Elizabeth Cady Stanton and Susan B. Anthony.

He also argues that there are several predictable acts in the stage life of a creative pair, the first of which is often an attraction of the familiar to the unfamiliar. And while the two partners must in some way merge, each partner losing his or her particular identity to the other as in the confluence of rivers, "creativity proceeds from dichotomous exchange," as Shenk says. Roles that become fixed or static signal a dying fire. This dichotomous exchange often involves an asymmetry of power in the partnership and consequent tension and unraveling. Those generative sparks can be extinguished without moments of what Shenk calls *repair*, moments of returning to the pure joy and delight of the original sparking.

To illustrate one of these moments, he played a clip of the Beatles' famous 1969 rooftop concert, their last live performance together. During their rendition of the song "Don't Let Me Down," John forgets the words to the beginning of the second verse and improvises several syllables of gobbledygook instead, exchanging bemused smiles with Paul. Shenk identifies this as a moment of repair in a torn relationship—by the time of this performance the friendship between John and Paul had frayed nearly to the breaking point—a recapturing of delight.

While Shenk didn't use the word "marriage," marriage easily qualifies as a locus for creative energy, although not necessarily marriage as it's envisioned today, with its focus on equal rights and equal workloads, of two people completing each other's deficits into some measurable whole. I hasten to add that fairness and equality, in some form, are necessary to any fruitful marriage; however, the asymmetries and tensions and inequalities that also occur within marriage are often the source of a relationship's generative genius. Shenk's taxonomy of creativity between pairs appealed to me instantly because I found immediate evidence to support his structure, not in the pairing of people but in the sparks that fly when unexpected disciplines are rubbed together.

One of the keynote speakers at the conference was Teri Rofkar, a native of Alaska and a member of the Tlingit people. She began her career as a traditional weaver making baskets from such materials as the roots of spruce trees, maidenhair ferns, and native grasses, an art taught to her by her grandmother and which she is now teaching her granddaughter. These baskets, aside from being beautiful, can last for hundreds of years and are woven so tightly they can be used as water vessels. When she took a class at a local community college on traditional methods of textile weaving, she realized that she already had most of the skills she needed to make the leap from weaving plants into baskets to weaving goat hair into traditional robes, a skill that had almost disappeared.

To practice her new craft, she needed mountain goat wool, and lots of it, so she befriended local park rangers who worked with a herd that had been introduced in 1923. The rangers informed her when they found spots where the animals had shed or when they found one dead. She became aware of a study of the genetics of the mountain goats, which discovered a herd genetically unrelated to the introduced herd and dated it to the last ice age, indicating that the species had not been "introduced" but was, in fact, native.

This genetic drama was unfolding as she was beginning work on a new robe. In addition to the traditional patterning, she added mathematically correct renderings of the distinctive DNA strands of the two herds. Although in some ways the addition was a design innovation, she knew from her many years of basket weaving that her ancestors had always transmitted a deep knowledge of the natural world through their art. On her website she writes:

> *Decades of weaving have opened my eyes to the pure science that is embedded in Tlingit art. The arts and our oral history together bring knowledge of ten thousand years of research to life. My goal is to continue that research, broadening awareness for the generations to come.*

She wore the robe as she presented her keynote speech, dipping each shoulder and spinning so the robe rose up like smoke around her. "Who knew science could dance?" she laughed. Her delight communicated itself to the audience as we witnessed a moment of repair between ancient art and modern science.

Martin and I returned to Austin just in time to attend the last day of the Texas Book Festival, a spectacular annual gathering of people who love to read and write. We attended a session facilitated by one of Madroño Ranch's first residents, Juli Berwald. She interviewed Alan Weisman, an environmental journalist and the author of *Countdown: Our Last Best Hope for a Future on Earth?* Fiercely researched and beautifully written, *Countdown* follows Weisman's travels through more than twenty countries asking four very loaded questions: how many people can the land carry? How robust must the Earth's ecosystems be to ensure our continued existence? What species are essential to our survival? What kind of economy would serve a stable human population, rather than the current exploding one?

Despite the complexities of the questions—which Weisman addresses with sensitivity and intelligence—a uniform answer presented itself in virtually every context: education of girls, which almost inevitably leads to lower birth rates and to fewer ecological pressures on the planet.

He tells a story about Esmail Kahrom, an Iranian ecologist whose interest in biology had its roots in the Persian carpets he saw in the museum his father took him to as a child, one in particular, dating back to 1416. It depicted a Tree of Life, and among its branches the boy found an extravagance of intricately woven birds, animals, and even insects:

> *The depictions were so detailed that zoologists could determine each species. He was looking, Kahrom understood, at creatures now extinct in his land. The eyes of ancient carpet weavers are how Iranian biologists know today what once lived there.*

One of the animals that has almost disappeared is the Asiatic cheetah, which exists now only in Iran. Visiting the United States for the first time, Kahrom found himself in a sixth-grade classroom in San Diego, invited by the teacher, who was married to one of Kahrom's cousins. She showed her students the Iranian flag and Iranian coins and then unrolled a Persian rug, one that Kahrom could tell immediately was ancient and expensive. She introduced him to the class as an ecologist, someone who studies the ways in which all life is connected.

Then the classroom door opened, and in walked a curator from the San Diego Zoo with a muzzled cheetah on a leash.

The teacher asked her astonished class what would happen if the endangered cheetahs disappeared altogether. Would the students suffer from the loss? Would they still be able to live their lives? The class agreed that they would, even though they thought the cheetahs should live. The teacher pointed to the beautiful rug she had brought in, noting that it was years in the making, with its more than one and a half million knots. What if someone came in and cut out one, or even two hundred, of the knots? Would you be able to tell? No, she said. You wouldn't even notice.

But what if you keep cutting, she asked, as her students and the cheetah watched her. Opening her arms to include the space beyond the classroom walls, she said:

> *All this is the carpet of life. You are sitting on it. Each of those knots represents one plant or animal. They, and the air we breathe, the water we drink, and our groceries are not manufactured. They are*

produced by what we call nature. This rug represents that nature. If
something happens in Asia or Africa and a cheetah disappears, that
is one knot from the carpet. If you realize that, you'll understand that
we are living on a very limited number of species and resources, on
which our life depends.

These stories weave together many things, but what struck me was the
union of the textile arts with modern science. So often the realm of women
and household, textiles claim a lower rung on any cultural-status ladder
than the hard sciences, but their marriage can strike all sorts of generative
sparks. Jewish mystical theology identifies the work of the chosen people
as the restoration of God's shining shattered dwelling place, associated with
the feminine principal, with God's exiled self: *tikkun olam*, or repair of the
world, whose signal marker is delight. In a culture that so often measures
itself by efficiencies of scale and measurable, predictable outcomes, I won-
der if we wouldn't be well served to seek out irregular marriages between
powerful and humble enterprises, between unlikely partners like science or
technology and the arts, rather than seeking to separate them, as so often
happens in times of economic stress. In these unlikely partnerings perhaps
we'll see some repair of our moth-eaten world.

POEMS

Invocation

How shall I begin? By whom shall
I be led? This journey through the realm
of blessing needs a guide. The kiln
of grief and violence, in which all,
at times, are tempered, can so bake
body, mind, and heart into rock-
hardness that we require some wreck,
some wrench, back to the humid ache
of stretching toward a supple life.
The leading can be gently done
as well, a whisper in the din,
the way a rhyme is often rife
with routes toward new and fruitful words.
My daily life is full of guides
that I ignore, although some goad
me to awaken, as shrill birds
shriek when snakes are near. In a dream
that was not mine, the guide appeared. Eyes
ancient, quiet, a babe at ease
upon her lap, she knew extremes
of grief and grace, and, gazing, blessed
the bank from which I watched my mother
drift along the tide of dying, tethered
for a while by will and then possessed
by faceless deep. I tried to dive
into the tide; that tensile gaze
contained my thrashing grief like gauze
on bleeding flesh and so contrived
to reel me back. Now I invoke
the presence from my girlhood bedroom

wall that I ignored, her eyes abrim
with love and future grief, to stoke
my memory's tinder, even if it burns
the constant trees, so that the grass returns.

Prophet

I hate it when this happens: walking down
a crowded city street I find my clothes
dissolving, my wobbly self exposed, and
though I squirm with shame and panic, no one
notices. So when I saw her wading
through oncoming waves of traffic, pulling
off her shirt and shorts and shouting CAN YOU
HELP ME, I thought: Wake up! Naked up
the street she strode, impervious to swells
of steel, indifferent glances, sniggering
patrons of the corner filling station,
her clarion lament unfurling over
swirling city tumult: CAN YOU HELP ME?
Poor thing, I thought, and kept on walking toward
the courthouse—traffic ticket—pondering
the recent devastation on the coast,
apocalyptic scenes of water poured
with vengeance, poured with fury, pouring to
reveal uncleanness: haughty thoughtlessness
of power, faces of betrayed forsaken
children, generations stranded long before
they clambered to their rooftops, marooned
and keening dogs, the earth and sea convulsing
under toxic muck. I woke to find her,
clothed for now and surging toward me. She had
me in her eye: CAN YOU HELP ME? I forced
myself to look at her and found my clothes
dissolving in that irritating way
they have, and there I was, exposed before

her clear-eyed gaze. No, I said, I cannot
help you, shame and panic flaming, NO FOOD
NO NOTHING? My hair in ashes, bald and
naked, I said No, I cannot help you.
Seeing who I was, she coursed ahead to
other mortals, invoking us to squirm
ourselves awake and mark the water rising
under sky so hot and hard it groaned.

Compunction

Who begs for a broken heart? Who begs
to be the river, pierced endlessly?
Look: the cypress with its knobby knees
plants its multi-jointed feet in the river's
innards. Cormorants dive down, thrust up,
stitching air to the water's skin with
their orange beaks. From underneath, carp
and bass blast through the surface, living
lances that with each thrust sting twice.
The slashing sun is fiercest, at
times slicing to the river's marrow.

Its pathos is concealed, most days.
Most days I row along as if
nothing grew beneath me or
looked up through the current, watching.
Some mornings, though, especially
in winter, a shaft of sun will
pierce the river's breast and I see
past my reflection into its
depths. Boulders, tiny shells, soft green
bones of fallen trees, thick stands of
pond-weed moving to an unheard
rhythm, and sometimes the snapping
turtle's plodding menace—this world

on which I glide so mindlessly
is illuminated, dazzling
in its deep prosaic presence.

Then I know with sorrow that
I often walk insensate on
the living earth, deaf to the life
beneath my feet, blind to the molten
center that upholds me. And I
pass by strangers on the street (or
by those beloved bearers of my
unwieldy heart) never noting
that they are rivers quick and rich
with arrows, with the messiness
of blessing. For a depthless moment
I beg to be the river, coursing
from my arid heart and down my face
full of silvery darkness, pain and grace.

What She Knew*

> *I saw four ways in which the body dried. The first was through blood-
> lessness, the second was the consequent pain, the third was that he
> was hanging up in the air as people hang up a cloth to dry, the fourth
> was that his physical nature needed liquid, and there was no kind of
> comfort ministered to him.*
>
> —Julian of Norwich, *Showings*, Chapter 17

She heard him say, All will be well, all will
Be well. But first she saw his sagging body
Like laundry hung to dry in parching wind,
Saw flesh's urgent need to fall, be still,

---

* Reprinted with permission of the *Anglican Theological Review*, where it was first published in
the fall 2002 issue (volume 84, number 4).

Denied by nails, saw weight detaching bone
From sinew, socket. She saw the body bruise,
His dripping blood congeal and dry. She saw
His desiccating skin. How could she—alone,
Immured, removed from daily chaos—know
That sin resides in us behovely, vital as
Dark blood and words? How in this aching vision
Did she find water, light, by which to grow?
She said: Without this sin and pain, God's delight
In us would burn like ulcers, sucked dry like blight.

Sacrifice

Ash Wednesday: one year I stood in thick cool
dust along with several others, waiting for
an ancient drama to begin again,
waiting as if I weren't an actor in it
too. Through the thorny brush the bison
entered, awkward bodies wary, dense beneath
the bulky wreath of muscle draped across
their shoulders. One shook her head—so massive
that her horns looked dainty—watching us with
eyes black as moonless snake-filled summer nights.
We climbed into the pickup, all except
the shooter, who moved with quiet purpose
as we sat in silence, waiting for the shot
that finally came—shocking, if expected—
and penetrated mercifully, the cow dead
before she finished sinking to the dust.
Another man performed the bleeding when
she was hoisted, limp, still warm, head down,
carotid artery cascading blood
a color and consistency I had
never seen before, a frothing cochineal
oasis in the thirsty dust. I asked
the shooter if and how he steeled himself

for harvest. Pray two days before, he said.
Sit quietly. We watched the hands prepare
her for the journey, another kind of life.
Her body, treasury of light and grass
and epic wanderings, will enrich
a larger body now, a body more than
body when it knows the incarnate cost—
be it hoofed, winged, scaled, or even rooted
life—of nourishing itself. Around us,
bushes burned in lilac, white, and yellow
flames, their incense rising toward the hawks
and caracaras, wheeling in mandalic arcs,
awaiting our departure so to gather
in the dust and then consume the bloody
pool, their bounden duty.

Proof

This warm November morning
so many butterflies are floating
on their enigmatic journeys;
so many leaves are drifting down
from elms and clattering cottonwoods,
spinning—spangled as the butterflies—
each side fusing for a flash
into a single surface;
the breeze so quick and shifting that
the heavy scent of blooming
loquat swells, recedes, at once
sinking, surging—so chatoyant is
this scene before me that I must
conclude
the surface of reality
comes unglued in autumn from
some thicker world beneath it,
curls at the corners and bids us

to consider this obvious
deduction: the shimmering is all
there is. So, too, on a summer
night cicadas' chanting throbs
in unison, dissolves into
a thousand separate beats, and
gathers, rising to a single
pulse once more, enjoining listeners
to hear a broken, seamless whole.
Hence be it known in soul and bone:
earth's divide from heaven is undone.

Within

Look! The world's lit from within by rays
we cannot see but always recognize
when heart's eyes
open. Praise,

gratitude, and love are debris
left by passage of their dark flames, dust
blown to blind so we must
blink and see.

With

Yes, yes, I know that
acorns grow to oaks,
that their potential stokes
the flaming path

teleology projects.
But what of *this* one,
wonderfully begun
and ended *now*? Annex

no future, just watch
this girl, fetchingly
hatted, squat as she
sorts through duds—cracked, blotched—

and finds it: pristine,
glossy, cap intact.
Watch: as it lacks
nothing, she rubs its sheen,

bites it, spits, and skips
away. Before
adorning acorn
or girl with ancient scripts

or prophecies—which is
vital, dazzling labor—
rest with them and savor
silence's chaotic riches.

Ordination

Ordinations take place every day
in this temple, performed when the holy
is born and released to irradiate, slowly,
this feculent world composed of its rays.
Who handles the holy? All who guess
that it stipples the whole etiology
marring creation, who courteously
dare to relieve its distress.

Ordination
Piedras Negras

Who is it that handles the holy,
contaminant of the mundane?
Those who are carefully trained
for invoking, inducing, extolling.
They're not hard to spot, devoted and worthy,
most of them. But invisible priests
venture unvested to work in the least
likely places. In cracked, earthy
vessels they offer unstable
reactive old elements, portending
arrival of radiant, upending
newness, foretold in odd stories and fables.

Sweaty and dusty, a cadre of priests
up to their chests in loud children
commanded the wild, surging tide into
straight lines. As they readied the feast,
few saw the emergence of clean sacred space
beneath the mesquite trees and ankle-deep
dust, in the casual trash heaps
festooned with barbed wire, in faces—
most bright with excitement, some
damaged by want—of the children before
them. An oblivious postulant poured
out the Kool-Aid in disciplined rhythm
and handed out snacks, seeming quite unaware
of the chalice she bore, of the paten
she carried. A girl wearing satin
blue bows and no shoes stopped and stared
at the ground. "Gracias," she murmured.
Startled awake, the server replied,
"No, gracias a tí," and walking inside
of the luminous space the small minister
showed her, she too was ordained to set

free chained love, to rejoice in love's
triumphs no matter their size. Her
movements—hospitable now, though less fluid—let
the holy arrive as she greeted
each child, asked every name, gave each
some food. The walls of the temple, soon breached
and cast down by the daily, receded.

Beside

At the river in the morning,
turtles peer and disappear,
their ancient, knobby heads mere
nods to more normal formings;

herons everywhere, though not
at first apparent. An errant
eye soon sees the careful stares and
languid legs laced to the knotted

hunters' trunks, tensed to shoot from thick
dark bank and branch. Mayflies sashay;
fish applaud with clapping jaws. Gray
shadows flick fey eccentric

shapes across pocked cliffs, shift bright
to view—cardinal, swallow, wren—
and, dopplering, recede again,
songs spraying like champagne. Site

of hidden, just-glimpsed stories,
the river, rived by writhing, leaping
lives, is mended endlessly, a steeping
scripture, breathing text of wordless glories.

Beneath

When I start to write, all things seem nude and need
covering, so I lay out the morning's scenes:
should I address the vitriolic screed
that jays pour down on my coiled cats? the green
sprouts that whisper up into the air unheard?
What about the footnotes trailing under
gestures, shrugs, eye-rolling sighs, or swallowed words
at breakfast conversation? Or I wonder
if the news itself needs shaping: what can
she mean, this woman calmly naming body
parts that showered on the burning bus when a man
climbing on exploded? It seems a haughty
task, basting words to things, but the unwritten
word undulates beneath events. I grope, smitten.

With her mother, Jessica
Hobby Catto, 2009.

With Martin, Point Reyes National Seashore, California, 2010.

With Martin and Isa,
Madroño Ranch, 2011.

Epilogue

Heather's sister Isa Catto Shaw, a visual artist who lives in Colorado, posted the following on her blog "Creative Rummage" in October 2016.

Soul Sister

You will lose someone you can't live without, and your heart will be badly broken, and the bad news is that you never completely get over the loss of your beloved. But this is also the good news. They live forever in your broken heart that doesn't seal back up. And you come through. It's like having a broken leg that never heals perfectly—that still hurts when the weather gets cold, but you learn to dance with the limp.

—Anne Lamott

This Monday marked the second year without Heather. She was part of my life on this ground for forty-nine years, and still is, of course, but is now part of an interior landscape of shades, yearning, and nostalgia. A great sister—and mine was—makes you visible, affirms you. Women tend to be listeners: we listen to our kids, to dinner partners, to the disgruntled parents at school, to the lonely contractor, to the dissatisfied soul at the post office, to the neighbor, to other members of the family. As an introvert with a powerful "look at me, don't look at me" dynamic, I find this a safe place, but an isolated one. Heather was the one who listened to me, and was interested in the quotidian details of my life, alongside the more opaque side of my inner life. She was honest when my paintings baffled her, or when I was prone to lazy thinking, and honest when she thought I was wrong. We would call each other when we were having "fat and ugly" days, or "poor poor pitiful me" days, or when we just needed a bitch session. We could move from the trivial to the complex with ease. She would call to ask if my daughter was over a cold, to learn of our son's antics, what I thought of a particular book or a Krista Tippett interview, or wonder if I was sleeping well since women in our family struggle with insomnia. There was never impatience, just a flow of conversation. And like all sisters, we shared a repository of family lore and drama. My husband is my best friend, but Heather was my North Star.

Initially my loneliness was so acute that I was simply functioning the first year without her. I felt invisible and small. These feelings have morphed, the way they always do, into a gentler, constant current. I eased back into the world of joy and light and delight, but the undertow remains. As Anne Lamott put it, "you learn to dance with the limp."

After Heather was diagnosed with cancer, I called her at least once a day. When I called she would pick up the line and ask, "Is this my daily harassment call?"

"Why, yes it is," I would respond.

And off we'd go. We fell into the good habit of telling each other "I love you" at the close of every call until the cancer moved into her brain and swept away her ability to communicate well over the lines.

For years, I worried that I loved Heather more than she loved me. I fretted that she disapproved of my wild-child ways, especially when she was grounded in the rigor of parenting small children; we led opposite lives and my freedom might have seemed unearned and carefree, while her domesticity seemed safe, respectable, and out of reach. She was an academic, a theologian, and lived in a world of reason. She harvested conclusions with discipline while my artistic world was more emotional, chaotic, and charged, relying on visual cues and sloppy mysticism. There was often no linear progression to my own career as a painter, no tidy accumulation of accomplishments. She harvested degrees like the dedicated academic she was. And though generous of spirit, she was more emotionally reserved and restrained than I. I lean toward impulsive thinking and speech, with a dash of hyperbole. She always took a more disciplined route to her conclusions. When I was young and much more literal, I mistook her reserve, her pointed glance over her reading glasses, and that wry smile below, as a form of censure.

When my life got upended by autoimmune disease after the birth of my first child, I finally realized how much her love bound us, filling in any crack in our differences. Heather went into motion and was my advocate-in-chief. She coaxed me out of many an emotional mouse-hole. When we lost our mother, we knew we lost a singular champion. But we still had each other, and we were closer than ever before. It took many years to really absorb the lesson embedded in poetry, in literature—in all of the arts: that unconditional love is not evaluated measure for measure, but is just a constant that we take for granted. That lesson never comes early enough.